Captain Cook and the
South Pacific

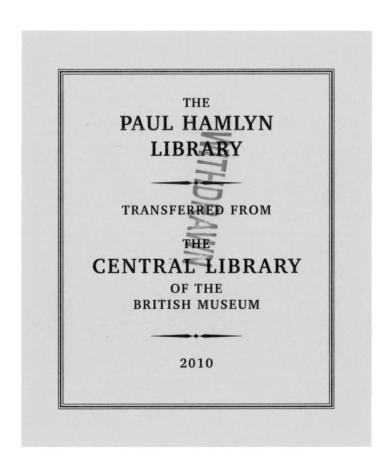

The British Museum Yearbook 3

Captain Cook and the South Pacific

Published for the Trustees of the British Museum by
British Museum Publications Ltd

2085

© 1979, The Trustees of the British Museum

ISBN 0 7141 0088 9

Published by British Museum Publications Ltd
6 Bedford Square, London WC1B 3RA

British Museum
   Captain Cook and the South Pacific/[British Museum]
   — (British Museum. Yearbooks; 3).
   1. Cook, James, b.1728 2. South Pacific Ocean
   I. Title II. Series
   910'.09'1648   G420.C65

Edited by T. C. Mitchell
Designed by Sebastian Carter
Set in Monophoto Ehrhardt with display in Photina
by Filmtype Services Limited, Scarborough
Printed and bound in Great Britain by
Jolly & Barber Ltd, Rugby

Contents

Preface

On 14 February 1779, Captain Cook was killed in an affray with Hawaiian natives. James Cook (1728–79), a Yorkshireman who had joined the Navy in 1755 after many years of commercial sailing off the east coast of England, now enjoys a reputation as one of the greatest explorers of all time.

This reputation rests on the three voyages to the Pacific which occupied most of the last ten years of his life. His First Voyage in the bark HMS *Endeavour*, which lasted from August 1768 to July 1771, had as one of its aims the setting up of an observatory in Tahiti to make observations of the planet Venus which it was known would pass across the face of the sun in 1769. This was successfully accomplished, and the expedition went on to explore the coasts of New Zealand and eastern Australia, returning to England by way of the Cape of Good Hope. With Cook on this voyage, in a private capacity, was a wealthy young man named Joseph Banks (1743–1820), who brought with him a staff of scientists and draughtsmen. Banks, who had studied botany at Oxford, was already a Fellow of the Royal Society at the time of the voyage, and later, as Sir Joseph Banks, he was well known for over forty years as the President of the Royal Society. In the first paper in this volume, Dr Averil M. Lysaght discusses the artists who accompanied Banks on Cook's first voyage and gives an account of the drawings by them which are now in the collections of the Department of Manuscripts of the British Library.

Cook sailed in the converted sloop *Resolution* on his Second Voyage of Pacific exploration, leaving England in July 1772, and not returning until July 1775. His party also included a smaller vessel, the *Adventure*, commanded by Lieutenant

7

Tobias Furneaux, and the two ships stayed together until November 1773, when, after he had missed meeting Cook at New Zealand, Furneaux returned to England on his own. During this voyage Cook carried out an extensive exploration of the southern Pacific, finally reaching England by way of Cape Horn in July 1775, a year later than Furneaux. Considerable interest was aroused at this time by a Polynesian from Tahiti named Omai who had come to England with Furneaux, and the second paper in this volume, by Dr Rüdiger Joppien, discusses one of the manifestations of this interest, the staging of a pantomime in London, based on the life of Omai.

Cook set out on his Third Voyage in July 1776, again in the *Resolution*, accompanied this time by the *Discovery*, commanded by Captain Charles Clerke. After Omai had been returned to Tahiti, attention was largely concentrated on the search for the North-West Passage, and exploring the northern coasts of America and Asia. In the central Pacific, Hawaii was discovered, and here Cook met his death, the command of the *Resolution* then being taken over by Clerke, with Lieutenant Charles Gore in command of the *Discovery*. When Clerke died of tuberculosis later in the voyage, Gore took over the *Resolution*, and Lieutenant King succeeded him in the *Discovery*. The two ships finally reached England, by way of the Cape of Good Hope in October 1780.

Captain Cook's voyages brought the existence of the island peoples of the Pacific very much to the attention of the western world, and this gave rise to speculation about how they came to be there. In the third paper Dr Brian Durrans discusses, in the light of modern ethnographic knowledge, some of the theories and misconceptions which arose over this question.

Several of those who accompanied Cook on his voyages brought back objects of local manufacture to England and some of these form part of the collections of the Department of Ethnography (Museum of Mankind). A special room, the Otaheite or South Sea Room, was opened for their exhibition in 1778 in Montague House, the old British Museum, and this proved very popular with the public. The last two papers in this volume, by Dr Adrienne L. Kaeppler and Professor Deborah Waite, discuss the Museum collections from Hawaii and the Solomon Islands respectively, with special reference to the material deriving from Cook's voyages.

With this volume, the Yearbook takes on a new, more compact, format, which it is felt will make it easier, both to handle and to accommodate on the bookshelf.

T. C. MITCHELL
Editor

8

Banks's Artists and his *Endeavour* Collections[1]

A. M. LYSAGHT

The Artists

The participation of Joseph Banks in Cook's first voyage round the world is a remarkable landmark in the history of biology. It was not the first time that a qualified scientist had sailed across the Atlantic, rounded South America, and continued west across the Pacific. Just before Cook made his famous circumnavigation in the *Endeavour* (1768–71), Bougainville had also sailed round the world. He was accompanied by Philibert Commerson, a doctor of medicine and an excellent biologist (he was sent down from the University of Montpellier owing to his raids on the university garden for specimens for his own herbarium); Commerson employed one intrepid collector, Jean (Jeanne) Baré, disguised as a man for most of the voyage. But the scientist disembarked at Mauritius on the return voyage to investigate the local flora and fauna and there was joined by an able draughtsman, Jossigny, who made detailed drawings of his South American and other collections before Commerson died from overwork. Many of his specimens were neglected; his fishes were said to have been kept in Buffon's attic for twenty years before being examined; a number of his drawings were stolen after his death by his rascally assistant, Sonnerat, who used them to embellish his own fictitious *Voyage à la Nouvelle Guinée*. It is the type of scandal that gradually emerges though it may take a century or more to do so. Cuvier knew of it but it was hushed up until recently when Sonnerat's extraordinarily improbable record of Antarctic penguins in New Guinea was solved.[2] The full story still remains to be told, but Banks, returning to England in the *Endeavour*, met Sonnerat at Cape Town and gave him at least one Australian bird[3], a Kookaburra, which was thus erroneously added to the New Guinea fauna. Ironically, Banks's Kookaburra was selected as a cover illustration by Madeleine Ly-Tio-Fane in her recent sympathetic study of Sonnerat[4], thereby underlining the dismal facts of his industrious plagiarism. The saddest fact is that Commerson's diary was lost and only recently rediscovered; it has not been published.

The perennial interest in Cook's accomplishments as a navigator, has at long last led to the recognition that Banks's contribution to the biological and other achievements of the three circumnavigations should be re-assessed, and that detailed catalogues of all his *Endeavour* collections, including the drawings, should be attempted. The late J. C. Beaglehole made the text of Banks's *Endeavour* diary available, although a certain amount of editing and a superabundance of footnotes tended to slow down for many readers the immediacy of the young scientist's response to his discoveries.

Meanwhile a certain amount of work has been carried out on the artists and drawings of that voyage, and the following notes may be regarded as an interim report on some aspects of the contribution made by Banks, Solander and their artists to the biological and ethnographical results of their years in the *Endeavour*.

The collections made during the voyage were, as far as possible, drawn and described at the time of their acquisition, or as soon after as was practicable. Banks engaged two well qualified artists, Sydney Parkinson and Alexander Buchan, for this purpose; unofficially he had a third, his secretary Herman Diedrich Spöring, formerly Solander's clerk in the British Museum.[5] Spöring was a talented draughtsman who produced, during the voyage, a varied collection of pencil sketches, both sensitive and accurate, of ethnographical and zoological subjects, landscapes and coastal profiles (Pls. 10–14).

During the voyage Banks also acquired a number of primitive water-colours by an artist hitherto unidentified; a pen and ink portrait by C. H. Praval, a seaman taken on to the ship's complement by Cook at Batavia – there is some reason to suppose that he may have been responsible for some curious composite copies of work by Parkinson which were attributed to Cook by Skelton and Beaglehole and have been discussed elsewhere;[6] and a small series of paintings of South Africans (Pl. 26). The technique of this last artist resembles in some respects paintings of South African animals by Colonel Gordon, examples of which may be seen in the Department of Prints and Drawings, British Museum.[7]

Banks's map collection, some folio volumes of which have been recently identified in the British Library by Mrs Sarah Tyacke, has never been catalogued. In the Department of Manuscripts there is a chart of the North Island of New Zealand drawn for him by Richard Pickersgill, Master's Mate (Pl. 28); and there is a very fully labelled map of the Society Islands by Banks himself, recently reproduced elsewhere,[8] both of which deserve mention in this summary of the *Endeavour* drawings.

On his return to England, Banks engaged another group of artists, the brothers James and John Frederick Miller, John Cleveley Jr., Frederick Polydore Nodder and various engravers, to complete and prepare for publication many of the drawings already collected and commissioned, as well as to make fresh studies of some of his material. The portrayal of the oddest animal of all that they had seen, the kangaroo, was entrusted to men of greater eminence; George Stubbs made a delightful oil painting from Parkinson's pencil sketches and the skin; Nathaniel Dance drew its skull,[9] rather less well-known than his portrait of Captain Cook.

In addition to the draughtsmen in the *Endeavour*, Banks employed four trained collectors, invariably and unfortunately referred to as his servants. We have precise information about their role from a letter Banks wrote to his old school-friend William Phelp Perrin, on the eve of his departure from London to Plymouth where he and Solander were to board the *Endeavour*.[10] He outlined the steps he had taken to secure a passage and continued: 'I take also beside ourselves two men to draw & four more to Collect in the different branches of Nat. Hist. & such a Collection of Bottles Boxes Baskets bags nets &c &c as almost frighten me who have prepard them'. These men were Peter Briscoe who had been with Banks in Newfoundland and Labrador; James Roberts, a younger man who eventually became steward of the Revesby Estates, dying six years after Banks; and two negroes, Thomas Richmond and George Dorlton, who died from exposure during the ill-fated midsummer expedition to the hills in Tierra del Fuego. Little is known about these last two men except for an entry in Banks's diary in early September, 1768, when Richmond was watching for plankton. 'A shoal of dagysa's [salps] were observd', wrote Banks, 'and he Eager to take some of them threw the cast-net fastned to nothing but his wrist, the string slippd from him & the net at once sunk into the profound never more to torment its inhabitants'.

I do not know whether it was the widow of Richmond or of Dorlton to whom Fothergill refers on p.6 of the 1784 edition of Sydney Parkinson's posthumously published journal: 'J. Banks very readily fell in with the proposal, and settled at the same time a pension upon a black woman, the wife of a faithful black servant who went out with him, and perished by the cold of Terra del Fuego'.

SYDNEY PARKINSON

Sydney Parkinson (he sometimes signed himself Sidney) was born in Edinburgh about 1745.[11] His father Joel was a brewer and Quaker who found it difficult to collect his debts; he died leaving his family in financial straits. 'His son Sydney was put to the business of a woollen-draper; but, taking a particular delight in drawing flowers, fruit, and other objects of natural history, he became soon so great a proficient in that stile of painting, as to attract the notice of the most celebrated botanists and connoisseurs in that study'. This passage occurs in his brother Stanfield's introduction to Sydney's posthumously published journal (Pl.18); Stanfield also states that his father Joel was well known and esteemed by men of all ranks in that city. Everything about Sydney Parkinson suggests that his education was broadly based, and that he had been professionally trained by an accomplished artist. Little has been traced so far of his family background but his mother Elizabeth was presumably also a Quaker, and he had a sister, Britannia. They were related to wealthy Quakers in Newcastle upon Tyne. Joshua Middleton (1647–1721), was imprisoned for his adherence to Quaker tenets.[12] One of his daughters, Hannah, a famous beauty, married Joseph Gurney of Norfolk; their progeny included families of eminent Quakers such as the Frys, Hoares and numerous Gurneys whose descendants are today noted for their intellectual accomplishments.

Hannah Gurney had a beautiful niece, Jane Middleton, who when very young was married to a much older man, Captain Gomeldon, from whom she fled, ultimately adopting men's clothing to escape her distracted husband's pursuit, and sailing off to France. There her impersonation was so successful that she nearly persuaded a young nun to flee with her from her convent. On Captain Gomeldon's death in 1751, Jane returned to Newcastle where she died in 1780. She and her cousin Sydney Parkinson were on excellent terms.

An obituary notice in the *Newcastle Chronical*, 15 July 1780, refers to her as 'a Gentlewoman of liberal Education, a great adept in Natural History and Philosophy, and a generous Benefactor to the Poor'. Other details are given in a newspaper cutting without adequate provenance attached to a copy of one of her books[13] in the Public Library at Newcastle upon Tyne: 'Mrs. Gomeldon had a portrait of herself engraved in size about 15 inches high, by 9 inches broad copies of which were distributed amongst her acquaintance. She had remarkably fine teeth which she carefully preserved as they fell out through age, and had their enamel set in rings which were presented to her immediate friends. She fell in love with the name of captain James Cook, and wished to accompany him round the world when he went on his first voyage'.

Some of her fifty-seven maxims foreshadow the haiku:

> The World in general is in a State
> Of Surprise
> Each wondering at the Conduct of their
> Neighbour.[14]

12

She says of herself in her earlier and longer book 'I was, my reader must know, a dry Joker'; she deserves to be better known as an early feminist.

In a letter to her from Batavia, 6 October 1770, Sydney Parkinson wrote: 'I have spared no pains during the voyage, to pick up every thing that is curious for thee; and I flatter myself that I shall make a considerable addition to thy museum'. Jane replied, hoping that he himself would come and arrange his treasures for her, and extending a warm invitation to Banks and any other of his friends to come north with him, and stay at Walknowles, her home.[15]

The reading list in Parkinson's little sketchbook in the British Library (Add. MS 9345) includes Chaucer, Spenser, Ossian, Gay, Pope, Dryden, Virgil, Homer and La Fontaine, as well as Hogarth's *Analysis of Beauty* and other works relating to painting. There is no direct evidence bearing on the details of his technical training as a draughtsman but the quality and variety of his work suggests that he may have been a pupil of William De la Cour, a gifted Frenchman who ran the first publicly maintained school of drawing and design in Great Britain. Set up in Edinburgh in 1760, largely on the initiative of Henry Home, Lord Kames (1696–1782), a Trustee of the Board for the Improvement of Fisheries and Manufactures in Scotland,[16] it fulfilled a need made plain decades earlier by the poor quality of design in industry. As early as 1729 the Edinburgh School of St Luke had laid stress on the importance of achieving a higher standard in textile manufactures, and about the middle of the century the Select Society of Edinburgh attempted to improve matters by offering premiums for a wide range of drawing competitions. The awards were unfortunately given not for original work but for copies of classical subjects. The names of the prize-winners were published in the local papers but it very soon became apparent that professional teaching was needed. De la Cour, an excellent draughtsman, well known for his portraits, theatrical designs, classical paintings and landscapes, was selected as the first instructor. He appears to have been born about the turn of the century and to have come to London to work as a theatrical designer and portrait painter in about 1740. Short biographical accounts have been published by John Fleming[17] and by Croft-Murray.[18] Some fragments of his booklets of decorative designs exist in the British Museum and in the Victoria and Albert Museum, but the Witt Library (that marvellous repository of facts relating to the arts in general) has an old cutting referring to a complete set of his booklets (1741–47) in the Cooper-Hewitt Museum, New York (now a part of the Smithsonian Institution), and this set is still intact. Within the last few months Mr Gavin Bridson of the Linnean Society and I independently discovered engraved sheets of superbly drawn Migratory Locusts (Pl.21a), one in the Linnean Library and the second in the Department of Prints and Drawings in the British Museum. These sheets (22.8 × 30.3 cm.) bear the caption, 'A true Representation of the Locusts that fell in England the 4th of Augst 1748. Price 6d. De la Cour delin.

etc. in Kathrine Street in ye Strand. N.B. the Green Bodies are the Females. R. White sculp.'. I am most grateful to Mr Peter Dance for sending me references to reports about the havoc caused in central Europe by huge swarms of these insects in 1747, 1748 and 1749. In 1748 they devastated areas near Bristol, Shropshire and Staffordshire. The following year a report came in from Germany and appeared in the *Gentleman's Magazine* (XIX:430):

'The empress queen is again pregnant, a large army is kept up, and in very good order. The locusts, after ravaging part of *Poland*, and the neighbourhood of *Vienna*, (where they killed multitudes with fire arms, but were obliged to desist by the stench of the carcasses) took their flight, darkening the air, towards *Bohemia* and *Bavaria*'.

None of the coloured engravings mentioned has yet been found but the plain sheets are of considerable interest in that the insects are shown in a variety of poses, and totally lacking in the stereotyped quality that mars so many entomological drawings; the same vitality is conspicuous in Parkinson's drawings of insects and other small invertebrates (Pl.21a,b).

No other natural history drawings by De la Cour have been discovered as yet. In London he is known to have designed sets for two operas, and in 1752 he set up as a portrait painter at The Sign of the Ship, a grocer's shop in Great Russell Street, Covent Garden. In 1754 he moved to Dublin to set up an academy but this plan was abandoned and, after working there as a scene painter, he went to Edinburgh in 1757. Some of his work still exists in public and private collections in Scotland. His portraits include one of Jane Pringle, daughter of John Pringle (1707–82). Taught by Boerhaave and Albinus in Leyden, Pringle became one of the great reformers of military medicine and public hygiene, and in 1766 he was knighted for his public services. He was a close friend of Joseph Banks who succeeded him as President of the Royal Academy in 1778. The Pringles were also friends of Captain Cook and his wife; after Cook's death his widow gave some of his trophies to the Pringles and some of these are now in the Royal Scottish Museum. It is plain that people with similar interests formed a close-knit society in Edinburgh.

When the School of Design was set up in Edinburgh, the Trustees selected a certain number of boys and girls apprenticed to various trades; they included engravers, gilders, calico printers and others.[19] Pupils of great promise had their fees paid by the Trustees, others were taken on easy terms. The classes were held for two or three hours daily, and four times weekly; the courses lasted four years. Lists of the students, specimens of and reports on their work were submitted annually. In the N.G.1 series at Register House in Edinburgh it is stated from time to time that these records were entered in detail in the General Precept Book.[20] It is vexatious to have to report that I have been unable to trace any such volume. It may be there nevertheless, but it is possible that it was lost with many of the other records in a disastrous fire in 1818.[21]

De la Cour received a salary of about £100, but he had adequate time to execute private commissions, and he received additional payments for providing patterns for damask manufacturers, being particularly noted for his decorative foliage designs. When the drawing school at Aberdeen was established 'William Mossman, the master applied to the Trustees for the use of patterns and drawings executed by de (sic) la Cour. The patterns were despatched to Aberdeen to be copied, and the Trustees granted de la Cour ten guineas for producing eighty six drawings of foliage for use by the northern school'.[22] None of these patterns seems to have survived; they were probably worn out from constant use.

The few examples of the French artist's work reproduced here (Pls.19–21a) give some idea of his range and quality; that Sydney Parkinson possessed a highly cultivated sense of design is apparent in the large series of botanical drawings in the British Museum (Natural History). Even when he lacked time to complete the whole drawing, which happened more and more frequently after the death of Buchan at Tahiti, his outline is placed most beautifully on the sheet; a small section was carefully coloured together with precise notes on variation in form or hue (Pl.23). Other details that suggest the influence of a teacher such as De la Cour are present in some of his landscapes and will be discussed later.

When Sydney Parkinson was nineteen or twenty he and his widowed mother left Edinburgh for London where some of his flower paintings were exhibited by the Free Society in 1765 and 1766. It is probable that the Parkinsons already knew another Quaker, James Lee of the Vineyard Nursery, Hammersmith, a native of Selkirk, near Edinburgh. Lee engaged Sydney Parkinson to give drawing lessons to his daughter Ann, then thirteen years old. Her highly accomplished paintings may be seen in the Library of the Royal Botanic Gardens at Kew; there is also one in the National Library at Canberra.[23] Early in 1767 Lee introduced Parkinson to Banks who in turn put him in touch with Pennant. Banks set the young painter to work on collections he had made in Newfoundland and Labrador in 1766[24] and to copy a number of paintings executed for Gideon Loten, a former governor of Ceylon, which were reproduced in Pennant's *Indian Zoology*. Parkinson also painted exotic birds and insects in Banks's possession. These early Parkinson paintings, including all those of the Newfoundland and Labrador material, remained in the British Museum when the bulk of the natural history collections, including Parkinson's sets of botanical and zoological paintings from the *Endeavour*, were transferred to the Natural History Museum, as it was then known, in South Kensington. Many of the drawings in the British Museum, Bloomsbury, have not been identified or listed save for those connected with Banks's voyage to Newfoundland and Labrador, and a set by a less competent artist, one of the several midshipmen who sailed on Cook's second circumnavigation.[25]

Before sailing in the *Endeavour*, Parkinson made his will (10 July 1768), describing himself as a painter in the Parish of St Anne's, Soho, about to set out on a long and hazardous voyage from which 'God knows I may never return'. He was to die within two days of his fellow artist Spöring, in late January, 1771, soon after the *Endeavour* had sailed from Princes Island.

I do not wish to recapitulate here the unpleasant accusations that Banks had appropriated Parkinson's journal and collections brought by Stanfield Parkinson after the return to England. It is important, however, to draw attention to the fact that some of Sydney Parkinson's paintings may still be in the possession of his brother's descendants. Stanfield had two children who were also named Stanfield and Sydney; they were minors when their father died, insane, in 1776, their guardian being Jane Parkinson whose relationship to them is not known. More than one hundred years later in 1896 a so-called self portrait in oils of Sydney Parkinson was presented to the British Museum (Natural History). In 1950 Mr F. C. Sawyer, then in charge of the Zoology Library where the portrait used to hang, wrote a paper about Sydney Parkinson.[26] There was then a label on the back of the painting stating that it had been donated by a Mrs Smith of Purser's Cross Road, Fulham. Mr Sawyer and I discussed the possibility that there might be other material relating to Parkinson still in the possession of descendants of his family, but we lacked the courage to investigate the innumerable blind alleys into which the name of Smith might lead us. It has always been at the back of my mind however that such a search should at least be initiated and a few months ago I looked again at the painting. It had been sent to the restorers, and the paper label on the back had disappeared. Mr Rex Banks then checked the acquisition records at the British Museum (Natural History) and found that apparently the portrait had actually been donated by a Mr G. S. Parkinson of 44 Purser's Cross Road, Fulham. The ratepayers rolls of Fulham show no house numbered 44 Purser's Cross Road in 1896 but in 1899–1900 a Mrs C. Smith lived in one with this number; a fine art dealer, Frank Partridge, lived at no.42. These houses were in fact only built during the last years of the century. Somerset House records the death of George Seaborn Parkinson, on 24 September 1898. He left no will but letters of administration were granted to Sophia Eliza Parkinson, spinster.

ALEXANDER BUCHAN (Pl.1)

Searches carried out intermittently over many years for any information on Parkinson's fellow countryman, Alexander Buchan, have not revealed that any work of his was exhibited in London before Banks engaged him as one of his artists in the *Endeavour*, with special qualifications in portraiture and landscape. Yet such work must have been available and finally it became obvious that he must have been connected with the Scottish circle of Banks's friends, a group to which little attention has been paid, partly because after Banks had visited the Hebrides, Iceland and the Orkneys in 1772, he handed his journal and many of the drawings made during the voyage to Thomas Pennant who published Banks's account of Staffa in his own *Tour in Scotland and Voyage to the Hebrides*, 1774, 1776, with profuse acknowledgements to Banks, but with most of the plates redrawn and signed by his own draughtsmen.

It is possible that Banks visited Edinburgh when he was studying at Oxford. At all events he knew John Hope (1725–86) before he sailed to Newfoundland in 1766. Hope had studied in Edinburgh, in Glasgow and in continental medical schools. He graduated as a doctor of medicine from Glasgow in 1750; eleven years later he was appointed Professor of Botany and Materia Medica in Edinburgh. On 17 April 1766 he wrote to Banks recommending that Adam Freer, one of his favourite students with medical and botanical qualifications, should accompany Banks to Newfoundland as an assistant, but Banks and his friend Phipps had already left London for Plymouth. There are twenty-three letters from Hope to Banks, including this one of 1766, and two replies from Banks in the Library at the Royal Botanic Gardens, Kew, and in the British Library, but nearly all the rest of Hope's correspondence has disappeared. This is greatly to be regretted, not only was he King's Botanist for Scotland, but also Superintendent of the Royal Gardens in Edinburgh. It was he who was responsible for moving the Botanic Garden from its rather marshy position, where Waverley Station was later erected, to its present site. He had many friends amongst whom was James Burnett, better known as Lord Monboddo, a title he assumed in 1767. Monboddo was an upright judge and brilliant advocate. Moderate in his own tastes, he was a warm-hearted and generous man and held fortnightly 'learned suppers' at which Hope was a regular visitor.

Monboddo is best known for his early views on the evolution of man and the origin of language. His first volume *On the Origin and Progress of Language* appeared in 1773. This contained a report on Thomas Braidwood's successful treatment of a deaf-mute, Charles Sherriff, who learnt to read, write and speak, and ultimately became a successful miniature painter in London, Bath, Brighton and the West Indies. Braidwood set up an academy in Edinburgh for deaf-mutes which gained Dr Johnson's favourable commendation when he visited it in 1773.

Another eminent member of Monboddo's circle was Henry Home, Lord Kames, an enthusiastic supporter of William De la Cour. In addition to a keen interest in gardening and in painting, Home was actively involved in far-sighted engineering projects such as Watt's canal for linking the Clyde and the Firth of Forth. Watt was closely connected with the Lunar Circle, members of which Banks had met during his winter tour of the Midlands in 1767–68.[27] Some of the members to whom Banks refers besides Matthew Boulton, the closest friend he made at that time, included James Keir (1735–1820), described by Watt as 'A mighty chemist before the Lord and a very agreeable man'. Keir, an orphan, was educated in Edinburgh by his mother's brothers, the Linds. One of his cousins, James Lind (1736–1812), a medical man and an astronomer, travelled with Banks to the Hebrides, Iceland and the Orkneys in 1772. Thus Banks had a wide circle of Scottish acquaintances, and it may have been through any one of them that he learnt of the extremely accurate work of Alexander Buchan who nowhere in his *Endeavour* paintings and drawings suggests any tendency towards the romanticism that is apparent even in Sydney Parkinson's version of the Tierra del Fuegians, although Parkinson certainly does not carry it to the extremes that are only too obvious in Cipriani's engravings of Buchan's paintings. Cipriani appears to have seen even the most poorly endowed members of the human fraternity in terms of Greek mythology (Pls.3a, b; reproduced in Hawkesworth's official account).

Although Parkinson, Spöring and Buchan all drew natural history subjects with delicate precision,[28] their treatment of coastal profiles, people, artefacts and landscapes in general are fundamentally different. Bernard Smith commented on this long ago: 'Even when Buchan drew a group of natives his vision was free from conventions of style, his approach being entirely ethnographical . . . . . But when Parkinson drew the Fuegians he disposed them according to the dictates of composition and placed them in a picturesque setting'.[29] The question arises, where did Buchan acquire his professional training, and how was it that his family allowed a sufferer from epilepsy to set out on such a hazardous voyage? I have found no record of his birthplace but I have not yet examined the parish records of North Berwick where one branch of the Buchans is recorded as an old-established family. This was apparently the side of the family traditionally attached to the army; one Major Buchan, of whom there is an unfinished portrait by Raeburn, for a time owned the portrait of Alexander Buchan. Members of the other branch of the family were yeoman farmers.[30]

According to John Martine, writing about North Berwick in 1890,[31] 'A signal station was erected on the top of the Law in 1803, when Bonaparte's invasion was threatened. The ruins still remain, and are interesting relics of a former time. Lieutenant Leyden, a naval officer, connected with the town by marriage with Miss Buchan, an old North Berwick family, was in command of the station'. He also notes on another page that the new and spacious churchyard contains the burying places of many old native families and others, Dalrymples, Yules, Crawfords, Buchans, Walkers. Unfortunately when I made a methodical search of

18

the old churchyard in December, 1977, I failed to find a single Buchan headstone.

Major Buchan was a founder member of the famous North Berwick Golf Club, which held notable dinners. At each of these a member present would intimate a special donation for the next feast; John Kerr in his *Golf-Book of East Lothian* (1896), noted 'Captain Buckle, being on the spot, furnished such luxuries as a fishing village could afford, lobsters, crabs, crabs' claws and sand eels – Major Buchan sardines and cucumbers'.

Raeburn, who died in 1823, painted a soldier brother of the North Berwick major, resplendent in his Waterloo uniform. Members of the family still own these two Raeburn portraits and that of Alexander Buchan. The penultimate owner of Alexander Buchan's portrait was named Christian Leyden Braidwood Anderson. There may be perhaps some connection with John Leyden (1775–1811), the great Oriental scholar from Roxburghshire who made such an immense contribution to the initial studies of the Indo-Chinese languages. I had thought too that she (Christian Anderson) might have been a descendant of Thomas Braidwood, the famous teacher of deaf mutes, but I was, however, mistaken in this and am grateful to Professor Christopher Crowder[32] who has written to tell me that she inherited property from a relation by marriage, James Braidwood, a prosperous grocer and evangelist about whom there is a memorial volume. He died in Balerno, Edinburgh, in 1884.[33]

I have set these particulars down since it seems possible that papers relating to the young artist may still be in the possession of members of the family living in East or West Lothian today. There is still another possible connection. The surgeon's mate on Cook's Second Voyage round the world, was William Anderson, who was surgeon and naturalist on the Third Voyage. His father was a highly respected schoolmaster at North Berwick. The son died during the Third Voyage, and a diary which he kept of the Second has never been found. Parts of his diary of the Third Voyage are in the Public Record Office; his natural history notes are in the British Museum (Natural History). Anderson left all his belongings, apart from his natural curiosities which were to go to Banks, to an uncle, William Melvill, living at North Berwick Mains[34], and to his two sisters. George Dempster, brother of Lord Hailes and a friend of James Boswell, acted for them. Anderson is a very common Scottish name but it may be significant that the recent owner of the Buchan portrait referred to above was also named Anderson.

There are few references to Buchan in the journals from the *Endeavour* but there is a very pleasant quality about his drawings, a modesty about his signature, as indeed there is in the drawings signed by Parkinson and Spöring, and a compelling truthfulness about his work.

The first mention of the fact that Buchan was an epileptic comes in Banks's account of the climb to the hills in Tierra del Fuego;[35] it was 16 January 1769, midsummer in the southern hemisphere. Banks remarked that:

'The weather has all this time been vastly fine much like a sunshiny day in May, so that neither heat nor cold was troublesome to us nor were there any insects to molest us which made me think the traveling much better than what I had before met with in Newfoundland.

'Soon after we saw the plains we arrivd at them but found to our great disapointment that what we took for swathe [sward?] was no better than low bushes of birch about reaching a mans midle these were so stubborn that they could not be bent out of the way but at every step the leg must be lifted over them & on being plac'd again on the ground was almost sure to sink above the ankle in bog. no traveling could possibly be worse than this which seemd to last about a mile beyond which we expected to meet with bare rock for such we had seen from the tops of Lower hills as we came this I particularly was infinitely Eager to arrive at expecting there to find the alpine plants of a countrey so curious our people tho fatigued were yet in good spirits so we pushd on intending to rest as soon as we should arrive at plain ground.

'We proceeded two thirds of the way without the least difficulty & I confess that I thought for my own part that all difficulties were surmounted when Mr. Buchan fell into a fit a fire was immediately lit for him & with him all those who were most tird remain while Dr. Solander Mr Green Mr. Monkhouse & myself advancd for the alp which we reachd almost immediately & found according to expectation plants which answerd to those we had found before as alpine ones in Europe do to those which we find in the plains.

'The air here was very cold & we had frequent snow blasts'.

Banks goes on to describe the alarming effect of the drop in temperature as they descended; and how, although Buchan was much better when they reached him and his companions, Solander and Richmond insisted that they were too tired to proceed and lay down in the snow. Since it was clear that they were to be benighted Banks sent five men on to prepare a fire in a suitable place; Buchan, already much better, formed one of that party. Banks himself stayed behind to try to keep the others warm. A fire was started about a quarter of a mile further down the hill, and Banks with great difficulty got Dr Solander to his feet, but was obliged to leave Richmond and Dorlton and a seaman behind; Solander eventually was able to reach the rough shelter. Further unsuccessful attempts to move the other men were made but Dorlton and Richmond had drunk copiously of rum which had inadvertently been left behind, and worsening weather made it impossible to carry them through the difficult terrain. Banks and some others made a shelter for them and covered them with boughs but it became plain that they would be unlikely to survive a night's exposure under such conditions.

20

'At 6 O'Clock the sun came out a little & we immediately thought of sending to see whether the poor wretches we had been so anxious about last night were alive. Three of our people went but soon returnd with the melancholy news of their being both dead – Peter [Briscoe] continued very ill but said he thought himself able to walk Mr. Buchan thank god was much better than I could have expected so we agreed to dress our vulture [which had been shot the previous day] and set out for the ship'.

Buchan and Briscoe were unwell the next day but soon recovered, Buchan then made some very interesting records of the Ona peoples living on the parts of that coast visited by the *Endeavour*, as well as some more general paintings.

Banks has described how, when they were at sea, he and Solander sat with the artists and secretary at the round table in the Great Cabin from eight in the morning until two, when they had dinner, and continued working again at four in the afternoon. Solander had 'a delicate stomach' and could not bear the smell of cooking that permeated the Great Cabin after dinner. When they were cruising along a coast Buchan was sometimes up at dawn; Banks has noted the time of day on the verso of some of the coastal profiles. Spöring must have been a special friend of Buchan's since he labelled many of Buchan's paintings and larger drawings with his characteristic printing.

One of the problems concerning Buchan is his small output after the *Endeavour* rounded Cape Horn, when he sketched a profile of the coastline dated 25 January 1769, until land was sighted again on 4 April; he then drew Lagoon Island, now Vahitahi, and made other sketches including a faint outline of Tahiti dated 12 April; this seems to be his last drawing. His death occurred on 17 April. Cook recorded it:[36]

'At 2 oClock this Morning departed this Life Mr Alex Buchan landscip Draftsman to Mr. Banks, a Gentlemen well skil'd in his profession and one that will be greatly miss'd in the course of this Voyage, he had long been subject to a disorder in his Bowels which had more than once brought him to the Very point of death and was at the same time subject to fits of one of which he was taken on Saturday morning, this brought on his former disorder which put a period to his life. Mr Banks thought it not adviseable to Enterr the Body a shore in a place where we was utter strangers to the Customs of the Natives on such Occations, it was therefore set out to Sea and committed to that Element with all the decencey the circumstance of the place would admit of'.

Banks himself wrote:

'Dr Solander Mr Sporing Mr Parkinson and some of the officers of the ship attended his funeral. I sincerely regret him as an ingenious & good young man but his loss to me is irretrevable my airy dreams of entertaining my freinds in England with the scenes I am to see here are vanishd No account of the figures & dresses of men can be satisfactory unless illustrated with figures'.

The Master, Robert Molyneux, added a little more:

'At 2 AM departed this life Mr. Alexander Buchan who was much esteemed ..... at 10 sent 2 Boats (with Proper Persons) out to the Offing to Bury the deceas'd'.[37]

Cook himself added in a first draft of his holograph journal, 'there are now none on board that understands this sort of drawing'.[38]

The number of drawings and paintings by Buchan now in the Department of Manuscripts of the British Library scarcely seems to justify these comments by Cook and Molyneux. Did Buchan work his Tierra del Fuegian sketches into paintings that were later lost or stolen? He must have been active for some of the ten weeks that passed between Cape Horn and early April. Did he keep a journal, and were any of his papers sent to his family at the end of the voyage?

HERMAN DIEDRICH SPÖRING

The same questions may be asked about Spöring's work and papers. Luckily we know more about him and his background than we do of Buchan. No list of Spöring's drawings has been published since I identified those in the British Library many years ago. Recognition that he was one of Banks's artists is primarily thanks to Mr Alwynne Wheeler who observed this when he and I were working on the identification of the fishes from the *Endeavour* voyage, in connection with the publication of the late J. C. Beaglehole's edition of Banks's journal. Mr Wheeler noticed that Dryander (a Swede who became Banks's librarian after Solander's death in 1782) had written 'Sporing' on the bottom left-hand side of a drawing, and we then found several very fine studies by him of fishes and some other marine animals. That sent me off to the Department of Manuscripts at the British Museum (now the British Library) where to my astonishment there were many of his drawings previously regarded as the work of Parkinson or Buchan.[39] Through a Swedish friend I was put into touch with Professor Bengt Hildebrand who told me that Herman Diedrich Spöring had been born in Åbo, then Swedish, where his father held the Chair of Medicine. Recently Dr Louis Perret of Helsinki[40] and Mr J. B. Marshall of the British Museum (Natural History)[41] have added to our knowledge of him. H. D. Spöring, who bore the same names as his father, was born about 1733. He was a student at Åbo from 1748–53 and then went to Stockholm to practise surgery. His family were close personal friends of Linnaeus who perhaps

22

persuaded him to study natural history. His father had died in 1747; his only sister, Hedwig Ulrika Spöring, married a clergyman, Vasa Petrus Hedman. About 1755 he seems to have left Stockholm for London where he worked as a watchmaker for eleven years; towards the end of this time he was employed as a clerk by Solander at the British Museum. This is known from a statement by Solander in a letter sent from Rio to Linnaeus.[42] Much precise information about Spöring's work at the British Museum and on board the *Endeavour* has recently been elucidated by Mr J. B. Marshall in his paper 'The Handwriting of Sir Joseph Banks, his scientific staff and amanuenses'.[43] He has shown beyond doubt that copies of various works of Linnaeus annotated by Spöring are in the British Museum (Natural History), and that a number of manuscripts hitherto ascribed to Solander were written by Spöring. The most interesting of all these sets are some interleaved copies of the *Species Plantarum* and Solander's own copy of the *Systema Naturae*. Matthews knew of this latter edition and used some of the manuscript notes contained in it.[44] These volumes, with notes inserted by Spöring from Banks's and Solander's descriptions actually drawn up during the voyage of the *Endeavour*, are in remarkably good condition. They make a most noteworthy addition to the late Professor Carey Taylor's list of books carried by Banks in the *Endeavour*.[45]

Spöring's drawings are a fascinating collection comprising his exquisitely detailed studies of fishes, his accurate coastal profiles, ethnographical studies and landscapes (Pls.10–14,16a). They are all in pencil and have survived the years remarkably well. His age, he was about ten years older than Banks, and there was an even greater disparity between himself and the other two draughtsmen, has perhaps given rise to the impression that he was of a graver and more thoughtful disposition than was really the case. He scarcely gets any mention in any of the diaries; Cook, in the first draft of his journal[46] on the 5 May 1769, after the ship's quadrant had been stolen in Tahiti, commented: 'set up both the Clocks and got everything ready for setting up the Quad^t as soon as damages is repaired it sustaind by the Natives when in their Possession which Mr Sporing one of Mr Bankes gentlemen is about, to this gentlemen we are obliged for repairing ma[n]y defects we find in several of our Instruments'. Francis Wilkinson, one of the two master's mates, added a little:[47] 'upon the Second Examination of the Quadrent it was found Repairable. Mr Sporing one of Mr Banks Ingenious Gentleman has under taken it to Repair. Mr Banks being fortunatly in Possession of a Set of watch Makers tools & These Happy Circumstances makes all Easy again'.

When the transit of Venus was actually observed, Spöring, Munkhouse, Gore and Banks were all at York Island (Eimeo) now Moorea, where Spöring and Munkhouse made independent observations which were in due course presented to Maskelyne by Cook,[48] but Mr J. B. Marshall's recent attempts to trace this manuscript have so far been unsuccessful.

Spöring is mentioned in an entirely different context when the *Endeavour* was at Tolaga Bay, New Zealand. 'While Mr Sporing was drawing on the Island', Banks wrote, 'he saw a most strange bird fly over his head he describd it about as large as a Kite & brown like one. his tail however was of so Enormous a [   ] that he at first took it for a flock of small birds flying after him he who is a grave thinking man & is not at all given to telling wonderfull stories says he Judgd it to be at least [   ] yards in lengh'.

A careful scrutiny of Spöring's drawings suggests a brilliant draughtsman and a man with a delicious sense of the ridiculous. He was never betrayed into the theatrical gestures that Parkinson is sometimes led to employ but seems to have possessed a power of perception similar to that shown by Buchan in some of his Tierra del Fuegian studies. This feeling for comic situations is noticeable only in some details of larger drawings (Pl.14), and in his selection of some of the Maori carvings (Pls.12a,b). Since he and Solander were both friends and students of Linnaeus I have wondered whether other drawings by Spöring, his papers and letters, were sent back to Sweden after the voyage by Solander himself? They may yet be found in private possession, and perhaps throw some light on the enigmatic nature of the Swedish artist.

When Banks and Solander fell so ill in Batavia (Djarkarta), together with Peter Briscoe and James Roberts, shortly before the death of Tayeto, the Tahitian lad, and his master, Tupaia, Banks took a house in the country where their physician hoped that better air and a more exposed position might benefit them. Spöring, Cook's own servant and a seaman went to help look after them, but Spöring very soon developed malaria himself, and Cook, too, fell ill so that Banks immediately sent his servant back to the *Endeavour*. They were very fortunate in having a good doctor, of whom Banks wrote: 'Dr. Solander had chang'd much for the better within these last two days so that our fears of losing him were intirely dissipated for which much praise is due to his ingenious Physician Dr Jaggi who at this Juncture especialy was indefatigable'.

In spite of his illness Banks accumulated a large amount of information about Java, the flora and fauna, vocabularies, trading systems and superstitions. Parkinson was able to sketch some of the native craft and he made seventy-one plant studies, none of which was completed. I think that his unsigned work should be very carefully examined, with a view to determining whether any of it can possibly be attributed to Spöring. It seems rather curious that anyone with such a range of gifts as the Swedish secretary should apparently have produced no drawings at all after the *Endeavour* sailed from Australia.

The horrific tragedy of the dysentery and malaria that spread so disastrously through the men in the *Endeavour* after she sailed from Java left Cook with so sickly a crew that they were scarcely able to man the ship. It was a doubly cruel ordeal for him, who, aided by Banks's and Solander's knowledge of anti-scorbutic plants, had been able to keep his crew remarkably free from scurvy on their long voyage.

It was this additional strain that perhaps accounts for Cook's terse records of the deaths of Spöring and Parkinson on 25 and 27 January 1771: 'Departed this Life Mr Sporing a Gentleman belonging to Mr Banks's retinue', and on the following Sunday, 'Departed this Life Mr Sidney Parkinson, Natural History Painter to Mr Banks'. There is apparently no record anywhere of his appreciation of the coastal views and profiles that they had contributed to the records of the voyage.

Solander was desperately ill again at Capetown but much better, though extremely emaciated, when they left for St Helena in mid-April. They spent three days on that island and finally sailed for England, landing at Deal on 12 July.

BANKS'S ARTISTS AFTER HIS RETURN TO ENGLAND

Banks had a magnificent collection of drawings, biological and ethnographical material to be dealt with. He immediately engaged a group of artists to complete the drawings of his botanical and ethnographical collections. First and foremost were the brothers James and John Frederick Miller (Pl.29b), two of the twenty-seven children of Johann Sebastian Müller, a professional engraver from Nuremberg, who came to England in 1744 and made a living engraving portraits of the royal family. Müller was a great admirer of Linnaeus and was chiefly interested in botanical illustration. With the Millers, Banks engaged John Cleveley, junior, whose father, a shipwright, sometimes painted nautical subjects; for this reason the son invariably added Jr. to his signature. In a few cases, persons unfamiliar with the family situation have changed the inscription below the drawing from Jr. to Jan^ry. Another son, James, was a carpenter on Cook's Third Voyage. He too, had a certain facility for drawing; some of his sketches were worked up into aquatints by his brother John and sold singly.

The Miller brothers and John Cleveley Jr. worked steadily and consistently for Banks, who also employed various other artists from time to time (Pl.30). These included James Roberts, a professional etcher, who probably had no connection at all with the young collector in the *Endeavour*; the Barralet brothers who made a number of copies of drawings by Parkinson and Spöring. John James Barralet (1747–1815) and J. Melchior Barralet (n.d.), appear to have both been born in Ireland. There are two examples of their work (one signed J. Barralet and another signed J. J. Barralet) in British Library Add. MS 15508, ff.4, 20 (Pl.17). I am inclined to think that other unsigned work in this volume can be attributed to them. Frederick Polydore Nodder completed many of Parkinson's botanical drawings; amongst the engravers was a rascally Sibelius, who had formerly been in the service of the great Dutch naturalist, Pierre Lyonnet, but who had fled, deserting his family (after prostituting his wife and daughter) and heavily in debt to his baker. Lyonnet wrote to Banks in January, 1775,[49] asking him to stop paying Sibelius until the debt was wiped out, or alternatively that he would take over the debt himself if Banks would send him some of the shells from the South Seas as he had promised.

The most famous artist of all those engaged by Banks at this juncture was George Stubbs, who painted the strangest animal of all those discovered during the voyage, the kangaroo. Using the skin, the skull and Parkinson's sketches he executed a charming oil painting which was engraved for the official account of the voyage. The engraving was printed as pl.20 in Vol.3 of the 1773 edition of Hawkesworth; it faces p.561, and lacks attributions to both painter and engraver. The painting was exhibited at the time and then disappeared from all the records. Then, oddly enough, it was shown at a Stubbs exhibition at the Whitechapel Art Gallery, where it was seen by my friend and neighbour, the late Eric Newton. He drew my attention to it, and we recognised the long-lost original of the engraving.[50]

The owner also possessed what purported to be a Stubbs painting of a dog from New Holland. Banks had mentioned that the Aboriginals had dogs but there was no mention of any having been shot; furthermore the painting was considered by Dr Peter Crowcroft, Miss Phyllis Mander Jones and myself to bear no resemblance to dingoes as we know them today. In the absence of any reliable records we decided that it had probably been acquired elsewhere and that we would not admit it to the scientific records. Just before Christmas, 1977, I was searching the Scottish newspapers at the Newspaper Library, Colindale, to see whether the deaths of the two able young Scottish painters in the *Endeavour* had been noticed, and found the following note in the *Edinburgh Advertiser*, 6 September 1771, p.157; it was printed in the *London Evening Post* a week earlier and was reproduced in the 1968 reprint of Beaglehole's edition of Cook's *Journals*[51], where I had failed to notice it; it originated from a letter written by someone in the *Endeavour*, dated Woolwich, 18 July:

'The savages were very troublesome in New Holland, attacking us very often; and by setting all the sea grass on fire round the ship at low-water, they were very near burning the vessel, and blowing up all our powder. Upon this barbarous shore we took an uncommon curious animal, which weighed upwards of 80 pounds; it was formed like a rat in the face and run erect upon its hinder legs . . . Upon this inhospitable shore I shot a large dog, which when we were at short allowance of provisions, we eat with great greediness, notwithstanding it had a most fishy taste – but hunger will bring the human stomach to any repast when deeply necessitated'.

The skin was probably brought back to England but it seems unlikely that Banks bothered about the skeleton which could account for the unconvincing nature of Stubbs's painting.

The general excitement over the safe return of the *Endeavour* to England was immense. For Banks himself there was the joyful reunion with his mother and sister, his numerous other relations and friends. He and Solander were presented to King George III, and both were awarded honorary degrees by the University of Oxford. At the same time they were busy with the mass of herbarium material to be carefully mounted and labelled, and with the arrangement of the zoological collections; Banks's chief assistant in this latter task was the neat-fingered Jenner,[52] later to be so famous for his work on vaccination. Any gardener will sympathise with Banks in the pleasure he must have felt in introducing numbers of exotic species of plants, presenting material to Kew and in giving away, with typical generosity, a large proportion of his treasures. A manuscript list of the institutions and persons to whom he sent seeds exists but has not been published. Finally there were the very substantial ethnographical collections to be labelled and exhibited.

Unfortunately two time-consuming ordeals of a much less agreeable nature had to be faced. Abandoning all his original prejudices against matrimony, clearly expressed in a letter to his old school friend William Phelp Perrin, March 1768,[53] Banks had, on the very eve of sailing, in a mood of over-excitement and too many farewell parties, rashly become engaged to a certain Harriet Blosset, a ward of his friend James Lee of the Vineyard Nursery, Hammersmith, who had doubtless encouraged the match. After all the delights of Tahiti, the deep interest of the voyage, and the kindness shown to himself and Solander at Capetown (where he went so far as to say that he thought that a Dutch girl would make a perfect wife if he were inclined for matrimony), Banks was appalled at the realisation that he had formally engaged himself to Harriet. He lost all the moral courage which he had so often displayed during the voyage, refused to meet her, then, forced to do so by his friends and family, did so, retracted, gave way and altogether behaved very badly before the engagement was finally broken off. Her feelings were somewhat soothed by a substantial payment, a circumstance there is no reason to doubt, since it was related by Lee's son in the Foreword to the 1810 edition of his father's *Introduction to the Science of Botany*.

Even more painful to Banks must have been the accusation by Sydney Parkinson's brother Stanfield that he had stolen the journal kept by the young artist with whom he had worked so closely for so long. The whole story has been related elsewhere several times. Its importance lies in the fact that Stanfield obtained a fragmentary version of the journal which was given to a hack writer and rushed into print in order to forestall the official version of the voyage. It was forcibly withdrawn from circulation and finally appeared in 1784 with full prefaces completely exonerating Banks and a Quaker, Dr John Fothergill, who had tried to act as intermediary and was then, in turn, accused by Stanfield who shortly afterwards became insane and died.[54]

In the meantime Banks had handed over, on loan, not only the fragmentary journal but also Sydney's collections and some of the paintings which undoubtedly belonged to him since he had commissioned them. Some things were never returned. In Parkinson's journal there are plates such as those of the Australian Aboriginals, and of Tayeto playing the nose flute, which are unrepresented in Banks's own collection; not only was there ample opportunity for loss and muddle here, but there was also the matter of Banks's assisting Hawkesworth with the preparation of the official account of the voyage. Hawkesworth borrowed Banks's journal, and many of the drawings for the engravers to work from. What Banks must have felt when the curious versions by Cipriani, Bartolozzi (Pls.3a,b) and others appeared, with their extraordinary distortions of his artists' careful work, and when the illustrations of his own carefully labelled ethnographical collections were published without any detailed captions, can be surmised from a comment written by Solander to the Earl of Hardwick in 1774:[55] 'Nothing is more certain', he wrote, 'than that the Publication of the South Sea Voyages at last became a *perfect Jobb* which has been extreemly disagreeable to Those who had in some measure a hand in it'.

There are very odd gaps to be accounted for when the collections of drawings are collated with the journals. There is for instance the loss of the original from which Will Byrne engraved the scene of the *Endeavour* on the beach at Cooktown (Pl.13). We do not even know whether this is based on work by Spöring or by Parkinson. The details of the anchors, the masts, ropes, stores and tents, suggest Spöring to me. Furthermore, some plates we know to be based on signed originals in the British Library, usually bear no attribution save to the engraver, and sometimes not even to him.

The absence of drawings by Spöring after his studies of Australian fishes is another curious gap. And even odder is the fact that we know that Banks collected New Zealand and Australian birds but only a sketch of the Banksian cockatoo survives. Some of the descriptions in Parkinson's journal make it possible to identify the species mentioned but the fact that he has noted the colouring of the soft parts suggests that he had uncompleted drawings which he intended to finish later (Pl.23). Some descriptions are muddled up so that New Zealand and Australian species are confused, a fact commented on long since.[56]

28

There are also some misattributions in the botanical and ethnographical material. Thus there are drawings clearly labelled 'Amsterdam Island', some folios of plants labelled 'The Friendly Isles', not one of which was visited on the First Voyage. The plants are from Tahiti and other Society Islands (individual plants are correctly localised). Some Polynesian baskets and other artefacts supposedly from Tonga were drawn by John Cleveley in 1774 (Pl.30), many months before Cook returned from the Second Voyage. They are clearly signed and dated.

There is one last comment I should like to make before going on to catalogue some of the drawings by Buchan, Spöring and Parkinson in the Department of Manuscripts, British Library, with which I have been particularly concerned over many years, since they complement the natural history drawings to which I was, so to speak, apprenticed by the late Sir Norman Kinnear when the publication of Cook's journals was initiated by the Hakluyt Society. In 1911 Edward Smith wrote *The Life of Sir Joseph Banks*; it was a scholarly work of over 200,000 words. He took it to twelve publishers before the Bodley Head accepted it on condition that he reduced it to just over half its original length, and made it suitable for the general reader.[57] Hence, eventually, it was published without documentation. On pp.15–16 occurs in quotes the well-known reply to someone suggesting that, instead of sailing in the *Endeavour*, Banks should make the Grand Tour of Europe: 'Every blockhead does that; my Grand Tour shall be one round the whole globe'. Endlessly quoted, without reference to context, it has inevitably strengthened the impression that Banks was a wealthy amateur in search of new scenes and excitements. Even Bernard Smith, who presents a much more sympathetic view of Banks in his *European Vision and the South Pacific 1758–1860*, (1969) than does the late J. C. Beaglehole in his many publications, comments (*op.cit.*p.17) that the landscape views and ethnographical illustrations that Parkinson made were chosen because they were curious enough to be interesting to a virtuoso, and goes on to quote Banks's description of a natural arch in Tolaga Bay, New Zealand, 24 October 1769. Smith continues, 'In this description Banks might satisfy the exacting requirements that a friend like Falconer might demand and also demonstrate as Falconer wished that nature was superior to art, but the language is nevertheless that of a young gentleman of taste vindicating his decision to go south with Cook. For Banks's description is carefully composed like a painting'.

I think that quite a different interpretation may be placed upon the whole of Smith's arguments on this page. England's greatest contribution to art in the eighteenth century is quite generally considered to have been the development of landscape gardening brought to perfection by William Kent, 'Capability' Brown and Humphrey Repton; this is reflected in the poetry and prose of the time, as J. D. Hunt and Peter Willis have shown in their delightful *The Genius of the Place; the English Landscape Garden 1620–1820* (1975). It is emphasised in William

Robin's rococo paintings of the middle of the eighteenth century, and Banks was steeped in the whole movement. His cousins at Burghley House were employing Brown to transform the famous Elizabethan gardens when he was in his teens; he had other cousins at Stowe where Brown was altering Kent's original achievements. In Lisbon in the winter of 1766–67 he was trying to persuade his friend, Gerard de Visme, to lay out a garden in the Cobham style; de Visme commented that Banks would be among the worthies in the niches.[58]

The language in which Banks described the view at Mt Edgcumbe at Plymouth when he was waiting to sail to Newfoundland in April, 1766 might have been written by one of his Scottish friends:

> 'Went today with a Party to Mount Edgecomb which I cannot say answerd my Expectation. tis situated on the side of a hill Looking down over Plymouth town dock & harbour My Lord Seems not to have Enough followed the Modern Taste as the Chief beauties you are carried to see are walks each Terminated by a tower 70 ft which you see from one situation the views are all of Buildings except that which Commanded the Mouth of the Harbour which being broken by a very *Bold Hill* Mewstone is as beautiful as any thing of that Kind can Possibly be ...'

That same summer Henry Home (Lord Kames) wrote to Mrs Edward Montagu of Denton, Northumberland about her recent visit to him saying [you have]:

> 'inspired me with most valuable hints for my rural embellishments ... That walk is to be extended over a great variety of ground, and to take in a variety of objects, so as to make a circuit of not less than four miles. One part is enchanting! The road sinks imperceptibly into a hollow, originally the bed of a river, lined on both sides with high banks covered with wood which hides every object from the sight but the sky. Emerging into open daylight, the first object that strikes the eye is the noble Castle of Stirling, situated on a rock, wild and Romantic!'[59]

That Banks placed scientific accuracy above all else in the work of his artists is supported by a careful comparison of some versions of the same scene in the folios catalogued below. Thus the accurate sketch by Spöring of a Maori Pa at Motuarohia, Bay of Islands,[60] New Zealand, was copied by Barralet for Banks in preference to the romanticised but less accurate version by Parkinson (Pls.16a, 17). There are many other instances; twenty years later, on 12 December 1793, the diarist Farington wrote: 'Sir Joseph Banks and Lysons called, and I showed them the sketches I had made at Valenciennes. Sir Joseph had his feet inclosed in large Stuff Shoes yet stood the whole time of his stay, as He said to avoid too much indulgence. *Accuracy of drawing* seems to be a principal recommendation to Sir Joseph', and the diarist underlined that key phrase.

30

In fact, Banks's rigorous search for accuracy, his insistence on professionalism in the carefully planned and documented scientific work carried out by his staff and himself in the *Endeavour*, was a prototype for such voyages from then on, culminating in the profoundly valuable work of research ships such as the *Challenger*, a century later, and in the establishment of marine biological stations all over the world, in all latitudes. This brief summary of the lives and work of Parkinson, Buchan and Spöring will perhaps act as a pointer to areas where further information about these artists may be found, and may help in the search for their missing sketchbooks and notes, many of which are very probably still in the possession of the descendants of their families. It is less than a year since the portrait of Buchan was traced, and only four months have elapsed since I was shown an unrecorded oil painting of a sea captain who had been an A.B. in the *Dolphin* when Tahiti was discovered.

The Drawings

The drawings by Banks's artists fall into two groups: most of those depicting the natural history collections are in the British Museum (Natural History); the bulk of the remaining material is in the Department of Manuscripts of the British Library. That there are others in private hands is almost certainly true, but our knowledge of these is fragmentary; one of the purposes of the essay preceding this catalogue is to stimulate a search for a number of originals which are known to have existed, and for others which circumstantial evidence suggests went astray both during and after the voyage.

The bird paintings from all three of Cook's voyages were catalogued in 1959 but there is no catalogue of the other zoological paintings from the *Endeavour*, including those by Buchan and Spöring, which, together with the bird paintings, are all bound together in three volumes attributed to Parkinson. The correct attributions were long ago noted by Dryander who wrote the artist's name on the lower left-hand corner of each plate; various manuscript lists confirm these names.

The botanical paintings by Parkinson are bound in eighteen folio volumes in the British Museum (Natural History). They need careful re-examination with a view to deciding whether any of the unsigned work could possibly be by Buchan or Spöring. Many years ago I made a note that ff.29, 32, 33 and 34 of the *Plants of Madeira* might perhaps be by Buchan.

It is hoped that detailed lists of all the zoological and botanical drawings will be published in the proposed facsimile edition of Banks's *Endeavour* diary. Documentation of all the identifications of plants and animals in the Hakluyt series of Captain Cook's journals was to have been published in a fourth volume but finally this was abandoned, to be replaced by the late J. C. Beaglehole's life of Cook. For this and other reasons the following lists of drawings by Buchan, Spöring and Parkinson will be confined to four volumes in the British Library, Add. MS 15507, 15508, 23920, and 23921. There will also be brief references to some curious copies of these drawings in Add. MS 7085. Parkinson's sketchbook, Add. MS 9345, is to be published in facsimile and is therefore not included here.

In the following lists annotations by Banks are indicated as J. B.; those by Spöring as H. D. S., and those by Buchan himself as A. B. Whether the notes are on the recto or verso is denoted by r. or v.

THE DRAWINGS BY ALEXANDER BUCHAN

Add. MS 15507

f.1a Watercolour drawing; five joined sections (right to left), each bearing the same annotation by J. B. on the verso: 'Bay on the Coast of S. America, Lat.21.29 Novr 9 1768'.

f.1b Wash drawing; two strips joined. J. B. v. 'Novr 12 1768 8 O'Clock in the Morn'.

f.2a Pencil and wash drawing; three strips joined. J. B. v. (left to right): 'Novr 12 1768 at Noon. Novr 12 1768 Noon. Novr 12 1768 At Noon the Land of Cape Frio appeared thus N 51 E is the Island which Lays off the Cape/A Cape Frio'.

f.2b Wash drawing. J. B. v. 'Thus appeard the Harbour of Rio Janeiro in the Evening of Novr 12 1768'.

f.3a Wash drawing; two strips joined. J. B. v. (left strip) 'Thus appeard the Entrance of the harbour of Rio Janeiro Novr 13 1768 at 6. in the morn Distant about two Leagues'.
(Right strip)   1 Sugar loaf
                2
                3
                4 The entrance within the Island No 2'.

f.3b Pencil drawing; three strips joined. J. B. v. 'a [right hand] No.1 Entrance of the harbour of Rio de Janeiro the ship supposd to be between the heads' No.2 The Entrance of the harbour of Rio de Janeiro
Fig.1 The Fort of Sta Cruz
    2 Ilhoa dos cobras

3 Benedictins convent

4 Sugar loaf

No.3 Entrance into the harbour of Rio de Janeiro.

f.3c   Pencil and wash drawing. J. B. v. 'Monte de St Jōā The Sugar loaf hill in the Entrance of the Harbour of Rio de Janeiro'.

f.4a   The Island of Teneriffe; three pencil sketches probably by Spöring q.v.

f.4b   Pencil and wash drawing; two strips joined. J. B. v. No.1 'Sierra de Sorgho a remarkable ridge of Mountains which appear almost opposite the town of Rio de Janeiro Cross the river & very far up in the Countrey'.
No.2 'Sierra de Sorgho'.

f.5a   Wash drawing; six strips joined. J. B. r. 'First sight of Terra del Fuego Jan 11 1769'.

f.5b   Wash drawing; four strips joined. J. B. r. 'Second Sight of Terra del Fuego Jan. 12 1769'.

f.6a   Pencil and wash drawing. J. B. v. [in ink] '1769 Jan^ry 12 Stood into this bay with the ship but found no likelyhood of shelter'; 'a bay in terra del Fugo [sic] Stood into with the ship Jan 12 1769' [in pencil].

f.6b   Painting in gouache, rather sombre, of the *Endeavour* against the hills. J. B. v. 'Jan.12 1769 Lat.'.

f.7a   Wash drawing. J. B. v. '1769 Jan^ry 13 $\frac{1}{2}$ past 10 Coast of Terra del Fuego from the Streights
     a Cape Gonzalez
     b the bay of Good Success
     c Prince Ruperts bay where we stopd tide
     d Snow on the hills which we attempted to reach Jan. & almost got to'.

f.7b   Wash drawing; two strips joined. J. B. v. 1 '1769 Jan^ry 13 at 11 O Clock Staten land appeard thus'; 2 '1769 Jan^ry 13 11 O Clock'
A. B. v. 'Staten Land Jan^ry 13 at 11 o'clock'.

f.8a   Wash drawing; two strips joined. Right hand strip A. B. r. '1,2,3 The brothers; 4 a hill like a shugar Loaf up the Country'. A. B. v. 'Terra dell Fuego the west entrance into Straits Le maire taken at 7 o clock Jan 13 1769'. J. B. v. '2 1769 Jan. 13 7 O'Clock'.
Banks repeated most of these notes in ink on the verso of the left-hand strip: 'Jan^ry 13 Terra del Fuego at the entrance of the Streights 1: 2: 3: Hills calld the three brothers

4 Sugar Loaf
5 Cape St Vincent
6 Entrance of the bay in which we landed Jan: 14
7 Cape St. Diego'
The drawing shows the *Endeavour*.

f.8b   Wash drawing. A. B. v. 'Staten Land'. J. B. v. 'Cape St. Bartholomew on Staten land appeard with the needle open thus soon after we enterd the Streights'.

f.9a   Wash drawing; three strips joined. J. B. r. 'South Side of Terra del Fuego Jan 23 1769'. A. B. r. 'N.53 W Dist 5 Leagues'.

f.9b   Wash drawing. Uninscribed; it shows the Sugar Loaf N.N.E.

f.10a   Wash drawing. J. B. v. '1769 Jan^{ry} 24 Small Island set round with pointed rocks' in ink, repeated in pencil! 'Small Island with rocks Jan 24 1769'.

f.10b   Wash drawing; two strips joined. J. B. v. (1) '1769 Jan. 25 11 O'Clock The southermost [sic] land we saw supposd to be Hermits Islands on which the french place cape Horn behind the Westernmost land we saw another headland which we supposd to be the cape but a mist coverd it before it could be drawn'. Also in pencil, 'Island in terra Fuego Jan 25' (2) '1769 Jan^{ry} 25 11 O'Clock'. (Pls.7a,b).

f.11a   Wash drawing; two strips joined. Lagoon island A. B. v. 'first view of the first Island'. J. B. v. 'No.1 Lagoon Island'. Another hand, '4th Apr. 1769' J. B. v. 'No.2 Lagoon Island first view of first Island'.

f.11b   Wash drawing; two strips joined. Left-hand strip. Anon. r. 'Lagoon island'. J. B. v. '2 view of first Island'. 'No.1 Lagoon Island'. unknown hand, '4th apr.' Right-hand strip. A. B. v. 'Second view of the first Is. J. B. v. No.2 Lagoon Island'.

f.12a   Wash drawing. ? H. D. S. r. 'Thrum-cap Island'.

f.12b   Wash drawing. ? H. D. S. r. 'Thrum-cap Island'. A. B. r. 'Distance one League Apr^l 4, 1769'.

f.13a   Wash drawing. J. B. r. 'Bow island'.

f.13b   Wash drawing. Unknown hand, r. 'The Groups'. (Pl.9) [A very pleasant sketch showing natives pushing off in their canoes.]

f.14a   Wash drawing. J. B. v. '6 of april 1769 The Groups'.

f.14b   Wash drawing; three strips joined. A.B.r. 'Distance 4 Leagues; No.3 Distance 1½ Leagues Distance 2½ Leagues'. J.B.v. 'April 8 1769 Chain Island' [very faint].

f.15a   Wash drawing. H.D.S.r. 'Osnaburgh island'. J.B.v. 'Mahitea April 9 1769 6 oClock p.m. osnabrugh Island'.

f.15b   Wash drawing. J.B.v. 'Mahitea Island april 10 8 OClock'.

f.15c   Wash drawing. J.B.v. 'Mahitea April 10 10 min past 12 Osnabrug Island'.

f.16a   Wash drawing; two strips joined. J.B.r. 'Otaheite'. J.B.v. 'Otahite april 11. 6 p.m.'

f.16b   Outline drawing; two strips joined. J.B.r. 'Otaheite'. A.B.v. 'G.I. April 12 10 a m'. [G.I. stands for George's Island.]

f.17a   Pencil outline drawing; three strips joined. This is the last of Buchan's coastal profiles. Two have a note in his hand on the verso of two of the strips: 'G.I. April 12 at 4 p.m.' The third has a note on the recto in Parkinson's hand 'a cascade of water'. On the verso Banks wrote 'Otaheite'. Buchan died on 17 April 1769.

The remaining coastal profiles and other views in this volume are by Spöring. There is one painting by Buchan in Add. MS 15508, the remainder are in Add. MS 23920.

Add. MS 15508

The single painting by Buchan in Add. MS 15508 is the first folio. This is a painting of necklaces worn by the Tierra del Fuegians; see also ff.20a and b, Add. MS 23920. A.B.r. 'A. Buchan pinxt! J.B.v. 'Necklaces of the inhabitants of Terra del Fuego'. Banks also collected bows and arrows there which he brought back and which were painted by J.F. Miller. See Add. MS 15508 f.2.

Add. MS 23920

ff.7–9   Three pencil drawings of Rio de Janeiro, the first is unsigned, the second and third are inscribed 'A. Buchan Delint. Nov. 1768', and 'A. Buchan Delint 1768'. The labelling is by Spöring in his characteristic printing, which may also be seen on his drawings of fishes in the British Museum (Natural History), as well as elsewhere in the British Library.

f.7. 'A. Ilha dos Cobros with the Sugar-loaf B appearing behind it. CC Fort

St. Sebastian. D Careening-place. E Way the Boats went to the Town'.
f.8 'View of the Town of Rio Janeiro from the Anchoring-Place'. (Pl.2)
f.9 F The Guard-Boat. G The Old Ambuscade. H Convent of Benedictines. I The Bishop's Palace. K A decay'd Fort. L Fishermens Houses.

f.11a   Pencil study of figures at the watering-place of the *Endeavour*, Tierra del Fuego. Unsigned. (Pl.5a).

f.11b   Painting, signed 'A. Buchan delint'. H. D. S. r. 'A View of the Endeavour's Watering-place in the Bay of Good Success'.

f.12   Wash drawing. Signed 'A. Buchan Delint'. Anon. r. 'An Indian Town at Terra del Fuego'.

f.14   Painting of hut, Tierra del Fuego. Signed 'A. Buchan delint'. Buchan's signature is on the lower right margin of the painting. H. D. S. r. 'Inhabitants of the Island of Terra del Fuego in their Hut'. (Pl.4a)

f.16   Painting of a Tierra del Fuegian. Signed on stone, 'A. Buchan'. H. D. S. r. 'A Man of the Island of Terra del Fuego'.

f.17   Painting, unsigned. H. D. S. r. 'A Woman of the Island of Terra del Fuego'. (Pl.6)

f.18   Five pencil sketches are mounted on this folio, four by Parkinson and a fifth by Buchan which shows a man in two different poses. J. B. v. 'Buchan not finished'. (Pls.5b,c)

f.20a   Water colour painting, signed 'A. Buchan Pinxt'. ? H. D. S. r. 'Ornaments used by the People of Terra del Fuego'.
Fig.I 'Necklace made of broken pieces of Shells, neatly polished.
Fig.II 'Do. made of broken pieces of Screw-Shells'.

f.20b   Unsigned water colour painting by Buchan. H. D. S. r. 'Ornaments used by the People of Terra del Fuego'.
Fig.I Necklace made of Birds-Bones.
Fig.II Do. of small Shells beautifully polished.
Fig.III Bracelet of Seeds and pieces of Shells'.

f.21a   Water colour 'A. Buchan Pinxt'. H. D. S. r. 'A Man's Head-Dress from Terra del Fuego'.

f.21b   Unsigned water colour, Buchan. H. D. S. r. 'Bow, Quiver & Arrows of the Inhabitants of Terra del Fuego'.

It is possible that Buchan drew some details of Chart 3 in Add. MS 7085. The top profile is very similar in style to his own record (Pl.7a) of that part of the coast of Tierra del Fuego; he or Spöring could have been responsible for the unusual form of Cook's name – Lieut. I. Cook instead of J. or James. See Pl.8c, but Mr J. B. Marshall and I have been unable to identify the actual printer.

This brings us to the end of Buchan's records other than the dozen zoological drawings which it is hoped will be listed in another publication largely devoted to Banks's records and collections.

THE DRAWINGS BY HERMANN DIEDRICH SPÖRING

All of Spöring's drawings in the Department of Manuscripts, British Library are in pencil; any exceptions are noted.

Add. MS 15507

f.4a   Island of Teneriffe; two pencil sketches on one sheet, probably by Spöring.
        ? r. 'Barga Leone'.

Although Spöring seems to have made no drawings other than this sketch until after Buchan's death at Tahiti he was certainly printing his beautifully professional labels on some of Buchan's work. He must have been very busy making fair copies of the zoological and botanical descriptions drafted by Banks and Solander on this first extensive survey of marine life to be carried out systematically during a voyage round the world. Banks had collected seaweed and some marine animals during his voyage to Newfoundland but here he had the specialised help of Solander, as well as of Briscoe, Roberts, Dorlton and Richmond and was better equipped with nets, fishing tackle, preservatives and containers.

f.17b   Pencil drawing. H. D. S. r. 'View of Åhiteråa, 5 miles distant Aug. 14 1769'. [Now known as Rurutu.]

ff.18a, 18b, 19a, 19b and 20a, are all coastal profiles of Poverty Bay, New Zealand, each labelled and numbered 1 to 5 on the recto, Taoneroa by Spöring. On the verso of 18a he has written 'New-Zeeland Oct. 8 1769'.

f.20b   H. D. S. r. 'View of Cape Kidnappers from the N.E.'.
        H. D. S. v. 'New-Zeeland Oct. 15th 1769'.

f.21a   H. D. S. r. 'View of Cape Kidnappers from the S.E.'.

f.21b   H. D. S. r. 'Table Cape'.
        H. D. S. v. 'New-Zeeland Oct 19th 1769'.

f.22a   H. D. S. r. 'Gable-end Foreland'.
          H. D. S. v. 'New-Zeeland Oct. 19th. 1769'.

f.22b   H.D.S. r. 'View of Gable-end Foreland from the N.N.E.'.
          H. D. S. v. 'New-Zeeland Oct 19th 1769 at Sun-set'.

f.23a   H. D. S. r. 'View to the N.ward near Gable-end Foreland'.
          H. D. S. v. 'New-Zeeland Oct. 19th 1769 at Sun-set'.

f.23b   H. D. S. r. 'Tegadoo Bay' 'No.1'.
          H. D. S. v. 'New-Zeeland Oct. 20 1769'.

f.24a   H. D. S. r. 'Tegadoo Bay' 'No.2'. (Pl.11)

f.24b   H. D. S. r. 'Tegadoo Bay' 'No.3'.

f.25a   H. D. S. r. 'Tegadoo Bay' 'No.4'.

f.25b   H. D. S. r. 'Tegadoo Bay' 'No.5'.

f.26a   H. D. S. r. 'Tolaga' 'No.1'.
          H. D. S. v. 'New-Zeeland Oct 23^d 1769'.

f.26b   H. D. S. r. 'Tolaga' 'No.2'.

f.27a   H. D. S. r. 'Tolaga' J. B. 'No.3'.

f.27b   H. D. S. r. 'Spöring's Islands Tolaga Watering Place' 'No.4'.

f.28a   H. D. S. r. 'Spöring's Islands Entrance to Tolaga Bay Dist. 5 miles'.
          H. D. S. v. 'New-Zeeland Oct 29th 1769'.

f.28b   H. D. S. r. 'The Island of Moutohora'.
          H. D. S. v 'New-Zeeland Nov.1st 1769'.

f.29a   H. D. S. r. 'View of the land on the S.W. side of Cape Runaway' v. 'New-Zeeland Nov 1st 1769 at 5 P.M'.

f.29b   H. D. S. r. 'The Court of Aldermen'.
          H. D. S. v. 'New-Zeeland Novr 3^d 1769 at 9 a.m.' (cf. Sydney Parkinson, Add. MS 9345 f.58b).

f.30a   H. D. S. r. 'View of the land to the S.E. of Opuragi'.
          H. D. S. v. 'New-Zeeland Nov 3^d 1769 at 3 P.M.'.

f.30b   H. D. S. r. 'Opuragi Mercury Islands' 'No.1'.
          H. D. S. v. 'New Zeeland Nov. 3^d 1769'.

f.31a   H. D. S. r. 'Opuragi' (Oyster River marked) 'No.2'.

f.31b H.D.S.r. 'Opuragi' (Watering place and Mangrove River marked). 'No.3'.

f.32a H.D.S.r. 'Opuragi' (Spöring's Grotto and Wharretouwa marked). 'No.4'.

f.32b H.D.S.r. 'Komotura, Opuragi Going out of the Harbour' 'No.5'.

f.33a H.D.S.r. 'Cape Colvill'.
H.D.S.v. 'New-Zeeland Nov 18th 1769 at 6 a.m.'.

f.33b H.D.S.r. 'Cape Brett & Piercy Island Motugogago'.
H.D.S.v. 'Motugogago This view appeared very nearly the same at the opposite ends of the compass New-Zeeland Nov 26th 1769 at 9 A.M.'.

f.34a H.D.S.r. 'Motuaro, [Bay marked] 'Here we landed' 'No.1'.

f.34b H.D.S.r. 'Motuaro' 'No.2'.

f.35a H.D.S.r. 'Motuaro The Hippa' 'No.3'.
H.D.S.v. 'New-Zeeland Nov 29 1769'.

f.35b H.D.S.r. 'East Cape Dist. 2 Leagues East-Island'.
H.D.S.v. 'New-Zeeland Nov. 30th 1769'.

f.36a H.D.S.r. 'The islands of Three Kings'.
H.D.S.v. 'New-Zeeland Dec 24th at 6 P.M.'.

f.36b H.D.S.r. 'The islands of Three Kings & Cape Maria van Diemen'.
H.D.S.v. 'New-Zeeland Jan 1st 1770 at 6 a.m.'.

f.37a H.D.S.r. 'Sugarloaf-Point'
H.D.S.v. 'New-Zeeland Jan 12th 1770 at 5 P.M.'.

f.37b H.D.S.r. 'The mouth of the Harbour Totaranui The Heppa Island'.
H.D.S.v. 'New-Zeeland Jan 12th at 5 P.M.'.

f.38a H.D.S.r. 'South Cape'
H.D.S.v. 'New-Zeeland March 9th 1770 at 12 P.M.'.

f.38b H.D.S.r. 'Solander's Island'. There is a very faint pencil note by Sydney Parkinson 'This Rock is dark brown'. The rest is indecipherable.
H.D.S.v. 'New-Zeeland March 11th, at 7 a.m.'.

f.39a H.D.S.r. 'Cape Five Fingers'.
H.D.S.v. 'New-Zeeland March 13th 1770 at 6 a.m.'.

f.39b H.D.S.r. 'Cape Five Fingers'.
H.D.S.v. 'New-Zeeland March 13th 1770 at 6½ P.M.'.

f.40a   H. D. S. r. 'View to the S.ward of Rocks-point'
         H. D. S. v. 'New Zeeland March 13th 1770 at 5$\frac{1}{2}$ P.M.'.

f.40b   H. D. S. r. 'View near Cascade-point'
         H. D. S. v. 'New-Zeeland March 17th 1770 at 2$\frac{1}{2}$ P.M.'.

f.41a   H. D. S. r. 'View to the S.ward of Rocks-point'.
         H. D. S. v. 'New-Zeeland March 23^{d} 1770 at 4 P.M.'.

f.41b   H. D. S. r. 'The entrance of Admiralty Bay.' J. B. r. 'The entrance to ——
         Harbour.' [This is very faint]
         H. D. S. v. 'New-Zeeland March 26th 1770'.

Add. MSS 15508

f.32b   Unsigned pencil drawing. Anon. r. 'Ornament worn round the neck. New
         Zealand'. This pencil drawing is almost certainly by Spöring, although the
         writing is not his. The three drawings on this folio are marked in pencil, 34,
         35, 35. The last, on the lower right has had 36 altered to 35; there are details
         of Maori designs on both sides and also a cross section of a canoe on the
         recto. These are all Spöring's work and should be compared with the
         drawings on f.24 in Add. MS 23921.

ff.33, 38, 39 and 40 These four unfinished pencil sketches of parts of carved Maori
         canoes are by Spöring.
         Cf. f.33 with f.78a in Add. MS 23920.
         Cf. f.39 with f.77a in Add. MS 23920.
         Cf. f.40 with f.79a in Add. MS 23920.
         No drawing has been found resembling f.38.

Add. MS 23920

f.32a   Anon. 'Inhabitants of the Island of Savu'. Two drawings by Spöring of
         girls, one carrying baskets, another with fruit on a pole. Initialled with an
         abbreviated signature he sometimes used.[61]

f.32b   Anon. 'A basket for collecting palm wine'. Two versions, unsigned but
         probably by Spöring.

f.38   H. D. S. v. 'The Watering-place with Spöring's Isles New-Zeeland
         Tolaga Bay'. It is signed with his abbreviated signature.

f.39　Anon. r. 'New Zealand. The arched Rock Tolaga Bay'. Unsigned pencil drawing, clearly by Spöring who wrote on the verso; 'The arched Rock Tolaga Bay New-Zeeland'.

f.42a　Anon. r. 'New Zealand a perforated Rock fortified on the top'.
H. D. S. v. 'Spöring's-Grotto Opuragi-Bay New-Zeeland'.

f.43a　Anon. r. 'Motuaro Bay of Islands'.
H. D. S. v. 'The Town on Motuaro-Island. New-Zeeland'. Mr Jeremy Spencer has surveyed this site and tells me that this drawing by Spöring is much more accurate than the same view as depicted by Sydney Parkinson. The current name is Motu-arohia. (Pl.16a)

f.48　Anon. r. 'New Zeeland War Canoe The Crew bidding defiance to the Ship's Company'.
H. D. S. v. 'Double War Canoe Nov^e 2^d 1769. New-Zeeland'. See Pl.14.

f.76a　H. D. S. r. 'New Zeeland. An Amulet'.
H. D. S. v. 'Hawkes-Bay, New-Zeeland Oct. 18 1769'.

f.77a　H. D. S. r. 'The Head of a Canoe'.
H. D. S. v. 'About 5 feet high. New-Zeeland'.

f.77b　H. D. S. r. 'The Head of a Canoe. 68$\frac{1}{2}$ feet in length'.

f.78a　H. D. S. r. 'The stern ornament of a Canoe'.
H. D. S. v. 'About 12 feet high. New-Zeeland'.

f.78b　H. D. S. r. 'The Head of a Canoe'.
H. D. S. v. 'About 3 feet high. New-Zeeland'. (Pl.12a)

f.79a　H. D. S. r. 'The Head of a Canoe'.
H. D. S. v. '2 feet high New-Zeeland'. (Pl.12b)

f.79b　H. D. S. r. 'The Head of a Canoe'.
H. D. S. v. '2 feet high New Zeeland'.

Add. MS 23921

f.1a　J. B. r. 'A View from the Point at Otaheite' Anon. 'The Bay where the Endeavour anchored with the Encampment on shore'. (Long unfinished folded strip).

f.1b　J. B. r. 'A View from the back part of . . . . .?' [very faint pencil legend.]
Anon. r. 'A View round the Point at the back of the Encampment'.

f.2a　Large faint unfinished drawing, unlabelled, of Fort Venus.

f.2b   Anon. r. 'Our little Encampment in Otaheite'.
         J. B. r. 'Our little Encampment in Otaheite'.
         H. D. S. r. (very faint) 'View of the Fort from the . . . .? Rock'.

f.3a   H. D. S. 4 strips, each labelled on recto 'View of Ajmähä'.
         J. B. r. 'Georges Island Higher land S 71° 30 E . . . .'. [top left, very faint.]
         Anon. r. 'View in the Island of Eimeo'.

f.3b   Four strips, 3 labelled by H. D. S., r., 'View of Uahäjnä, fourth unlabelled
         Anon. r. 'View in the Island of Huaheine'.

f.4a   This consists of six strips.
         1 H. D. S. r., 'View of Uahäjna from Ulaitaea'. 2,3,4,5 and 6 'View of
         Ulaitaea'. Anon. r. 'View of the Island of Uleitea'.

f.10a   Anon. r. 'Otaheite' 'Paihea's Long House'. Unsigned but unmistakably by
         Spöring; note canoes on right within the boat-house; these are drawn in
         detail on f.24 where the annotations by Banks, Solander and Spöring
         enable them to be identified as Ulietean, i.e. from Raiatea, Otaheite being
         used for the Society Islands in general in both cases. (Pl.22)

f.23a   Anon. r. 'Oboreahs Canoe'.
         H. D. S. v. 'Canoe about 30 feet in length belonging to Öbalhoea'.

ff.24a and b. These drawings by Spöring show one of the Ulietean canoes visible in
         the boat-house of f.10a. The upper drawing is a detailed sketch with a 50-
         foot scale and many measurements. H. D. S. r. '50–6 The length of the
         gunnel from the head to the stern'. Solander, 'Pahie no Ulaietea'. The
         lower figure is annotated, by Banks: 'An Ulaitaea Canoe Paihaea's Long
         house Otaheite'. Compare the t.s. with that sketched in Add. MS 15508,
         f.35, and see Banks's detailed description in vol.I, pp.319–320 of the 1962
         edition of Banks's diary (note 54).

f.27   There are three drawings on this sheet, a and c by H. D. S.
         a. H. D. S. r 'Ewhale re Eatua Uahaine', with pen and ink scale of 4 feet on
         one side.

f.27c   Anon. r. 'A Morai or Temple of a Pyramidical shape'. Also 'Morai no
         Tuttaha, Otaheite'.

f.29a   Anon. r. 'A Whatta at Otaheite'. Pen and ink scale of 6 yards.

f.32   Anon. r. 'Dress of the Chief Mourner'.
         H. D. S. r. 'Profile of The Head Dress'.

42

There are no drawings in Add. MS 15507 that can be ascribed to Parkinson although some of the places depicted by Buchan and Spöring in this volume were sketched by him in his personal collection, Add. MS 9345.

Add. MS 15508

f.3   This large wash painting is inscribed by J. B. 'Otaheite View at the back of Point Venus towards Pathos Long House'. Anon. bottom right 'Drawn by S. Parkinson'; this attribution seems correct. A double canoe with Tahitians fishing is shown in the foreground.

f.21   Probably Parkinson.
J. B. r. 'Man of New Zealand'.

ff.34, 35 These rough sketches of tattoo patterns are too scrappy to be attributed with any degree of certainty.

Add. MS 23920

f.13   Unsigned wash drawing, Anon. r. 'Natives of Tierra del Fuego with their Hut'. (Pl.46)

f.18   Four of the pencil sketches of Tierra del Fuegians on this folio are by Parkinson. Two of these show the painting of the faces and were used in the engraving that forms plate I in his posthumously published journal. Banks has written 'T. del F' on three of these sketches.

ff.29, 30 These large unsigned pencil sketches of Malay boats look like Parkinson's work but they are unsigned. The initials E J appear on the bottom right hand corner.
Anon. r. 'Savu Malay Boats'.
29 v. 'Serigas'; 30 v. 'Anatacan'.

f.31   Anon. r. 'Savu' 'A Chief's house in the Island of Savu near Timor'. Unsigned wash drawing, with the attribution in another hand 'Drawn by S. Parkinson'.

f.37   Large faint pencil sketch
Anon. r. 'Nests of the White Ant Endeavours River'.
S. P. 'White ants nests', [very faint bottom right.]

f.40b   Unsigned wash drawing; an oval vignette, clearly by Parkinson. Anon. r. 'A perforated Rock in New Zealand, Tolaga Bay'. This is one of the paintings that strongly suggest the probable influence of De la Cour.

f.41a   Wash drawing of a bay, New Zealand. Signed very faintly at bottom, just right of centre. 'S. P. Australiae 1769'. J. B. v. 'New Zealand'.

f.41b   Wash drawing, Bay and Maori meeting house. Signed, very faintly bottom left-hand corner. 'S. P. Australiae 1769. J. B. v. 'New Zealand'.

f.43b   Wash drawing of Motu-arohia, Bay of Islands, New Zealand. Unsigned but Parkinson has written on the verso 'View of the Hippa upon the Island of Motuaro in the Bay of Islands New Zealand'. This is less accurate than Spöring's drawing of the same scene, 43a q.v.

f.44   Wash drawing Anon. r. 'New Zealanders fishing'. Unsigned. J. B. v. 'New Zealand'.

f.46   Unsigned wash drawing. Anon. r. 'New Zealand War Canoe'.

f.49   Large unsigned wash drawing. Anon. r. 'New Zealand War Canoe'.

f.50   Unsigned, Anon. r. 'New Zealand War Canoe bidding defiance to the Ship'.

f.51   Anon. r. 'New Zeeland Canoe The Crew Peaceable'. (Pl.15)

f.52   Two series of pencil sketches, unsigned but probably by Parkinson. Anon. r. 'Sketches of Embarkations of New Zealand'. Some indecipherable initials at bottom right of lower drawing.

f.54   This seems to be a copy of one of Parkinson's wash drawings of a Maori head.

f.55   Wash drawing of a Maori, unsigned. Probably by Parkinson. It resembles in general Plate XVI, facing p.90, in his posthumously published journal.

f.56   Pencil sketch of Maori head, unsigned. This appears to be a preliminary study for f.55.

ff.60–65   These are unsigned pencil sketches by Parkinson of, Maori men and women in their cloaks, in boats etc., showing facial contortions and other details. Several have N.Z. inscribed on the bottom right corner. There are

44

also sketches on the versos of 62a, 63a and 64a. This last looks like a drawing of a Scottish woman spinning.

f.66   Four pen and ink sketches of tattooing. Unsigned
Anon. r. 'Black stains on the Skin called tattoo New Zeland'. Unsigned but Parkinson wrote on the fourth 'on the calf'.

f.67   Anon. r. 'Black stains on the skin called Tattoo'.
Four unsigned pencil sketches, 3 heads, and one finger nail which is labelled 'A finger nail in length $1\frac{3}{4}$ inch', but the writing is unfamiliar.

Add. MS 23921

f.6a   Unsigned wash drawing.
Anon. r. 'The Tree on one Tree Hill'. J. B. r. 'Done by Parkinson'.

f.7a   Unsigned wash drawing.
Anon. r. 'Otaheite, View of the Coast and Reef in the district of Papavia'.
J. B. v. 'View of the coast and reef in the district of Papavia'.

f.7b   Unsigned wash drawing.
Anon. r. 'View up the River among Rocks'.
J. B. v. 'Otaheite View up the River among Rocks'.

f.8a   Wash drawing signed 'S. P. Australiae 1769'.
Anon. r. 'View of Otaha', J. B. v. 'View of Otaha'.

f.8b   Wash drawing. Signed 'S. P. Australiae 1769'.
Anon. r. 'View between Ulietea and Otaha'.
J. B. v. 'View between Ulietea and Otaha'.

f.9a   Unsigned wash drawing.
Anon. r. 'View along shore'.
J. B. v. 'Otaheite View along shore'.

f.9b   Wash drawing. Signed 'S. P. Australiae 1769'.
Anon. r. 'Taroro' or Water Yams (left). Breadfruit tree (right).
J. B. v. 'Otaheite'.

f.10b   Signed wash drawing. 'Sydney Parkinson pinx. 1770. Marae Australiae'.
Anon. r. 'House and Plantation of a Chief in The Island of Otaheite'.
J. B. v. 'Otaheite'.

f.11   Unsigned wash drawing.
Anon. r. 'View in Ulietea'.
J. B. v. 'Ulietea'.

f.12　　Unsigned wash drawing.
　　　　Anon. r. 'Society Islands Double Canoes'.

f.16　　Unsigned wash drawing.
　　　　Anon. r. 'View of the Island of Otaha'.
　　　　J. B. v. 'Otaheite'.

f.17　　Unsigned wash drawing.
　　　　Anon. r. 'Society Islands Vessels of the Island of Otaha'.

f.19　　Unsigned wash drawing.
　　　　Anon. r. 'Society Islands'.

f.20　　Unsigned wash drawing.
　　　　Anon. r. 'Society Islands. Canoes of Ulietea'. J. B. v. 'Ulietea'.

f.21　　Unsigned wash drawing.
　　　　Anon. r. 'Society Islands. A War Canoe'.

f.23b　Drawings of canoes. One signed 'Canoe awning S. P.' Anon. r. 'Construction of Canoes'.

f.25a　Signed wash drawing. 'Sydney Parkinson pinx. Australiae 1770'.
　　　　Anon. r. 'View in the Island of Huaheine wt. an Ewharra and a small altar wt an offering on it'.
　　　　J. B. v. 'Huaheine'.

f.25b　Unsigned wash drawing.
　　　　Anon. r. 'View of an Ewharra Tree'. J. B. v. 'Otaheite. View of an Ewharra tree'.

f.27b　Parkinson. Sketch of houses and trees. There appears to be a signature. 'S. S. Copy'.

f.28　　Unsigned wash drawing.
　　　　Anon. r. 'a Morai with an offering to the Dead'. Banks's writing has been almost completely erased.
　　　　J. B. v. 'Huaheine'.

f.29b　Unsigned wash drawing.
　　　　Anon. r. 'A platform for supporting the offerings made to the Dead.'

f.31a　Unsigned wash drawing.
　　　　Anon. 'Otaheite' 'a Tupapow in the Island of Otaheite'.
　　　　S. P. v. 'Cabralla no te tuabapaow'.

f.36   There are five pencil drawings on this sheet, two men and three girls, one of which is labelled 'Heiva Dancing girl S.P.'.
Anon. r. 'Otaheite' 'Sketches of Inhabitants'.

f.37   These unsigned sketches of dancing girls, one partly coloured.
Anon. r. 'Otaheite' 'Sketches of Dancing girls'.
J.B. v. 'Ulhietea Dresses of Indian Dancers'.

f.38   Two unsigned sketches.
Anon. r. 'Otaheite' 'sketches of Dancing Girls'. There is a charming sketch on the verso of the upper drawing with notes on colour by Parkinson.

f.39   Two drawings by Parkinson, with his notes.
Anon. r. 'Otaheite'. 'War head dress'. The top one labelled 'Whow S. P.' is unfinished. The lower one is carefully marked to show materials used: 'Tropic Birds Feathers. Sharks Teeth. Basketwork. Pale brown Feathers of Pigeon's neck'. On verso of 39a is a pencil sketch of a heiva. On the verso of 39b Banks has written 'Ulheitea Indian Dancer'.

f.49   Four pencil sketches, one signed S. P. They depict a girl, a man with a spear, a woman and child, and a man's head with a wreath.
Anon. r. 'Otaheite, Sketches of Inhabitants'.

f.50a   Signed pencil drawing. 'S. P.' 'woman scraping bark to make cloth'.
Anon. r. 'Otaheite' 'girl scraping the Bark to make Cloth'. (Pl.25a)

f.50b   S. P. r. 'Woman beating cloth'.
Anon. r. 'Girls beating out the Bark with their Cloth beaters'.

f.51   Four unsigned pencil sketches.
Anon. r. 'Otaheite' 'Distortions of the Mouth used in Dancing'. On the verso of the two lower drawings are three pen and ink drawings of tattooing on the buttocks. On the verso of the top left hand sketch is a similar pencil drawing.

Notes

1 Once again my warmest thanks are due to the Librarian and Staff of the Lyon Playfair Library, Imperial College of Science and Technology, for the abundant facilities I have enjoyed while continuing this work on Sir Joseph Banks and his artists. I should also like to thank Professor Rupert Hall and Dr Marie Boas Hall of the Department for the History of Science and Technology, for their kind encouragement and Dr Norman Smith of the same department, once again, for helpful criticism of my manuscript. Mr James Holloway of the National Gallery of Scotland helped me initially in the search for Buchan's portrait, and in tracing some of De la Cour's work. My special gratitude goes to Professor Christopher Crowder, the present owner of Buchan's portrait, for his great kindness in allowing me to reproduce it, and for scholarly assistance in helping me to unravel the history of the Buchan family and its descendants, Mr Brian Gall, Librarian, Haddington, provided me with the notes on Major Buchan and the North Berwick Golf Club dinners as well as with the details of the Leyden-Buchan connection in the Napoleonic wars. Miss Joan Gladstone traced the obituary notices of Jane Gomeldon, Sydney Parkinson's cousin, in Newcastle upon Tyne. Mr Jeremy Spencer has generously allowed me to use his archaeological observations on the relative accuracy of the drawings by Parkinson and Spöring of Motu-Arohia.

Thanks are also due to the Trustees of the British Museum (Natural History) for permission to reproduce plates 23 and 24, and to the many members of the staff of that institution who have helped me over many years. I am especially grateful to Mr J. B. Marshall for expert assistance in identifying handwriting.

I am much obliged to the Duke of Hamilton for permission to reproduce De la Cour's painting of 'Flora' and to His Grace the Duke of Buccleugh and Queensberry, V.R.D., for the drawing of Old Edinburgh.

2 Lysaght, A. M. 'Manchots de l'Antarctique en Nouvelle Guinée', *L'Oiseau et R.F.O.* 22 (1952), pp.120–4.

3 Lysaght, A. M. 'Why did Sonnerat record the Kookaburra *Dacelo gigas* (Boddaert) from New Guinea?', *The Emu* 56 (1956), pp.224–5.

4 Ly-Tio-Fane, Madeleine. *Pierre Sonnerat 1748–1814.* Mauritius, 1976.

5 Beaglehole, J. C. Addenda and Corrigenda to *The Journals of Captain James Cook. I. The Voyage of the Endeavour.* Cambridge, 1968. See p.688 for Uggla, A. H. 'Daniel Solander och Linne', *Svenska Linné Sällskapets Arsskrift* XXXVI (1953); Marshall, J. B. 'Daniel Solander' in James Cook, *The Journal of H.M.S. Endeavour 1768–1771.* Facsimile edition. Guildford 1978, pp.49–59; and 'The handwriting of Sir Joseph Banks, his scientific staff and amanuenses', *Bull. Brit. Mus. (Nat. Hist.)* Bot. Ser. 6 (1978).

6 Lysaght, A. M. 'A Note on the Admiralty Copy of Cook's Journal in the Endeavour', in James Cook *The Journal of HMS Endeavour 1768–1771.* Facsimile edition. Guildford 1978. See also captions to plates XXa, XXb and XXI, *ibid.*, p.116.

7 Lysaght, A. M. 'Some eighteenth century bird paintings in the collection of Sir Joseph Banks 1743–1820', *Bull. Brit. Mus. (Nat. Hist.)*, Histor. Ser. 1, (1959) No.6, pp.263–5, 345–7.

8 Cook, James. *The Journal of HMS Endeavour 1768–1771.* Facsimile edition. Guildford, 1978, Pl.XV.

9 For Stubbs: Lysaght, A. M. 'A clue to the mystery of Captain Cook's Kangaroo', *New Scientist* 17 (1957), pp.17–19; For Dance: Morrison-Scott, T. C. S. and Sawyer, F. C. 'The identity of Captain Cook's Kangaroo', *Bull. Brit. Mus. (Nat. Hist.)* Zool. 1 (1950).

10 Lysaght, A. M. 'Some early letters from Joseph Banks (1743–1820) to William Phelp Perrin (1742–1820)', *Notes & Records, Royal Society* 29 (1974), No.1, p.955.

11 Sawyer, F. C. 'Some natural history drawings made during Captain Cook's first voyage round the world.' *J. Soc. Bibl. Nat.* 22 (1950), pp.190–3; Lysaght, A. M. *Joseph Banks in Newfoundland and Labrador 1766.* London, 1971, pp.101–107;

48

Lysaght, A. M. 'Banks's artists in the *Endeavour.*' in James Cook, *Journal of HMS Endeavour* (n.8 above), pp.37–48.

12 *Dictionary of National Biography*. London, 1894, 37, pp.354–5.

13 Gomeldon, Jane. *The Medley.* Newcastle upon Tyne, 1766. Some of Jane's correspondence and poems to her cousin were prepared for certain copies of the 1773 edition of Parkinson's posthumously published journal which was intended to forestall the official account of the voyage and forcibly withdrawn from circulation; one of these editions with her poems and letters may be seen in the British Museum.

14 Gomeldon, Jane. *Maxims.* Newcastle upon Tyne, 1779.

15 Parkinson, Sydney. *A Journal of a Voyage to the South Seas in His Majesty's Ship the Endeavour.* London, 1773, 1784. The 1784 edition includes much fuller introductory material. See also note 13 above.

16 Irwin, D. and F. *Scottish Painters at Home and Abroad.* London, 1974, p.91.

17 Fleming, John. 'Enigma of a Rococo Artist', *Country Life*, 24 May, 1962, pp.1124–6.

18 Croft-Murray, E. *Decorative Painting in England 1537–1837.* London, 1970, 2, p.199.

19 Register House, Edinburgh. Series NG1/7/5–6. Appendix to the Report to the King at Christmas, 1761, f.150.

20 Register House, Edinburgh. Series NG1/17; 17 March, 1762; 15 Feb., 1764, f.161, etc.

21 Gordon, Esmé. *The Royal Scottish Academy.* Edinburgh, 1976.

22 Mason, John. 'The Edinburgh School of Design', in *Book of the Old Edinburgh Club* 27 (1949), p.68.

23 See also Cook, *Journal of HMS Endeavour* (n.8 above) pl. VII.

24 Lysaght, A. M. *Joseph Banks in Newfoundland and Labrador 1766*, London, 1971, pp.101–7.

25 Lysaght, A. M. *Bull Brit Mus (Nat. Hist.)* Hist Ser. 1 (1959), No.6, pp.310–22.

26 Sawyer, F. C. *J. Soc. Bibl. Nat.*, 22 (1950), pp.190–3.

27 Broadbridge, S. R. *The Midlands Diary of Joseph Banks*, (awaiting publication, n.d.); Lysaght, A. M. *Joseph Banks, the Years of Discovery* (awaiting publication, n.d.).

28 Cook, James, *Journal of HMS Endeavour* (n.8 above), pl. XXXVII.

29 Smith, Bernard. *European Vision and the South Pacific.* Oxford, 1969, p.21.

30 Crowder, F. Jeffries. Personal communication, 1978.

31 Martine, John. *Reminiscences and Notices of 14 Parishes in the County of Haddington.* Edinburgh, 1890.

32 Crowder, Christopher M.D. *In litt.* 23 March, 1978.

33 Scott, William. *Memoir of James Braidwood, Leith.* Edinburgh, 1885.

34 Lysaght, A. M. 'Some eighteenth century bird paintings . . .', see full reference in note 7 above, pp.260–2.

35 Banks, Joseph. The quotations given here are taken from the holograph manuscript in the Mitchell Library, Sydney. The late J. C. Beaglehole's edition, 1962, reprinted 1968, differs only in details of spelling and punctuation.

36 Beaglehole, J. C. *The Journals of Captain James Cook on his voyages of discovery. The Voyage of the Endeavour 1768–1771.* Cambridge, 1955, p.81.

37 Beaglehole, J. C. *op. cit*, p.552.

38 Cook, James. Incomplete draft of his *Endeavour* journal. British Library Add. MS 27955.

39 Smith, *op. cit.* note 29, above, p.17n.

40 Perret, Louis. 'Herman Diedrich Spöring d.y. Medicinare, naturvetare och forskningsresande'. *Nordisk Medicin Historic Arsbok* (1968), pp.147–57.

41 Marshall, J. B. in Cook, *Journal of HMS Endeavour* (n.8 above), and *Bull. Brit. Mus. (Nat. Hist.) Bot. Ser.* 6 (1978).

42 Beaglehole, J. C. Addenda to *Journals* 1 (n.5 above).

43 Marshall, J. B. *Bull. Brit. Mus. (Nat. Hist.) Bot. Ser.* 6 (1978).

44 Lysaght, A. M. *Bull. Brit. Mus. (Nat. Hist.)*, Hist. Ser. 1 (1959), No.6, pp.255–6.

45 Taylor, A. Carey, 'Charles de Brosses, the Man Behind Cook', *The Opening of the Pacific – Image and Reality.* Maritime Museum Monographs and Reports, No.2, National Maritime Museum, Greenwich, London.

46 Cook, draft of *Endeavour* journal (n.38 above).

47 Wilkinson, Francis, in Addenda to Beaglehole, *Journals*, I (n.5 above), p.89 n.

48 Beaglehole in Addenda to *Journals*, I (n.5 above), p.694.

49 Lyonnet, Pierre, Letter to Banks. British Library Add. MS 8094, f.97, 16 Jan., 1775.

50 Lysaght, A. M. *Bull. Brit. Mus. (Nat. Hist.)*, Hist. Ser. I (1959), No.6 (see n.7 above).

51 Beaglehole, in Addenda to *Journals*, I (n.5 above), p.654.

52 Lysaght, A. M. *Joseph Banks in Newfoundland and Labrador 1766*, p.255.

53 Lysaght, A. M. *Banks, the Years of Discovery*.

54 Beaglehole, J. C., *The Endeavour Journal of Joseph Banks*. Sydney, 1962, I, p.61.

55 Solander, Daniel, Letter to Lord Hardwick. British Library Add. MS 35350, f.55. 1774.

56 Lysaght, A. M. and Serventy, D. L., 'Some Erroneous Records in Parkinson's Journal of a Voyage to the South Seas, 1773', *The Emu* 56 (1956), pp.129–30.

57 Lysaght, A. M., 'A granferised copy of E. Smith's *Life of Sir Joseph Banks*, *Journ. Soc. Bibl. Nat. Hist.* 4 (1964), pp.206–9.

58 Lysaght, A. M. *Joseph Banks in Newfoundland and Labrador 1766*, p.244.

59 Tytler of Woodhouselee, A. F., *Life of Henry Homes, Lord Kames*. 2nd ed., Edinburgh, 1814, Vol.2, Book 3, pp.44 ff.

60 Spencer, Jeremy. Personal communication, 1977.

61 See n.15 above, reproduced on p.38.

1 Alexander Buchan, d.1769. Oil painting,
   Courtesy Professor Christopher Crowder.

2 Pencil drawing of Rio de Janeiro by Alexander
Buchan, labelling by Herman Diedrich
Spöring. One of a set of three; the lettering is
explained in the other two. British Library,
Add. MS 23920, f.8.

3a Daphne and Apollo. An engraving by
  Bartolozzi of a drawing by Cipriani. Private
  collection.

3b Cipriani's drawing, engraved by Bartolozzi,
  after the painting by Alexander Buchan of
  Tierra del Fuegians in their hut. See Pl.4a.

54

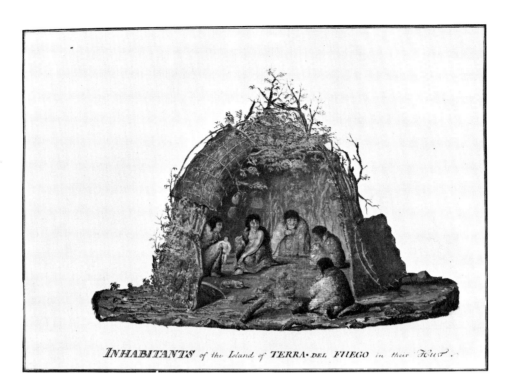

INHABITANTS of the Island of TERRA·DEL·FUEGO in their Hut.

4a Tierra del Fuegians in their hut. Painting by
Alexander Buchan, labelled by Spöring.
British Library, Add. MS 23920, f.14.

4b Tierra del Fuegians in their hut. Wash
drawing by Parkinson. British Library, Add.
MS 23920, f.13.

5a Cartoon by Buchan for a painting of natives
and sailors from the *Endeavour* at the Bay of
Good Success, Tierra del Fuego. British
Library, Add. MS 23920, f.11a.

5b,c Two pencil drawings by Buchan of a Tierra
del Fuegian man. British Library, Add. MS
23920, f.18. Two of five pencil sketches, the
others by Parkinson.

A WOMAN of the Island of TERRA DEL FUEGO

6 A Tierra del Fuegian woman painted by
Buchan, the labelling by Spöring. British
Library, Add. MS 23920, f.17.

W ½ N.

1 1769. Jan. 25. 11 O'Clock
" The southermost land we saw
supposd to be Hermits Islands
on which the french place cape Horn
behind the Westernmost land we saw another headland
which we supposd to be the cape but a mist coverd it
before it could be drawn

7a,b Wash drawing by Buchan of the coast in the
vicinity of Cape Horn. Banks's inscription
on the *verso* is reproduced beneath. British
Library, Add. MS 15507, f.10.

58

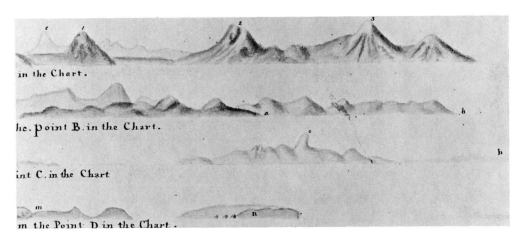

in the Chart.

he. point B. in the Chart.

int C. in the Chart

m the Point D in the Chart.

References to the Views.

a. Cape S.ᵗ Diego
b. C. S.ᵗ Vincent
c. Sugar Loaf
d. Middle Cape Staten L.ᵈ
e. C.S.ᵗ Bartholomew
f. Entrance Succeſs Bay
g. New Island

h. C. Good Succeſs
i Cape Horn
k. S.ᵗ P Hermites Iſles
l. Hermites Iſles
m. Barnevelts Iſles
n. Evouts Iſles
1. 2. 3. Three Brothers

A CHART OF THE S.East.PART OF TERRA DEL FUEGO INCLUDING STRAIT'S LE MAIRE AND PART OF STATEN LAND BY Lieut. I. Cook.   Jan.ʸ 1769.

8a–c Three details from a chart of Tierra del
Fuego, usually attributed to Cook, but
remarkably similar to work by Buchan.
British Library, Add. MS 7085, f.3.

9 Pencil and wash drawing of a cluster of islands, the two groups known as Marokau and Ravahere; the drawing is dated by Banks 6 April, 1769. The enlarged detail shown here suggests that it may be a composite work by Buchan and Spöring. Cf. Pls.10a and 10b. British Library, Add. MS 15507, f.13b.

10a,b Enlarged details from a pencil drawing by Spöring of the watering place in Tolaga Bay, New Zealand. The young man on the extreme right in Pl.10a is clutching a large crayfish, supposedly as an offering to the girl who is looking at him. British Library, Add. MS 23920, f.38.

60

Watering places

Tegad

11 Another enlarged detail of a drawing by
Spöring, showing Maori plantations in
Poverty Bay, New Zealand. British Library,
Add. MS 15507, f.24.

12a,b Carved Maori canoe prows drawn by
Spöring. British Library, Add. MS 23920,
ff.78, 79.

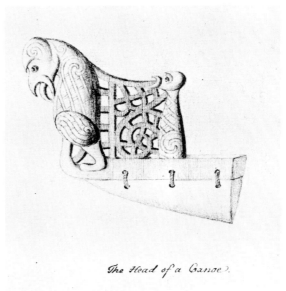

The Head of a Canoe.

Endeavours River with the Vessel hauled on Shore

13 Part of an engraving showing the *Endeavour*
   beached for repairs, plate 19 in the third
   volume of Hawkesworth, facing p.557. This
   appears to be by Spöring but only the name
   of the engraver is given, and the whereabouts
   of the original drawing seems to be unknown.

14 Maoris in their canoe, bidding defiance to the
   crew of the *Endeavour*. This detail of
   Spöring's drawing may be contrasted with the
   enlarged detail shown in Pl.15, a similar type
   of drawing by Parkinson. British Library,
   Add. MS 23920, f.48.

15 Enlarged detail from a drawing by Parkinson
   of Maoris peacefully fishing from a canoe.
   British Library, Add. MS 23920, f.51.

16a,b Two drawings of Motu-arohia, Bay of
Islands, New Zealand. The upper drawing
by Spöring is more correct and was copied
by Barralet for Banks, See Pl.17. British
Library, 23920, ff.43a and b.

17 Wash drawing by Barralet of Motu-arohia.
See Pls.16a and b above. British Library,
Add. MS 15508, f.20.

18 Sydney Parkinson as a boy. From the
engraving that forms the frontispiece to his
posthumously published journal. The frame
bears some resemblance to that of the self-
portrait of him presented to the British
Museum (Natural History) by a descendant
of his family.

19 View of Old Edinburgh from the north. Grisaille on panel, by William De la Cour who probably taught Parkinson at the Edinburgh School of Design in the early 1760s. By courtesy of His Grace the Duke of Buccleugh and Queensberry, V.R.D.

20 'Flora', a romantic oil painting by De la Cour; see Pl.19. By courtesy of the Duke of Hamilton.

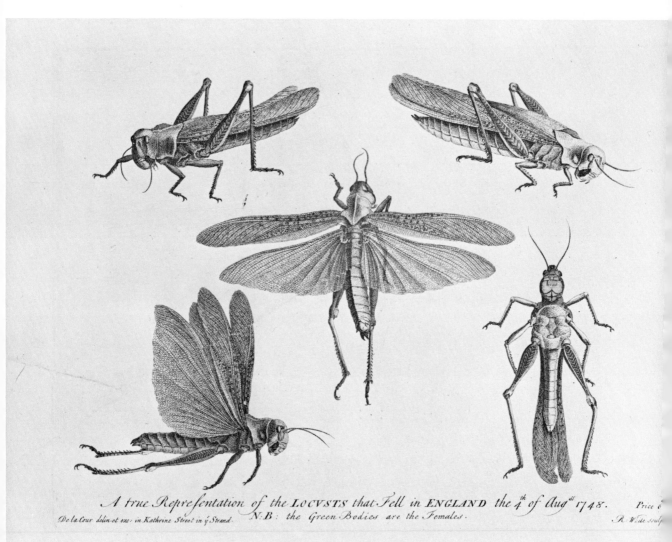

A true Representation of the LOCVSTS that Fell in ENGLAND the 4th of Augst 1748. Price 6
De la Cour delin et exc in Kathrine Street in ý Strand. N.B: the Green Bodies are the Females. R. Wade sculp.

21a Engravings of the Migratory Locust by William De la Cour. British Museum, Dept. of Prints and Drawings.

21b,c Newfoundland insects. Enlarged drawings by Sydney Parkinson of two species of insects collected by Banks in Newfoundland and Labrador in 1766: *Trichiosoma arcticum* Kirby and *Capnodis tenebrionis* (L.).

70

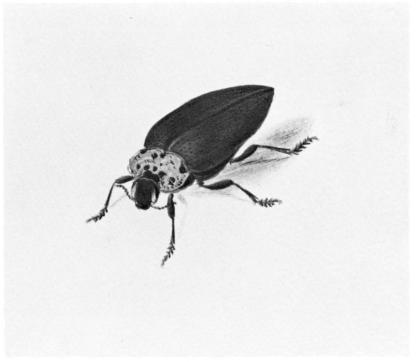

22 Spöring's drawing of 'Paihea's Long House',
Raiatea. British Library, Add. MS 23921,
f.10a.

23, 24 Parkinson's unfinished drawing of *Banksia serrata* Linn. f., annotated by Banks on the verso 'Botany Bay'; Parkinson has written his note for completing the drawing: 'The space below the flowers to be fill'd up wt dark Colour'. J. F. Miller

made the finished painting and almost certainly had a dried specimen to work from, though it has not been located recently. *Plants of Australia*, vol. VII, f.32, Botany Library, British Museum (Natural History).

25a Drawing by Parkinson of a Tahitian girl scraping bark to make Tapa cloth. British Library, Add. MS 23921, f.50.

25b Engraving from a drawing by Parkinson showing details of the head-dress worn by the girl in Pl.25a. One of several studies of Polynesian heads in plate VIII of his posthumously published journal.

26 Drawing by C. H. Praval of a Melanesian.
British Library, Add. MS 15508, f.13.

27 Maori and sailor, by an unidentified artist.
British Library, Add. MS 15508, f.11.

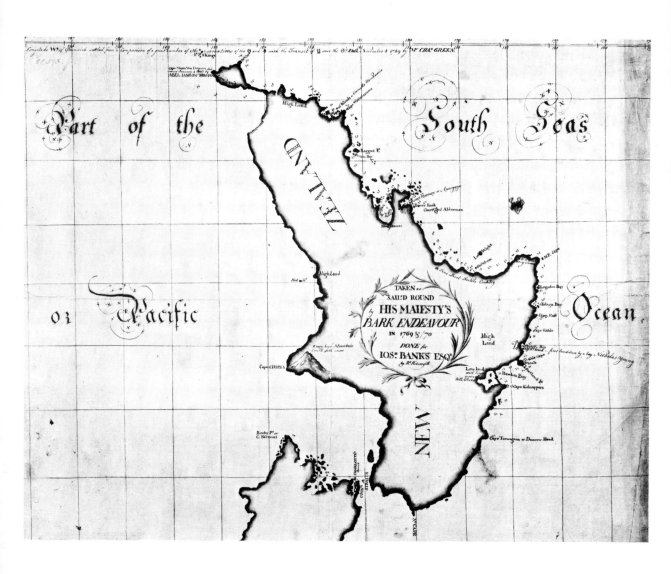

28 The North Island of New Zealand. Drawn
for Banks by Richard Pickersgill. British
Library, Add. MS 21593, map F.

29a,b Detail from a view of the Rogefeldt from
the Hantum. Probably by Colonel Gordon,
and probably also commissioned by Banks
when he was at the Cape of Good Hope.
Compare the detail of the painter at work
which constantly crops up in his artists'
work, with the example from the Orkneys
where J. F. Miller drew the Stones of
Stennis for him in 1772 (below) Plate 29a:
British Library Add. MS 23920, f.23; Plate
29b: Add. MS 15511, f.7.

78

30 Drawing by John Cleveley in 1774 of a basket
from Tonga, which is still in the British
Museum. Banks mistakenly wrote Amsterdam
Island on it which is Tongatapu, an island in
the Tonga Group visited by Cook on his
Second Voyage round the world, 1772–75.
British Library, Add. MS 23920, f.107.

Philippe Jacques de Loutherbourg's Pantomime 'Omai, or, a Trip round the World' and the Artists of Captain Cook's Voyages

RÜDIGER JOPPIEN

Kunstgewerbemuseum, Cologne

Omai — the Production

The pantomime *Omai, or, a trip round the world*, almost totally forgotten today, was hailed with great applause when it was first performed at Covent Garden on 20 December 1785[1]. A galaxy of distinguished artists had collaborated to make this production one of the most successful of the decade, if not the century: Philippe Jacques de Loutherbourg (1740–1812) was the designer of the show, William Shield its composer, John O'Keeffe the author of the libretto, John Webber a consultant on dresses and decorations, Matthew William Peters, John Inigo Richards, and Robert Carver painted the scenery, while popular actors of the London stage like Mrs Inchbald, Mr Delpini, Mr Edwin and Mr Kennedy gave life to the characters (Pl.31). The story was inspired by the life and adventures of Omai, the first Polynesian visitor to England and a well known character of the time, whose fate was strongly connected with the history of Captain Cook's Second and Third Voyages round the world. In fact, the pantomime *Omai, or, a trip round the world* was a travelogue, a stage-edition of Captain Cook's voyages. In some way dedicated to the memory of Cook, it was performed a year and a half after the official accounts of the Third Voyage had been released by the Admiralty, when the impact of Cook's achievements as an explorer had begun to grow upon a larger public.[2]

Omai was both a pantomine, in which the customary Harlequin and Colombine appeared, as well as an exhibition of South Sea scenery and dresses. Its conception, mixing the whimsical and the noble, the entertaining and the didactic, illustrates the role and importance which the stage played in disseminating topical knowledge in eighteenth-century England.[3] To the inhabitants of London in 1785 this production exercised a powerful attraction, if one is to believe the frequency of performances which it attained.[4] Combining the dramatic and the pictorial arts with great success, it illustrated and animated one of the most notable incidents in British and indeed in World history: the European exploration of the Pacific.

This process had been largely performed during Cook's three voyages of 1768–71, 1772–75, and 1776–80. Drawings of landscapes and peoples of the South Seas, examples of their culture and industry, specimens from the animal and plant kingdoms were brought back to England on all three occasions and amply demonstrated the existence of a world which was entirely new and strange. However, the greatest 'wonder' of all was the Polynesian Omai, a native of Raiatea who visited London from 1774 to 1776 and who made a lasting impression.[5]

Captain Tobias Furneaux, commander of Cook's second ship *Adventure*, had taken Omai to England, where he was placed under the care and protection of the Earl of Sandwich, First Lord of the Admiralty, and Joseph Banks, the naturalist who had accompanied Cook on his first circumnavigation.

Omai caused a sensation. His looks were found pleasing and his manners graceful. Banks and his fellow naturalist Solander gave him lessons on a range of customary subjects, whilst London Society eagerly watched his progress in mastering the conventional forms of civilized living. Incessantly lionized, Omai was presented to their Majesties (Pl.32), taken to balls and entertainments, and was soon renowned as one of the most exciting figures in the metropolis whom every hostess wished to present in her salon. Fanny Burney gives some glimpse of this when she talks about Omai in her diary, where she also records some of his conversations and opinions.

Omai was a curiosity, a visually striking personality, and a living experiment. His whole cultural background made him a provocation to Western society and a welcome test for those who believed in Rousseau's ideas about man's happy and morally superior existence in the state of nature; he was the perfect example of the 'noble savage'. Interest in Omai was shared by almost all quarters of philosophy and learning, and some of the leading artists of the day, including Sir Joshua Reynolds and Nathaniel Dance, made him the subject of their portraits (Pl.33).[6]

After Society, and the worlds of learning and the arts had taken the opportunity to study this most unusual specimen of the human race, Omai was taken back to his native country. Cook assisted him to install himself on the island of Huaheine. To heighten his prestige and to demonstrate British friendship, he was supplied with household goods, tools, domestic animals and a box of toys. When Cook had finished his mission on 30 October 1777 he wrote in his diary: 'The history of Omai will perhaps interest a very numerous class of readers more than other occurrences of the voyage, the objects of which do not in general promise much entertainment'.[7]

Cook was certainly right in his prediction about Omai. It may have been this very sentence which gave P. J. de Loutherbourg (1740–1812) the idea for a theatrical spectacle that was based on the history of the Tahitian. Already in 1775 it had been Garrick's intention to bring Omai on to the stage, though Garrick had thought more of a satire on London Society than of a vehicle for South Seas scenery and costumes.[8] But since Garrick's time, exotic settings of places in the Middle East, India or South America, often based on authentic sources, became increasingly popular.[9] In catering for the unknown and in opening new worlds of geographical discovery, the theatre's pictorial expansion to the Pacific was only logical. In John Webber (1750–93), who had accompanied Cook's last expedition for four years as the official draughtsman, an expert eye-witness was available, whose portfolio was filled with many fine unpublished views.[10] If Webber guaranteed authenticity and topographical verity, Loutherbourg promised superb execution of all designs and decorations. As principal scene-designer at Drury Lane from 1772–81, first under David Garrick then under his successor Richard Brinsley Sheridan, he had introduced several scenic innovations which were directed towards improving the stage illusion. After a dispute with Sheridan he gave up his career in 1781, never to work in the theatre again except for the sole instance of Omai.[11] It is certainly a testimony of the tribute paid to his ingenuity and experience that the permanent scene-designers at Covent Garden, John Inigo Richards and Robert Carver, whose rival he had been a few years before, agreed to work under his direction for this one production.[12] In Thomas Harris, the manager of Covent Garden Theatre, Loutherbourg met an enterprising producer who was known to advance large amounts of money for decorations which looked promising.[13] Thus Loutherbourg devised, together with Webber, a show which he may well have considered the final triumph of his career.

The realisation of Omai profited from Loutherbourg's longstanding acquaintance with Webber, which seems to have extended back to the time before Webber left for the South Seas.[14] It is tempting to think that when Cook's ships returned in 1780 Loutherbourg was among the first to receive a first-hand report on the incidents of the voyage. On this occasion he would have seen the sketches which Webber had done during the last four years, and which by order of the Admiralty he was now finishing and preparing for publication as plates in the official account.[15] Loutherbourg's tried commercial instinct and Webber's need for greater artistic reputation may well have tallied in giving the decisive idea for the production of Omai Webber's financial position during the preparation of the plate illustrations from 1780 to 1784 was perhaps not so satisfactory as he had hoped. It was stipulated that he make no public use of his drawings before Cook's account had been published, and, though the Admiralty paid him a salary of 200 guineas per annum, he may have looked for further benefit. In a letter of 28 September 1782 Sir Joseph Banks had proposed to the Earl of Sandwich that Webber be excluded from the royalties of the forthcoming publication in favour of the dependants of the late Captains Cook and Clerke, as well as of Captains Gore and King.[16] Webber was certainly eager to publicise the substantial part that he had played in the documentation of Cook's last voyage. From 1784 onwards he exhibited South Sea paintings at the Royal Academy and later began to publish a series of views of the Pacific.[17] To him *Omai* was an enterprise in which he saw another opportunity for gaining some benefit from his former years of labour. Webber's considerable contribution to *Omai* can be established from various sources. The dramatist John O'Keeffe reports: '. . . the dresses and scenery were done from drawings of Mr. Webber, the artist who had made the voyage with Captain Cook'.[18] Also, some of the designs for scenery which Loutherbourg did on the basis of Webber's drawings appear in the catalogue of the sale of Loutherbourg's estate, and bear witness to Webber's contribution.[19] When O'Keeffe says that he had 'with Mr. Webber . . . much conversation'[20] on the South Seas, he further points to Webber's capacity as consultant and adviser during the preparation of the show. For the considerable assistance which Webber afforded, which also included the painting of one scene decoration, Covent Garden paid him £123.[21] This figure was well below the £620 which Loutherbourg netted according to the theatre's accounts books.[22] It is possible, however, that Loutherbourg's salary included a reimbursement for the use of Webber's designs.

Omai was the joint achievement of two artists. While it had been Webber's role to supply a collection of extremely rare and attractive visual material, it was Loutherbourg's practical experience with scenery, his talent for organisation and his conception of the pantomime as a whole, that transformed Webber's drawings into the reality of the stage. He designed the sets and tested their technical practicability. He also supervised the execution of the decorations.[23] Under his guidance about a dozen scene-painters worked for three months, and this seems to have set an absolute record at the time.[24] Special stage machinery was shipped in from France,[25] and every possible care, including effective advertisement, was taken to ensure the success of the production. When it was finally staged, press and audiences alike expressed their complete approval, and one newspaper wrote that the scenes 'are presented and all of them finished in a style so superior to that of ordinary stage exhibition that they appear the product of a new effort in the art of painting, untried before.'[26]

The action of *Omai* can be extracted from several sources. The earliest of these is a manuscript in the Theatre Museum of the Victoria & Albert Museum, which

84

bears the title *Harlequin Omai, a Pantomime design'd by Mr. Loutherberg* (sic) *1785*.[27] A hand-written note on the front page says that this manuscript belonged to William Shield, the composer of the pantomime;[27a] several annotations in the text marking the place of airs, recitatives and songs are probably in Shield's hand. A later version of the text, in which the original protagonist, Harlequin Omai, has changed into the separate figures of Omai and Harlequin, is offered in the printed editions of *A Short Account of the New Pantomime Called Omai, or A Trip round the World*, with words written by O'Keeffe.[28] Both sources can be checked against the sometimes very detailed descriptions of the pantomime in the daily papers. From them it is possible to follow changes in the production in the *post-première* nights, which were introduced to improve the element of entertainment. The structure of the plot and the choice of scenery was, however, largely maintained throughout all texts and different accounts.

When the play opens the scene of action is a *marae*, a sacred ground on Otaheite, by moonlight. Otoo (Pl.34), father of Omai and descendant from the legal kings, is seen among the tombs invoking the spirits of his ancestors that his son may be seated on the throne. A sacrifice blazes up and Towha, the supreme god of the island appears in the disguise of a Chief Mourner (Pl.35), accompanied by showers of hail and an eclipse of the moon. Towha promises his support for Omai but proposes that he should first go to England to woo Londina, daughter of Britannia. At this point the scene changes to a vision showing Britannia sitting on a rock and holding her daughter Londina by the hand. The next scene is played inside a sacred hut of the Grand Chiefs, which is adorned with life-size statues of the gods. Here Otoo instructs Omai concerning his mission, but they are disturbed by the appearance of Oedidee, another pretender to the throne, who is backed up by Oberea, a powerful enchantress (Pl.36). Omai disembarks at Plymouth, followed by Harlequin as his servant. In the haughty Spaniard Don Struttolando who happens to arrive in Plymouth at the same time, Omai meets a rival for the hand of Londina. The action then proceeds to London where the two parties meet again in Kensington Gardens. During this scene, Hyde Park is seen in the background with horses, gigs and pedestrians. Omai meets Londina and they fall in love at first sight. As her father is opposed to their union Omai carries her away. Harlequin likewise manages to elope with Colombine, servant to Londina, and from this moment the action of flight and pursuit, the trip around the world, begins. The first stop on the journey is the shores of Kamtchatka, with the summer habitations of the natives in the background. The scene changes to the interior of a *jourt*, the winter habitation of the Kamtchadales. With the two parties still pursuing each other, Harlequin escapes by jumping through the mouth of an idol. After this he waves his wand and the scene changes to a dreary island. Here Clown is attacked by a white bear. A boat appears and takes Omai's people to a village in the Friendly

Islands, where natives sing a rondeau and busy themselves with making feather garments. The pursuit continues to the Sandwich Islands where Omai's and Londina's steps are suddenly intercepted by the enchantress Oberea. Perceiving the danger, Omai changes the scene to an ocean where he appears in a war canoe in the centre of the Tahitian fleet. The scene changes yet again to a delicious shrubbery by moonlight, where Omai and Londina fall asleep. Londina is then carried away by Oberea's evil spirits, Omai himself taken prisoner and shut up in Oberea's magical cavern. As Oberea is about to kill Omai, a convulsion of the elements is heard and Towha the powerful god makes his entry in martial dress (Pl.37). He rescues Omai and sets Oberea's palace on fire. A happy ending follows: Omai is installed upon the throne of Otaheite with Londina as his queen. The last scene reveals an extensive view of the great bay of Otaheite. A procession is staged in which representatives of all quarters of the Pacific participate: six men of Otaheite take the lead; then follow a group of natives from New Zealand (Pls.38–42); after them come people from Tanna, the Marquesas, the Friendly Islands, the Sandwich Islands and Easter Island. They are followed by Asians, men and women from Tchutzki Peninsula (Pls.43–44) and Kamtchatka (Pls.45–47); and the American peoples, inhabitants from Nootka Sound (Pl.48), Oonalashka and Prince William Sound (Pls.49–50) bring up the rear. After they have been placed at either side of the stage, Tahitian dancers of both sexes make their entry (Pls.51–52), followed by a Tahitian girl wearing precious feather objects as presents (Pl.53). Then Omai is hailed as king and saluted as an ally of Britain. An English captain steps up to Omai and presents him with an English sword addressing him as follows

> 'Accept from mighty George, our sovereign lord,
> In sign of British love, this British sword'.[29]

Here a mad prophet appears who, being possessed by the spirit of a superior being, predicts eternal friendship between Great Britain and the Kingdom of Otaheite (Pl.54). To complete this patriotic finale, an enormous painting of the apotheosis of Captain Cook being crowned by Britannia and Fame, is lowered from the clouds. Then all those on stage raise their voices and sing a song of homage to the great circumnavigator and explorer.

O'Keeffe's scenario is a concoction of names and incidents from Cook's voyages which reveals much artistic licence on the part of the playwright. Omai, who in reality was a native of comparatively low distinction, is made King of Otaheite in the play. Cook had not always regarded Omai as the best representative of his native people and would have preferred Oedidee, who was of a more respected family, to have gone to England instead. Additionally, Omai's resettlement at Huaheine in 1777 was quite different from the way it is presented in the play, for there was no idea of him being accepted as a leader of his people. On the contrary, owing to Omai's imprudent behaviour towards his countrymen and his showing off as a travelled man, Cook was anxious about Omai's safety after the ships had left the island. But if Omai's triumphal coronation in the play was pure fiction, it was at least true that his safety was guaranteed by Britain's power, for Cook had warned the chiefs of retaliation if Omai was molested. It had been Cook's intention to foster good relations between Omai and the other inhabitants of Huaheine, so that Omai could tell what he had seen and experienced in England. He was seen in the role of Britain's 'ambassador' on the Society Islands, as formerly he had represented the Polynesians in Britain. Wishful thinking in this vein is reflected in the last scene of the pantomime, when Omai is made an ally of Britain. Despite much artistic licence on the part of the playwright, the last scene, however exaggerated, comes near the truth. The end of the play with its patriotic overtones was certainly aptly chosen, for it kindled Britain's self-esteem as a naval power and underlined that in this new age of discovery and exploration she was to play a decisive role by peaceful means.

Incorrect, if not nonsensical, though entertaining, as O'Keeffe's scenario was, it served as a broad platform for some striking phenomena of Pacific geography. Never before had a stage attempted a fuller representation of a particular quarter of the globe, never had so many different climates, vegetations, animals, and costumes, all totally new and strange, been exhibited. This didactic element was well taken. The *Rambler Magazine* characterised the production poignantly as 'a school for the history of man', whereas *The Times* recommended the show to the attention of both the philosopher and the child.[30]

Omai – Scenery and Costumes

The elements which were most liable to convey a sense of realism and authenticity, were naturally scenery and costumes. The production required twelve different exotic settings with individual costumes for about fifty native people.

Loutherbourg's sale catalogue lists a number of scene-models or maquettes for this play, the majority of which seem to have been lost.[31] Fortunately for our knowledge of *Omai*, two sets of maquettes representing the scenes of *Kensington Gardens* (Pl.55), and *Inside a Jourt* (Pl.56) have survived in the Department of Prints and Drawings in the Victoria & Albert Museum.[32] They are among the most instructive and detailed model sets of the eighteenth-century English stage. The model of the Jourt scene, though incomplete, is of some importance, as it gives an idea of Loutherbourg's practice of design. From descriptions of that scene as they appear in press-reviews, it can be deduced that three different illustrations by

Webber were employed to create a decoration that was both practicable and visually attractive.[33] Moreover, all individual pieces of the model set bear annotations on their reverses which mark their act and scene number as well as their respective positions on the stage as wings, flats and borders.[34] Additionally there is Loutherbourg's hand-written note 'Mr. Hodgins' on the back of a border piece, thus stipulating that this part of the decoration should be executed by the artist of that name.

Students who have previously worked on this pantomime have made a number of suggestions which have helped to reconstruct the scenery of *Omai*.[35] As designs were largely missing they were inclined to approach their subject from the illustrations in Cook's narratives. Little account was taken, however, of the fact, that designs did not necessarily have to correspond to published engravings. This point is attested by a watercolour drawing in the British Museum, which has never been studied as an element of the scenery for *Omai*. It was catalogued by Laurence Binyon as a *South Sea Island Scene, for Pantomime of Captain Cook* (Pl.57) and attributed to Hodgins.[36] There is no inscription indicating the act for which it was designed, or what scene it represented. No such scene appears among the prints of Cook's narratives, so the student with no knowledge of ancient Polynesian culture was deprived of any means of identification. The drawing represents a South Sea landscape in which exotic shrubbery surrounds a clearing with grave stones and sacred poles. The sea comes in on the right, and there is a mountain in the background. The view is strikingly similar to an oil sketch on paper in the Yale Center of British Art, Paul Mellon Collection, which has been convincingly attributed to Webber (Pl.58).[37] Both drawing and oil sketch represent what was meant to be a *heiau*, a sacred ground or temple in Hawaii, with objects which very much resemble those in Webber's drawing of *The heiau at Waimea, Kauai*.[38] Since both Webber and Hodgins participated in the decoration of *Omai*, their sketches can be expected to tally with the scenery of that show. The probable clue for the identification of their scene is given in Shield's libretto: with the scenery of Act 2, scene 6 described as 'A View in the Sandwich Islands. A large rock on one Side – A morai on the other'. In this scene Omai, Londina, Harlequin and Colombine are closely pursued by Londina's father and his party; upon striking a rock they run into it. When the pursuing party attempts to follow them, they are frightened by a flock of penguins and a wooden idol; thereupon they try to escape into a 'morai', or *marae*, but are stopped by Oberea who reproaches them for their unhallowed intentions. Thus the *marae* was not really entered, and therefore was probably not a set scene. The circumstance that it was seen at the back of the stage, behind the opening rock, suggests that it was hung up as a prospect. This is supported by the distanced view into which the foreground of the *heiau* develops. The measurements of the British Museum drawing corresponds with those of the other maquettes which have survived from the show,[39] and it seems possible that it served as a design. With no work firmly established by the hand of Hodgins there is no actual evidence for the attribution to this artist. It seems equally conceivable, if not likely, that the view was drawn by Loutherbourg himself; but he may have intended Hodgins to execute it, as indeed he had done on other occasions.

As has now frequently been pointed out, Webber's drawings of South Sea scenery were the main source for the decoration of *Omai*. However, they were not the only ones. It was perhaps with the idea of bridging illustrative material from both Cook's Second and Third Voyage that Loutherbourg also made use of material by William Hodges (1744–97), the artist who had accompanied Cook during the Second Voyage of 1772–75.[40] In 1777 Hodges had exhibited a large oil painting of the *War Boats of the Island of Otaheite* at the Royal Academy, and during the same year a similar scene was engraved by Woollett as the *Fleet of Otaheite assembled at Oparée* and published in the official account of Cook's Second Voyage (Pl.59).[41] A comparison between these depictions and a description of the Ocean scene in the second part of *Omai* – where according to the *London Chronicle*, 'Omai appears in a war boat in the centre of the Otaheite naval power which at length is shut up amidst the confusion of battle and clash of arms'[42] – very strongly suggests Hodges' representation as the principal source, even more so since Webber had not witnessed this spectacle during his voyage. No design of this scene, however, has come to light.

The only other scene in the pantomime which can be visually documented is the *Apotheosis of Captain Cook* in the last scene of the show. Cook is 'crowned by Fame and Britannia, with the Medallions of Several celebrated English naval officers in the background'.[43] Both *The Times* and the *London Chronicle* refer to this representation as the work of the Revd Matthew William Peters.[44] The British Museum possesses an unpublished pencil drawing of an apotheosis of Cook by P. J. de Loutherbourg, which fits the description of the papers (Pl.60).[45] Cook rests on clouds and is surrounded by the allegorical figures of Britannia and Fame; there are also the outlines of medallions sketched in. A later and more accomplished version of this scene in watercolour appeared in the salerooms some years ago (Pl.61).[46] Because it is of irregular shape it looks very much like a cloud piece which could have been part of the design for this scene. It was perhaps identical with a drawing which Webber owned and which was sold on his death in 1793.[47] The new buyer at that time may have hoped for some commercial gain when, a few months later, he published an etching of the apotheosis in which the allegorical trio of Cook, Britannia and Fame hover above a view of Kealakekūa Bay and the scene of the murder of Cook (Pl.62). The etching identifies the representation of the apotheosis as 'being from a design of P. J. de Loutherbourg, R.A.'.[48] Against this background one would not hesitate to claim Loutherbourg as the designer of the apotheosis for the last scene in *Omai*, had not two papers given contrary evidence. It can only follow that either Peters designed the allegory which in turn inspired Loutherbourg's representation, or that Loutherbourg himself invented it and Peters executed the figure group in his well established painterly manner. If Peters may be identified as the 'celebrated artist' to whom the play-bills refer, among the phalanx of executers of scenery,[49] the second alternative and thus Loutherbourg's authorship gain more weight.

The small number of designs for scenery for *Omai* is to some degree compensated for by the lucky survival of twenty-one costume designs (Pls.34–54 and 63), most of which are today owned by the National Library of Australia.[50] The majority of these are new to Cook studies and only a small number have ever been reproduced.[51] They are of paramount interest both for the history of theatre as well as for ethnology. Apparently they are the earliest original costume designs which have survived from the eighteenth-century English stage. The nature of *Omai* with its obligation to depict the characters in a manner true to life was such that almost every figure which appeared on the stage had to be newly designed; this was a rare circumstance for the time. It may well have been this, as well as the connection with the voyages of Captain Cook, which saved these designs from disappearing like the rest of Loutherbourg's costume designs.[52] For a study of *Omai*, and the sources used in the preparation of it, they are of very high value, since they illustrate both fidelity to authentic models provided by Cook's artists, as well as a number of interesting deviations. These were probably introduced in the interest of visual variety.[53] In a limited study like this no picture-by-picture discussion can be given, nor can it be expected exhaustively to deal with the ethnographic problems which these designs present. Instead, some more general remarks are made as to their attribution and relevance to the pantomime.

Taken as a group the number of designs can be divided into two series. The first includes costumes of the main characters in the plot: Otoo (Pl.34); Towha in the dress of a Chief Mourner (Pl.35); Oberea (Pl.36) and Towha in martial dress (Pl.37); to this belongs a figure similar to Towha in martial dress which is inscribed both with the names of Towha and Oedidee; it is henceforth referred to as Towha-Oedidee (Pl.63). The other series consists of sixteen figures from the final scene and the procession in honour of Omai (Pls.38–54). The designs have continuous running numbers in their top right corner, from Towha in martial dress who is no.1 to the mad prophet inscribed no.46. As the prophet enters last in the play it apparently follows that forty-six different exotic dresses had to be designed. With the aid of O'Keeffe's libretto, numbers can be attributed to those designs which have been lost. Among them one expects the costume design for Omai who probably figured as no.3 as well as those of the other native characters who took part in the procession.[54]

Webber's influence upon these designs seems to have been conspicuous. The figures of the natives of New Zealand (Pls.40–41), the chief and the common man of Kamtchatka (Pls.45–46), the native of Nootka Sound (Pl.48), the couple of Prince William Sound (Pls.49–50), and the three natives of Tahiti (Pls.51–53) are strongly indebted to Webber's drawings.[55] In several cases the correspondences between the designs and Webber's earlier drawings are in fact so close that it should be considered whether some of the costumes were drawn by Webber himself. Significantly, two styles of colouring may be noticed among the designs.[56] In the drawings of the man of New Zealand (Pl.41), the Tchutzki woman (Pl.44), the three Tahitians (Pls.51–53) and Towha-Oedidee (Pl.63), the watercolour is soft in tonality and thinly applied on paper. By comparison the rest of the drawings are characterized by stronger strokes of the brush and their figures are more forcefully and solidly conceived. An attribution of styles to either artist, Loutherbourg or Webber, is however extremely problematic. The latter group includes the designs of Otoo, Oberea and Towha in martial dress, which bear witness to considerable artistic licence and a decisive adaptation for the stage. Their costumes combine factual and imaginative elements in the draping as well as in the colourful patterns of their cloaks. There is, for example, no authentic drawing from Captain Cook's voyages which could serve as a model for Oberea's dress. Though it makes use of feather pendants, which can be linked with the Tahitian mourning costume, it is pure fiction. It is therefore reasonable to expect that Loutherbourg himself designed these figures, taking more than usual trouble to verify the details.

The question is, would the figures of lighter execution in the first group then have to be regarded as being by Webber? The duplication of dress in the designs of Towha (Pl.37) and Towha-Oedidee (Pl.63), is puzzling for both show the same kind of breast-plate and head dress. This congruence could well suggest Loutherbourg and Webber both designing costumes side by side. It is the drawing of Towha-Oedidee (Pl.63) which on stylistic grounds one would rather like to attribute to Webber. Ethnographically speaking it is also the more reliable of the two. This shows in a number of details of which only the longer shaped head dress and the lack of ornament and fringes on the cloak need to be mentioned. Though correct, it later seems to have been superseded by the more fictitious version of Towha (Pl.37), who looks more theatrically sublime and who by virtue of his long white beard and wand comes nearer to the conception of this figure as an awesome god and magician.[57]

Unfortunately a comparison of what appears to be Loutherbourg's and Webber's hand-writing – Loutherbourg's possibly being the one in the inscription 'Oedidee', Webber's in 'Toha Chief of Otaheite' – gives no final clue, as both hands show up indiscriminately among both groups of drawings.

The question of attribution becomes even more complex when it is realised that for some of the dress designs Webber supplied no models. The figure of Towha (Pl.37) seems to be one of these, since no corresponding drawing appears among his *oeuvre*. It is rather more likely that this figure was copied from Woollett's engraving of the *Fleet of Otaheite, assembled at Oparée* (Pl.59),[58] after a drawing by Hodges, in which Towha the admiral of the Tahitian fleet is distinguished by the enormous size of his head dress and the martial appearance of his breast-plate adorned with shark teeth. Another figure for whose appearance Loutherbourg consulted an engraving after Hodges (Pl.39), is the Chief of New Zealand (Pl.38). The head of the native with tattoo marks, feathers and white bunches of bird down, not only show ethnographic idiosyncracies of a Maori as portrayed in Hodges' *Man of New Zealand*,[59] it also follows its model in the three-quarter position of the head.

It was Loutherbourg's vision of the total presentation, his feeling for colour and variety of dress, that determined him to look for pictorial sources outside Webber's *oeuvre* and even outside the context of Cook's voyages. The dresses of the Chief of the Tchutzki (Pl.43), the Tchutzki woman (Pl.44) and the woman of Kamtchatka (Pl.47), bear no relation to people whom Cook had met. The design of the Tchutzki chief was certainly inspired by some drawing of a Red Indian or composed on the basis of dress elements which Loutherbourg had studied in some collection in London.[60] For the two other figurines Loutherbourg used Thomas Jefferys's important costume book *A Collection of the dresses of different nations* (London, 1757 and 1772) which, for theatre costumes, was the indispensable standard work at the time, and of which Loutherbourg himself owned a copy.[61] Both representations can be identified as *Habit of a Tatarian Woman in Kasan* and *Habit of a Samoyed Woman and Child*.[62] In 1768 the celebrated French astronomer L'Abbé Chappe d'Auteroche had published his *Voyage en Sibérie* with illustrations by Jean-Baptiste Le Prince, the artist who had accompanied him on his journey through Russia.[63] It is from this source that Jefferys had copied his illustrations.[64] As a travelling artist, Le Prince had received instructions similar to those given to Hodges and Webber ten to fifteen years later, and there is no reason to mistrust his authenticity. But it seems odd that in these two cases Loutherbourg should have preferred the drawings of Le Prince.[65] Not only are they out of keeping with dresses worn by the Tchutzki and the inhabitants of Kamtchatka, they also discard Webber's drawings.

This evidence almost necessarily leads to the attribution of these designs to Loutherbourg himself; it seems unreasonable for Webber to have voluntarily deviated from his own drawings which he knew were ethnographically the more correct ones. If Loutherbourg then executed the Tchutzki chief and the Tchutzki woman and thus adopted two different styles he could certainly have done the other costume designs as well. In the absence of more conclusive evidence, all

92

designs must be attributed to Loutherbourg, since he was the organiser of the show, who planned and supervised its entire visual presentation.

The British Museum Drawings – A study of Weapons

After this survey of designs for scenery and dresses for *Omai* some other drawings, all of which are illustrative of South Sea subject matter, must be brought into the discussion. They are kept in the British Museum and are contained in an album of drawings which are mostly by, and once belonged to P. J. de Loutherbourg.[66] They were catalogued by Laurence Binyon in 1902, but since then do not seem to have received any attention. To facilitate discussion each item is listed in the sequence of its appearance in the album; Binyon's titles have been retained and his numbers are cited in parenthesis:

271 *Prow of a New Zealand canoe.* Pencil, 21.5 × 38.4 cm (No.86).

272–75 *Four studies of heads of savages.*

272 Pencil, 8.8 × 8.0 cm (No.87a).

273 Pencil, 6.5 × 6.3 cm (No.87b).

274 Pencil, 13.1 × 9.7 cm (No.87c).

275 Pen over pencil, 11.0 × 9.7 cm (No.87d).

276 *One whole-length study of a savage,* pencil, 21.2 × 17.0 cm (No.87e).

277 *Savages in a canoe.* Indian Ink, 5.0 × 17.8 cm (No.88a).

278 *Savage weapons from the Sandwich Islands, New Zealand, etc.* Pen and ink, 18.9 × 28.9 cm (No.88b).

279 *A man addressing a group seated on the ground.* Indian ink, 8.8 × 33.0 cm (No.88c).

280 *Head of a savage.* Watercolours, 6.6 × 5.2 cm (No.89a).

282 *Savage with a tomahawk.* Red chalk, 20.1 × 7.6 cm (No.90a).

283 *Woman of the same tribe, carrying a child.* Red chalk, 17.0 × 8.7 cm (No.90b).[67]

Of the twelve works listed, only two can be attributed to Loutherbourg himself. The first, the sketch of a *Head of a Savage* (Pl.64) is attributed tentatively on the basis of stylistic comparison with another drawing on the same page.[68] The hair of the native is black and his face of a swarthy yellowish colour. His features could well be Polynesian and one could speculate as to whether this portrait was drawn in connection with *Omai*.

The second sketch, a pen and ink study of *Savage weapons from the Sandwich Islands, New Zealand, etc.* (Pl.65) may be safely ascribed to Loutherbourg. The flow of the line and the writing underneath some of the artefacts are suggestive of

Loutherbourg's hand. The geographical descriptions across the sheet specify the provenances of the Objects as North America, New Zealand, the Sandwich Islands, Otaheite and the Friendly Islands. These are all places which Cook had visited during his Third Voyage; only in 1778 did he discover the Sandwich Islands and it was in the same year that he sailed along the North-west Coast of America. Not only do the drawings of weapons derive from areas that Cook had visited, but the sharpness of some of the detail and the annotations of measurements strongly suggest that they were drawn from actual specimens brought back to England. As Miss Adrienne Kaeppler has shown, many artefacts were officially collected by Captain Cook and his successors on the Third Voyage as well as privately by various members of the expedition.[69] Many of these were sold again in England to private collectors and it is interesting to note that Loutherbourg himself acquired a considerable number of artefacts. When his estate was sold in 1812 various objects from the South Seas and from North-west America showed up, such as 'two War Bludgeons from the Friendly Isles', 'a capital long Wood Spear from the Sandwich Islands', 'two Bows from North America', or 'A Bone Pattopattoo [from New Zealand]'; objects like 'a Helmet, Mantle, and other curious Ornaments, composed of Feathers, from the Sandwich Islands', or 'A curious Gorget from Otaheite, composed of Feathers, Hair and Shark's Teeth' were also included.[70] They were comparatively rare specimens and would have done honour to any collection of weapons of his time. It is not known when or from whom Loutherbourg acquired these objects. He was known as a keen collector of weapons,[71] and probably would have tried to purchase some soon after the return of Cook's ships. For him the most likely vendor seems to have been John Webber, who owned one of the most extensive private collections of 'artificial curiosities'.[72] If Loutherbourg did not buy objects early after the return of the expedition his later co-operation with Webber over the designing of scenery and costumes for *Omai* would have given him another opportunity to extend his collection.[73]

Loutherbourg's ambition to present *Omai* in the guise of curious and spectacular realism, with particular regard to ethnography, made it necessary for him to study his material as extensively as possible. An opportunity to do so was offered to him in Sir Ashton Lever's *Holophusikon*, a private museum of natural history and ethnographic specimens in Leicester House. Lever, one of the great collectors in eighteenth-century England, had obtained the bulk of the ethnographic material from Cook's Third Voyage in 1781.[74] He already possessed a substantial collection of artefacts and curiosities from Cook's two earlier voyages, thus when he put his new acquisitions on display, the *European Magazine* commented that there was no spectacle in town that was 'more worthy of the attention of a curious and intelligent person than the Holophusikon'.[75]

94

In February 1781 when Lever's museum had been open to the public for six years, Loutherbourg set up a show-room for a model-stage without figures to imitate the various conditions of nature; it had an equally unusual name, the *Eidophusikon*,[76] and within a short time became one of the most successful entertainments in London. These two centres of learning and entertainment were in close promixity to each other in Leicester Square.[77] In part, Loutherbourg's choice of a name so similar to Lever's 'Holophusikon' for his little theatre was perhaps no coincidence. These two enterprises though so different in character, both pursued the idea of embracing the whole of nature, one by exhibiting natural and artifical productions, the other by imitating natural phenomena of day and night, light and shade, or changes of weather. Both Lever and Loutherbourg aimed at exhibiting nature on a global scale; the first by incorporating thousands of specimens of natural history and man's ingenuity, the other by displaying attractive scenes from overseas: places like Tangier, North America or Japan on his model-stage.[78] For several months both men were almost next-door neighbours, and although there are no actual documents to prove their relationship, it is most likely that they were acquainted, if only as rivals for public attention.

There can be little doubt that Loutherbourg actually visited Lever's museum, since a number of weapons in his sketch were exhibited there.[79] In 1783 the woman artist Sarah Stone was a daily visitor to Lever's museum where she made watercolour copies in great detail of the most outstanding and precious objects from Lever's Cook collection.[80] The sketch books in which she drew ethnographic objects are a most valuable record of the artefacts which Lever owned,[81] and it is with their aid that the weapons sketched by Loutherbourg can be identified as most probably Leverian objects.[82] A case in point is Loutherbourg's sketch of a Tongan club (sixth club from top, on the right, in Pl.65). This was a unique object in Lever's collection which has luckily been preserved and which is now owned by the University Museum for Archaeology and Ethnology, Cambridge.[83]

Ethnographic objects obviously played a vital part in the preparation of *Omai*, as an inspiration for both colour and shape as well as for the material used for stage replicas. Many of the characters in the play carry artefacts or natural products of their countries. In a number of instances the male figures in Loutherbourg's dress designs carry weapons. The figure of Towha-Oedidee (Pl.63) and the Maori of New Zealand (Pl.41) both hold a spear, while the Chief warrior of New Zealand (Pl.40) is armed with a *taiaha*, a two-handed striking weapon, and a *patoo patoo*. In addition, the natives of Tchutzki, Nootka and Prince William Sound are armed with a different kind of arrow, quiver and tomahawk. It is no coincidence that several of these objects or, rather, specimens of identical shape, are depicted in Loutherbourg's study of weapons, for they are the ones which the impersonators of the natives carried on stage. If one accepts the Tongan club as sufficient proof, then

Loutherbourg copied specimens in Lever's museum. One imagines that subsequently he passed his study on to the prop-maker in the theatre to have replicas made. This suggestion is supported by the measurements noted against the drawings, and the attention which Loutherbourg paid to individual shapes and ornamentation, though it must be admitted that from an ethnographical point of view the latter are not specific but general.

A sketch of very similar character and of almost identical measurements is in the Alexander Turnbull Library, Wellington (Pl.66) representing an altar, god images from Hawaii, Tahitian drums, paddles and a pipe tomahawk.[84] Related features such as the distribution of the artefacts on the paper and the annotations of the objects according to geography and measurements suggest that this drawing, equally, was used for the production of *Omai*. All the objects depicted were required in the production. The altar and drums were probably copied from drawings, others, like the idols and paddles, could have been drawn from actual specimens.[85] A very interesting alien element in this assemblage of South Sea artefacts, is the pipe tomahawk at upper left. As an ethnographical object it belongs to the Red Indians of the Plains and Eastern Woodlands.[86] It is as unexpected within this group of South Sea artefacts as the Red Indian outfit of the Tchutzki chief among Loutherbourg's dress designs (Pl.43). The pipe tomahawk which the chief carries under his belt is of the same type as the one depicted in this sketch. This circumstance lends additional weight to the assumption that the sketch in the Alexander Turnbull Library is indeed a preparatory study for the production of *Omai*. Lever is known to have possessed a similar tomahawk in his museum and there is thus good reason to believe that the depiction was made from an actual specimen.[87]

Further sketches of this kind may have existed and are perhaps still awaiting discovery. This can be surmised from a large red quiver which is represented in Loutherbourg's costume design of the native of Prince William Sound (Pl.49). Only one such quiver – a unique specimen – can be identified from Cook's voyages, and this is known to have been on display in Lever's museum also.[88]

The British Museum Drawings – Studies from the South Seas

The remaining drawings of South Sea subject matter in Loutherbourg's album may be divided into three distinct groups on grounds of style and content: first, *The prow of a New Zealand canoe* (Pl.67); second, the *Savage with tomahawk* and the *Woman of the same tribe, carrying a child* (Pls.68–69), the *Whole-length study of a savage* (Pl.70), and *Four studies of heads of savages* (Pls.71–74); and third, *Savages in a canoe* (Pl.75) and *A man addressing a group* (Pl.76). The drawings of both the

96

second and the third groups give an impression of professional work by an artist who was versatile in several media, pencil, pen, chalk and Indian ink. His draughtsmanship is competent and rapid in execution, and is totally different from the style in which the study of the New Zealand prow is rendered. The latter, distinguished by great accuracy in the delineation of the ornamental carving, appears to be quite different from the rest of the drawings. It should therefore be considered first.

New Zealand was visited during all three voyages by Captain Cook, the longest stay being the first, from 9 October 1769 to 31 March 1770. Among the drawings that the artists and naturalists of the first expedition made while in New Zealand, there are six pencil studies of heads and stern ornaments of canoes.[89] They are the work of Herman Diedrich Spöring, Banks's Swedish secretary and assistant naturalist, who drew them at Tolaga Bay on 29 October 1769.[90] On Spöring's death, during the return voyage to England all his drawings fell to Banks.[91] They were later bequeathed by Banks to the British Museum, together with many other drawings mainly from Cook's First Voyage, and they are now kept in the Department of Manuscripts of the British Library.[92] Among Spöring's drawings there is one particular representation of a canoe head that is almost exactly like the study in Loutherbourg's album.[93] An original idea that one was a tracing of the other was invalidated by measurements of the objects in the drawings. The representation of the prow in the drawing in Loutherbourg's album is 21.0 × 37.7 cm, as opposed to 22.5 × 36.0 cm in the other. Neither did it seem probable that one was a copy of the other, since both drawings show minute details which are individually more accurate than their counterpart. A major difference can only be noted in the drawing, formerly in the Banks collection, which shows measurements of the length and the height of the canoe written neatly alongside the prow.[94] Otherwise, in point of style, the two drawings are so similar that both must be regarded as the work of Spöring.

This conclusion is of consequence, for it could mean that Loutherbourg received his drawing, if not directly, then perhaps indirectly, from Sir Joseph Banks. There is no evidence of an actual relationship between the two men, but in the light of Loutherbourg's production of *Omai*, and of the fact that Banks also owned a large collection of South Sea artefacts, Loutherbourg may be presumed to have visited his house.[95] Alternatively, the drawing could have been transmitted by Webber who had dealings with Banks when, between 1780 and 1784, he produced the illustrations for the journals of Cook's Third Voyage.[96]

What role did a New Zealand canoe play in the production of *Omai*? In one description of the last scene of the pantomime there is an allusion to the appearance of a New Zealand canoe. The *London Chronicle* reports, on the last scene in the pantomime: 'It is a most extensive view in the great bay of Otaheite at sun-set, with a view of *ships at anchor* . . . A fine view offers itself of all the *boats* of the islands entering the bay with Ambassadors from all the foreign powers'. [Author's italics].[97] According to O'Keeffe's libretto, the first group of 'ambassadors' who arrived on stage were the Maoris of New Zealand and there is good reason to believe that there was a New Zealand boat among the ships and boats that entered the bay. While a canoe used for such purpose would certainly not have been made up with intricately carved ornaments of the type depicted in Spöring's drawing, the representation of the prow may well have served as a basic inspiration for a simpler structure that was suitable for the stage.

The second group of South Sea drawings in Loutherbourg's album contains studies of heads and figures of South Sea islanders. Among them is a drawing in red chalk of a woman carrying a child on her back and leaning on a spear-like stick (Pl.69). When this is compared with extant works by Cook's artists, its medium and the treatment of the figure in sketchy outlines, are most suggestive of the style of William Hodges. Very conveniently our idea can be confirmed by a figure of similar appearance in Hodges' painting of a *Maori Family at Cascade Cove*.[98]

The picture belongs to a group of South Sea landscapes which Hodges did for the Admiralty shortly after his return from the Pacific in 1775, and it seems most likely that for the representation of the mother and the child in the left hand corner Hodges availed himself of his earlier study described above.

Cook had visited Cascade Cove in Dusky Bay on 11 April 1773. The presence of a waterfall gave grandeur to that 'wild romantic spot', which the natural historian George Forster emphatically describes in his journal.[99] However, no natives were met with on this occasion. The incident depicted by Hodges had taken place a few days earlier on 6 April on Indian Island, opposite Cascade Cove. While Cook established friendly relations with the Maori family which he met there, Hodges began to make drawings of them.[100] The encounter was only brief, but the next morning Cook returned to the spot, bringing a number of presents with him, such as hatchets and nails. Meanwhile the family had increased to eight members, and now consisted of 'the man, his two wives . . . , the young woman . . . and a boy about fourteen years old and three small children, the youngest of which was at the breast. . . .[101] Hodges again made drawings of the natives, and it would have been on this occasion that he drew the woman carrying her child (Pl.69) and the man with an adze (Pl.68).[102]

The fact that both drawings are placed alongside the study of weapons in Loutherbourg's album, makes them susceptible to an association with the production of *Omai*, and indeed there is a striking similarity between Hodges' drawing of the woman and Loutherbourg's costume design of the same subject (Pl.42). Loutherbourg maintained Hodges' conception of the figure as seen in profile from left to right and the positioning of its parts. The corresponding

98

position of the child on his mother's back and the woman leaning upon a stick leave little doubt that a direct relationship exists between the two drawings. One can not be absolutely certain that Loutherbourg did not copy his design from the figure in the painting of the *Maori family at Cascade Cove*, but when it is considered first, that the picture belonged to the Admiralty and was thus less accessible, and second that Hodges' sketch appears among a collection of Loutherbourg drawings, it seems much more likely that Loutherbourg had Hodges' drawing before him when he designed his costume.

Unlike the drawing of the Maori woman with the child, that of the man with the adze can not be connected with the production of *Omai*, and judging from the extant group of Maori costume designs, it was not used at all. Neither is there any evidence to suggest that the drawing of a seated native in a cloak (Pl.70) had any bearing on the show. The drawing can safely be attributed to Hodges, and is thus revealed as a visual document of the Second Voyage. Unfortunately the ethnographic identity of the sitter is difficult to establish,[103] and because of this it remains unplaceable in terms of the production of *Omai*.

The last two drawings remind us that Hodges' influence upon the pantomime, though beyond doubt, is less clearly defined than Webber's. Not only was Webber active in the preparation of the show, he also seems to have owned more appropriate and variegated illustrations. Besides, Hodges' contribution appears to be more difficult to define because fewer drawings from his hand are known. Where actual drawings are missing, indirect evidence may be brought forward in his favour. It could, for example, be suspected that his illustrations served as design material for Loutherbourg's costumes of the natives of Tanna, the Marquesas or the Easter Islands. These islands were only visited during the Second Voyage, when Hodges was the accompanying artist.

The four studies of natives' heads included in group two are believed to have been made on two of these islands. They are of the same 'unfinished' quality as the previous drawings and were probably done on the spot. Their slight pencil and pen work, and the small size of the sheets, suggest that they once formed part of a sketch-book from which they were subsequently cut out.

A drawing which lacks any elaboration of pencil work but still makes a charming study is the portrait of a young girl with a roundish face and protruding cheeks, looking left (Pl.71). As some faint lines around her head seem to indicate, she wears a high head dress similar to a turban, with a piece of cloth (or tapa?) falling down upon her shoulder. This outfit makes her resemble Hodges' drawing of the *Woman of Sta Christina*[104] and it is upon this representation that she is tentatively identified.

The two other sitters can be recognized as natives of Easter Island. Of the frontal portraits of the man and the woman (Pls.72–73), Hodges made more accomplished versions in red crayon, which were included in the illustrations to Cook's narrative.[105] The drawing of the man was begun in pencil and subsequently worked over in pen, in order to accentuate ethnographic details such as the diadem of grass and feathers which he wears as a protection against the sun. For the same reason the woman wears a conical straw bonnet. Both sitters possess extremely large perforations of the ear-lobe, a feature about which Cook commented in his journal. Cook noticed that inside the hole, the natives wore 'the white down of feathers, and rings . . . made of some elastic substance, rolled up like a watch-spring; I judged this was to keep the hole at its utmost extension'.[106] This observation is illustrated in Hodges' second portrait study of a woman of Easter Island (Pl.74), this time represented in profile. This drawing is of particular value since it gives additional ethnographical information which is not found in any of his other works.

Next to these portraits there are two more sketches of South Sea subjects in Loutherbourg's album. Binyon had entitled these *Savages in a canoe* (Pl. 75) and *A man addressing a group seated on the ground* (Pl.76). Though they are rendered in Indian ink and thus differ from the drawings discussed so far, they can also be attributed to Hodges. They show Hodges' free and spirited handling of the medium and reflect a professional fluidity of style.[107] In each of the two sketches, only a few brush strokes indicate the darker parts of the figures and boats, leaving it to the eye to complete the full shapes. A few pencil lines and an occasional outline in pen add to the reality of the scene. It would have taken only a few seconds for a small impression like the *Two natives in their canoe* to be created, with one thick stroke for the boat and some wash for the surface of the sea. The ability to sketch strange and unexpected phenomena rapidly was no doubt a necessity for an artist who, like Hodges, saw the South Seas for the first time.

The significance of these sketches as evidence of Hodges' method of working in the Pacific is enhanced by their historiographic value as documents of Cook's Second Voyage. The *Two natives in their canoe* were possibly drawn in October 1773 when Cook's ships visited the Tongan or Friendly Islands, and they may have formed part of a group of approaching canoes of which Forster gives a lively description.[108] The Tongan character of the boat is stressed by the torpedo-shaped, equal-ended hull and outriggers.[109] To the seaman, the Polynesian boats were a constant source of curiosity, and Cook and others commented on their construction as well as on their nautical prowess.

The other sketch which represents a group of natives in their boat can be more firmly linked with a particular incident on the voyage. From the feathers on the natives' heads, as well as from the shape of their garments, the figures can be identified as Maoris. After Cook had spent April 1773 in Dusky Bay, where he had encountered the Maori family mentioned above, he proceeded to Queen Charlotte

Sound where a pre-arranged meeting with Captain Furneaux of the *Adventure* took place. During the three weeks from 18 May to 7 June, when both ships stayed in the Sound, there was much contact with local natives. On the morning of 4 June, a few days before departure, a double canoe approached from the north armed with 28 men. It was the largest boat so far seen. It stopped opposite the *Resolution* and two members of its party, apparently chiefs, stood up to address Cook's ship. According to George Forster the first man held a green flax plant in his hand and thus symbolized his peaceful intentions. The second chief was remarkable for his temperament, and accompanied his speech with wild movements of the arms.[110] Both these circumstantial details appear in Hodges' sketch but are fused into one figure. In the light of Forster's description it becomes obvious that the squatting figures are not being addressed by the speaker, as Binyon assumed, but are, in fact, looking towards the *Resolution*, following the direction of the chief's speech. This impression is verified by a larger and more finished drawing of the same incident which Hodges did in watercolour and wash, now owned by the La Trobe Library in Melbourne (Pl.77).[111] On the right hand side of this drawing a part of the *Resolution* is included as a *repoussoir*-element, and this illustrates the situation more convincingly than the sketch. Some time after their address the Maoris were invited on board. Of the objects which they traded the Forsters acquired a rare worked shell trumpet. This seems to be identical with one which they gave to the naturalist Thomas Pennant on their return to England; it is now at the University Museum of Archaeology and Ethnology, Cambridge.[112] Thus this sketch by Hodges is not only important for the history of Captain Cook's voyages, it also documents the circumstances in the acquisition of certain precious Maori artefacts.

The last two drawings certainly lie outside the topic of *Omai*, for their execution was too sketchy and the objects represented too indistinct to offer much help in the preparation of the pantomime. Yet one wonders why they were kept together with other drawings, such as the study of weapons of Hodges' woman of New Zealand, which in all probability served as design material for the show. One would like to know whether the ethnographic drawings in Loutherbourg's album reflect a collection which was once much bigger, and out of which only some drawings were used as suitable models for *Omai*. The other drawings in Loutherbourg's album representing such subject matter as military costumes, naval actions, details of ships, landscapes, etc., suggest that they once belonged to Loutherbourg's studio collection. This was auctioned after the artist's death in 1812 and registered in his sale catalogue.[113] Comparing the original amount and the remnants in the album it is obvious that the contents in the album now only represent a fragment. Fragmentation may also have seriously affected the South Sea drawings. If we suppose that a good many sketches from the South Seas by Hodges were included among the many missing Loutherbourg drawings and stage-designs, this would indeed explain why hardly any drawings made on the spot during Cook's Second Voyage are known today.

The assumption that Loutherbourg owned a number of Hodges' South Sea drawings is a tempting one though it can not be corroborated by any further evidence. The only indication that this may have been so is the fact that both Loutherbourg's and Hodges' drawings have been preserved together since, at least, the middle of last century.[114] However this may be, the ultimate value of these newly discovered drawings – apart from their possible connection with *Omai* – lies in their historic and ethnographic importance to Cook studies. As field-sketches, which they appear to be, they increase the documentation of Polynesian people from the time of Captain Cook's voyages. For Hodges' *oeuvre* the drawings are of exceptional interest since they include representations of whole-length figures and of groups. They tell against the common verdict that Hodges had no talent for figure drawing, and that because of this inability his representations of natives were 'confined to the head, or head and shoulders'.[115] It is true that Hodges' strength was not in figure but in landscape painting, however, the work he was committed to do also required records of people. Cook's and Forster's journals reveal that on several occasions Hodges drew multi-figure groups in which whole-length figures were certainly included.[116] The German traveller Georg Christoph Lichtenberg saw drawings of this type when he visited Hodges in London near the end of 1775.[117] Hodges' work as it has survived in public collections most commonly represents landscapes and bust portraits,[118] but it could well be that larger numbers of his figure drawings are still to be retrieved.

In the course of the foregoing discussion a number of documents, designs for scenery and costumes, have been referred to which illustrate that the production of *Omai* was an extraordinary event on the eighteenth-century English stage. It was an exhibition and travelogue of Cook's voyages, and a considerable number of artists, explorers, and natural historians were directly or indirectly involved in its realisation. As literary and graphic sources have shown, it was carefully planned and much attention was paid to realistic detail.

In the attempt to point out models which may have been of some consequence for the preparation of *Omai*, a number of drawings with South Sea subject matter have been referred to. These can reasonably be attributed to William Hodges, and they add to the number of his drawings and enlarge our knowledge of the people of Polynesia in the time of Captain Cook's voyages.

Notes

The composition of this text goes back to autumn 1975 when, on a scholarship of the Humanities Research Centre of the Australian National University, I had the opportunity to visit the National Library of Australia, Canberra, and study their important group of costume designs for *Omai*. At the time and frequently since Miss Margaret Murphy of the NLA has been most obliging in her assistance, for which I am very grateful. The complex of Sir Ashton Lever treated in this paper owes many helpful suggestions to Dr Peter Whitehead of the British Museum (Nat. Hist.). He not only gave active encouragement, but was also instrumental in introducing me to Dr Adrienne Kaeppler, Hawaii, and Peter Gathercole, Cambridge. Both of them followed the writing of my paper with keen encouragement and saved me from many errors. Their help is gratefully acknowledged. Finally, my special thanks go to the previous editor of the Yearbook Richard Camber for inviting me to contribute this paper, as well as to the present editor, T. C. Mitchell, for his valuable corrections of style.

1 Reviews appeared in a number of London papers: the *European Magazine* (December 1785), the *London Chronicle* (20–22 December 1785), the *Morning Chronicle* (20, 22, 24, 26 December 1785), the *Morning Herald* (29 December 1785), the *New London Magazine* (supplement to Vol.1, December 1785), the *Rambler Magazine* (January 1786), *The Times* (22, 23, 24, 26, 27, 28, 31 December 1785, 4 January 1786), the *St. James Chronicle* (20–22 December 1785), the *Universal Magazine* (December 1785).

2 For the numerous editions of Cook's Third Voyage which appeared shortly after 1784 see Cook-Bibliography (1970: 298–303); for the anthropological interest in the Pacific immediately following Cook's voyages see Joppien (1978b).

3 For an account of topical subjects on the London stage during the second half of the eighteenth century, see Thomas (1944) and Allen (1965).

4 During the season of 1785–86 *Omai* was performed fifty times and a further eight times in each of the following seasons, see Hogan (1968: seasons 1785–86, 1786–87, 1787–88).

5 On Omai's life, including his sojourn in England, see the following works: Angelo (1830: Vol.2, 55); Boswell (1935: Vol.3, 8); Burney (1832: Vol.2, 2–8); Burney (1907: Vol.1, 331); Colman (1830: Vol.2, 152–202); Cook (1777: Vol.1, 169–71); Cook/King (1784: Vol.1, passim); Dawson (1958: passim); Gardiner (1838: Vol.1, 5); Lichtenberg (1971: Vol.2, 633–35); Thrale (1951: Vol.1, 48); a guide to several MSS sources on Omai is also given in the Cook-Bibliography (1970: 221, 297, 666, 668, 764); for later historical studies on Omai see Alexander (1977); Clark (1941); Fairchild (1928: 71–73); McCormick (1977); Tinker (1922: 75–89, and 1938: 56–58); McCormick's study, the latest and apparently the most critical could not be utilised before this article went to press.

6 Several drawings and paintings were made of Omai, the most important ones being those by Dance, Hodges, Parry, and Reynolds, see Cook-Bibliography (1970: 766–69). Another portrait not recorded in the bibliography which is presumed to represent Omai, is in the Hunterian Collection of the Royal College of Surgeons, see Le Fanu (1960: 81). The pencil drawing of Omai (Pl.33), in the National Library of Australia, is attributed to Reynolds and seems to be a study for the portrait at Yale University Art Gallery; its measurements are 36.2 × 26.2 cm.

7 Cook/King (1784: Vol.2, 103).

8 Garrick (1963: Vol.2, 1031).

9 Earlier productions with exotic settings had been, for example: *The Fair Circassian* (Drury Lane, 27 November 1781); *Robinson Crusoe* (Drury Lane, 29 January 1781), or *The Choice of Harlequin* (Covent Garden, 26 December 1781). The decorations of the last production were based on Indian drawings by Tilly Kettle who had brought these back with him to England.

10 Webber, whom Martin Hardie has called a 'good draughtsman and a delicate colourist' (1967: Vol.1, 236), has never been studied as

an artist. An introduction to his South Sea works is given in Beaglehole (1967: Pt.1, CCXI–CCXIV).

11 Joppien (1972).

12 For these two artists see Rosenfeld/Croft-Murray (1964: Vol.XIX, No.1, 15–17, and Vol.XIX, No.4, 142–45).

13 Boaden (1825: Vol.1, 312).

14 In Loutherbourg's painting *A Winter Morning in Hyde Park, with a Party Skating* (1775/76) Webber, according to a tradition which was handed down with the picture, is portrayed alongside Mr and Mrs Loutherbourg, the engraver V. M. Picot and the dancing master J. G. Noverre(?). Webber appears to be the young man on the chair, facing the spectator, and there is indeed a great deal of likeness between this and the portrait of him painted some years later by Johann Daniel Mottet, now in the Historisches Museum, Berne (Joppien, 1973: No.22, and for Mottet's portrait: Beaglehole, 1967: Pt.1, Pl.7b). Both Loutherbourg and Webber had Swiss ancestors. Webber's father, who lived in London as a sculptor, was a native of Berne, whereas Loutherbourg's family on his father's side had originated from Basle. Both artists spoke German and both had at one time lived in Paris and belonged to the circle of J.-G. Wille. Thus one would expect them to have had opportunities to meet. For a short bibliography of Webber see Henking (1955–56: 325–29).

15 For Webber's work for the Admiralty see Joppien (1978a). It seems that, though the Admiralty controlled Webber's graphic work from the voyage for a number of years, his sketches were available to a select number of people. This is suggested by Fanny Burney's visit to Webber in March 1781. Fanny was the sister of Lt James Burney who had accompanied Cook on his Second and Third Voyage, see Burney (1904: Vol.1, 466).

16 Dawson (1958: 618).

17 From 1784–91, with the exception of 1790, Webber exhibited 29 works with subject matter from Cook's Third Voyage at the Royal Academy (Graves, 1905: Vol.4, 186–87). Between 1786 and 1792 he issued a number of aquatint drawings from the South Seas which apparently were sold individually. A complete series of 20 of these prints was published after his death by John Boydell as *Views in the South Seas* (London, 1808).

18 O'Keeffe (1826: Vol.2, 114). *The Times* makes a similar statement: 'Mr. Webber who was with Captain Cook in his last voyage, gave the information how to dress the characters in the new Pantomime of "Omai"; and it is from that gentleman's drawings, done on the spot, that many of the scenes are taken'. (23 December 1785).

19 Coxe (1812: 27). Among the section 'Paintings by De Loutherbourg' the following lots are listed: lot 64: 'Ditto [an oil sketch on paper] of a Summer Residence of Otaheite: the Design by Webber, for the Pantomime of "Omai"'; lot 65: 'Ditto, of a Burial Place, on the same Island, the Design by Ditto'; lot 66: 'Ditto, a View in Otaheite, for the same entertainment'; lot 67: 'Ditto, ditto'; lot 68: 'Ditto, Ditto, – A Moon Light'; lot 69: 'Ditto, Ditto, – the Entrance to a Burial Place'; lot 70: 'Ditto, – A Dusky Scene and Moon Light, – his own Design'.

20 O'Keeffe (1826: Vol.II, 114).

21 *The Times* (23 December 1785) states: 'The moonlight [scene] particularly, which was much admired, we are informed, was wholly painted by Mr. Webber'. This service may be connected with an entry in the Covent Garden Ledger, Egerton MS 2287, Vol.XV (September 1786–September 1787) for 4 December 1786: 'Paid Mr. Webber on account of last season £123'. British Library, Department of Manuscripts.

22 The Covent Garden Ledgers, Egerton MSS 2286, Vol.XIV and 2287, Vol.XV (September 1785–September 1786–September 1787) list that several payments were made to Loutherbourg on 17 October 1785, 15 November 1785, 15 December 1785, 23 January 1786, 20 December 1786, which total £620.

23 Credit to Loutherbourg as the organiser of the show is given on the title-page of the printed libretto, see O'Keeffe (1785), and on the front-page of William Shield's musical scores (1785). The advertisements for the pantomime which were printed in several London papers, such as *The Times* (21 December 1785) and the *Morning Chronicle*

(21 December 1785) make this point equally clear: 'The pantomime and the whole of the Scenery, Dresses etc. designed and invented by Mr. Loutherbourg and executed under his superintendence and direction by Messrs. Richards, Carver and Hodgins, Mr. Catton Jr. and Mr. Turner, assisted by two other celebrated artists'. *The Times* additionally states: 'The ideas of the pantomime and the designs of the scenes are announced to have originated with Mr. Loutherbourg'. (22 December 1785). Loutherbourg's authorship of the production must be emphasised, as O'Keeffe gives the impression (1826: Vol.2, 114) that he, as the playwright, was more entitled to credit. He belittles Loutherbourg's achievements, when he says that both of them received a fee of £100. His assertion is reflected by an article by Huse (1936), the first student of *Omai*, who thought of O'Keeffe as the creator of the pantomime and of Loutherbourg only as the scene-designer who transferred O'Keeffe's ideas into visual terms.

24 During the period from October 1785 up to March 1786 the following artists responsible for the execution of decorations are referred to in the Covent Garden Ledger: Banson, Blackmore, Catton Jr., Carver, Cooper, Dallas, Hodgins, Luny, Lupino, Melbourn, Mullins, Richards and Turner. Another artist employed was Matthew William Peters (see below). Payments of fees seem to have begun on 17 October 1785. It may have been the original intention of Covent Garden also to employ a number of more notable artists to add lustre to the show, but these attempts seem to have been abortive. In this vein the *London Chronicle* reported some weeks before the first night that 'the new pantomime at Covent Garden will be aided by some of the greatest painters in the Manner of the *Jubilee* to which Dance, Cipriani, Angelica, etc. all contributed. Thus with Loutherbourg, Peters is already at work, and it is hoped that Gainsborough, Cipriani and Farington will also be volunteers'. See Whitley (1928: Vol.2, 353).

25 *The Times* (26 December 1785) announced the arrival a few days before of new machines for the accomplishment of 'several humorous tricks and deceptions for the new pantomime of "Omai" by the celebrated Monsieur Bouverie, principal mechanist to his Majesty of France'.

26 *London Chronicle* (20–22 December 1785). Whitley informs us that Sir Joshua Reynolds sat in the orchestra on the first night and 'expressed the utmost satisfaction at all the landscapes' (1928: Vol.2, 354). It seems that to some extent the renown of *Omai* survived its own day. Thus James Boaden later wrote, 'the success of this elegant entertainment seems to have stampt a character upon the theatre itself, which has since constantly adhered to it'. (1825: Vol.1, 311). O'Keeffe's recollections, in 1826, of the performance, have been noted. A tribute to Loutherbourg's scenery for *Omai* is also paid in *Arnold's Library of Fine Arts* (1831: Vol.1, 328).

27 The manuscript gives a description of the individual scenes as well as of the construction of the plot. It has no dialogue or 'words'. The pantomime is divided into two acts with nine and ten scenes each. The manuscript was made available to me through the very kind services of Miss Dorothy Moore of the Society of Theatre Research, London. Another manuscript of *Omai* is kept in the Huntington Library, San Marino, Larpent Collection (LA 713), see MacMillan (1939:118). This version I have not seen; according to Mr William Ingoldsby of the Huntington (letter 3 September 1975) it 'does not contain any mention of scenery or costumes'.

27a Shield's musical scores for *Omai* have survived in the British Library, see Shield (1785).

28 There are various editions of O'Keeffe's libretto. According to Allen, the second student to write on *Omai* after Huse, the Yale University Library possesses two slightly different versions of the libretto: the 'second edition' which 'describes the action as it was performed on opening night' and the 'new edition' which includes some subsequent alterations, see Allen (1962: 209). No first edition has come to light yet. The Yale's second edition seems to be the only one of its kind, whereas of the new edition more copies are held in the British

Library and the Huntington Library, San Marino.

29 O'Keeffe (1785: 23).

30 *Rambler Magazine* (January 1786) – *The Times* (22 December 1785) says of *Omai* that it 'may be considered a beautiful illustration of Cook's voyages – an illustration of importance to the mature mind of the adult and delightful to the tender capacity of the infant'. 'To the rational mind, what can be more entertaining than to contemplate prospects of countries in their natural colourings and tints. To bring into living action the costumes and manners of distant nations. To see exact representations of their buildings, marine vessels, arms, manufactures, sacrifice and dresses. These are the materials which form the grand spectacle before us – a spectacle the most magnificent that modern times has produced and which must fully satisfy not only the mind of the philosopher but the curiosity of every spectator'.

31 Under the heading 'Sketches, Models and Designs for Scenery' (Coxe, 1812: 26), lot 44: 'Seven, Interiors, etc. of Huts of the Sandwich Islands'; lot 45: 'Seven, Scenery of Sandwich Islands'; lot 46: 'Two, Ditto'; lot 47: 'Six, Ditto'; lot 48: 'Four, Ditto'; lot 49: 'Thirteen, Ditto'; lot 50: 'Three, Ditto'; lot 52: 'Nine, Ditto'; lot 60: 'Six, Interior of an Otaheitan Cave'.

32 Both models were exhibited at the Loutherbourg exhibition at Kenwood, London, see Joppien (1973: Nos.85, 86). For a colour reproduction of *Kensington Gardens* see *Enciclopedia dello Spettacolo*, 1958, Vol.5, p.1583. See exhibition catalogue *The Georgian Playhouse* (Hayward Gallery, London, 1975, No.287) for a reproduction of *Inside a Jourt*. For a discussion of the respective scenes see Allen (1960: 288–90) and Joppien (1972: 303, 308–12). In an abbreviated form, Allen commented on these models in his article (1962: 201–4).

33 Allen was the first to note that Loutherbourg combined elements from several of Webber's drawings. He sums up by saying that 'in fact . . . De Loutherbourg was quite willing to abandon a "truthful" picture in favour of a more theatrical one', (1962: 204). A description of this scene in

The Times (22 December 1785) shows that in this case Loutherbourg borrowed elements from three of Webber's illustrations; these were published in the atlas of the third voyage: *The Inside of a House in Nootka Sound* (Pl.XLII); *The Interior of a Winter-House in Oonalashka* (Pl.LVIII); *The Inside of a Winter Habitation in Kamtchatka* (Pl.LXXVIII). Their respective drawings are in the Peabody Museum, Harvard University (the first two) and the National Library of Australia.

34 For measurements and verso inscriptions in artist's hand see Joppien (1972: 470–71, 472–73).

35 So far Huse, Allen and Joppien have dealt with this production. Huse, though his article is of considerable interest, was not aware of the scene-models of *Kensington Gardens* and *Inside a Jourt*; he rather approached and examined the libretto of the pantomime. He conceded that Loutherbourg might have seen sketches brought back by Webber but concluded: 'curiously enough . . . there is relatively little in the pantomime that cannot be accounted for by the engraved plates [of Cook's second and third voyages]'. (1936: 311). Allen (1962) rightly disputes this point, suggesting that Loutherbourg probably did not copy straight from the published prints but employed elements of several of Webber's representations for each of his designs. Allen was the first to discuss the two scene-models. While Huse had seen O'Keeffe as the author of the pantomime, Allen focuses on Loutherbourg. He gives an idea of Loutherbourg's previous stage work and examines the action and the scenes of the play from various newspaper reviews. His approach was to a great extent adopted by myself (Joppien 1972: 279–327) to which I added information on Webber, who appeared to have played a greater part than had been realised before. Attention was directed to drawings from Cook's voyages in the British Library (Department of Manuscripts), to documentary evidence concerning the decoration in the sale catalogue of Loutherbourg's estate, to costumes, and to a curious collection of maquettes by the English watercolour artist

Paul Sandby Munn which appear to be related to the scenery of *Omai*. As an adolescent Munn had studied and presumably copied some of the decorations from the production. In some cases these maquettes followed the description of scenery by the theatrical press extremely well, or they matched illustrations from the atlas of Cook's Third Voyage. In other instances however, their reliability as representing the actual scenery of *Omai* was questioned. In my thesis they were referred to as the 'Tunbridge Wells maquettes' after their then location in private possession. They have since been sold at Sotheby's, during the early 1970s, to an unknown American collector.

36 Binyon (1900: Vol.2, 315). The drawing measures 22.8 × 32.4 cm. Binyon gives no particulars about the artist whom he spells Hodgkin. Henry Hodgins worked as resident scene painter at Covent Garden from 1779 to his death 1796, see Rosenfeld/Croft-Murray (1964–65: Vol.XIX, No.2, 62–63).

37 Oil on paper, 23.5 × 29.8 cm. The picture comes from the collection of Sir Bruce Ingram, sold at Sotheby's on 18 March 1964, lot 161, and purchased by Mr and Mrs Paul Mellon. Its former title was *Place of the Dead. Hamilton Bay, with Mitre Hill in the background, New Zealand*, but this was later changed to *Coastal landscape in the Sandwich Islands*.

38 British Library, Add. MS 15513 fol.27 (reproduced Beaglehole 1967: Pt.1, Pl.31). *Heiau* is the Hawaiian word for sacred ground or temple. Heiaus, as well as the Tahitian *maraes* were normally enclosed by a stone wall – a characteristic which is lacking in the oil sketch at the Yale Center. Two oil sketches of burial places of Otaheite from designs by Webber were listed in Loutherbourg's sale catalogue (Coxe 1812: 27, lots 65, 69). Since two sacred grounds were required in the production it is just possible that one of the two mentioned designs represented a Hawaiian *heiau*, but was wrongly identified.

39 The height of the maquettes from the scene models of *Kensington Gardens* and *Inside a Jourt* were about 23 cm, the breadth about 30–32 cm. Compare measurements note 36.

40 For Hodges' work on the Second Voyage and for a list of his works, see Beaglehole (1961: CLVIII–CLXI). For a most illuminating discussion of Hodges' artistic achievements in the South Seas see Smith (1960: 39–54).

41 For Woollett's engraving see Cook (1777: Pl.LXI); the original painting is in the National Maritime Museum, Greenwich (oil on panel, 24.1 × 47.0 cm). The other painting of the *War Boats of the Island of Otaheite* is at Admiralty House (oil on canvas, 178.0 × 301.0 cm).

42 *London Chronicle* (20–22 December 1785).

43 *Universal Magazine* (December 1785: 334).

44 *The Times* (22 December 1785) and *London Chronicle* (20–22 December 1785).

45 Pencil, 14.8 × 17.8 cm, Department of Prints and Drawings, 201 c.5, No.252.

46 Irregular shape, approx. 15.0 × 25.0 cm. Sold Sotheby's 17 June 1970, lot 177. Compared with the pencil drawing there are minor changes in the figure of Cook, for example in the position of his legs.

47 Webber (1793: 8, lot 41). According to an annotated copy of the sale catalogue which Messrs Christie's own, the drawing was bought by Sequin.

48 The whole legend of the etching (26.2 × 22.0 cm) runs 'The APOTHEOSIS of CAPTAIN COOK/From a Design of P. J. De Loutherbourg, R.A. The View of Karakakooa Bay/Is from a Drawing by John Webber, R.A. /the last he made in the Collection of Mr G. Baker/London. Pub^d Jany 20 1794 by J. Thane, Spur Street, Leicester Square'. It should be noted that the sword which Cook holds in the pencil and in the wash drawings, has been exchanged for a sextant in the etching.

49 See play-bill for *Omai*, Pl.31.

50 The National Library of Australia owns seventeen of these (Acc. Nos. R.142–158). They were bought at Sotheby's on 10 May 1949 (lot 419). The content of this lot was described as 'A Unique Collection of 317 plates to illustrate the three voyages of Captain Cook' and 'of 17 coloured wash drawings of costumes, many originals (portraits and charts included) in 4 vols half cow-hide gilt, from the Scottowe Hall Library . . .'. They bear the following

measurements and inscriptions:

1. *Towha*, 32.0 × 20.0 cm, inscr. in ink: 'Toha. No.1';

2. *Oberea*, 32.3 × 20.0 cm, inscr. in ink: 'obereyaa Enchantress. No.2';

3. *Otoo*, 31.4 × 19.0 cm, inscr. in ink: 'Otoo King of Otaheite. No.4';

4. the *Chief Mourner*, 31.1 × 19.0 cm, inscr. in ink: 'Chief Mourner Otaheite. No.5';

5. *Towha-Oedidee*, 30.8 × 18.7 cm, inscr. in ink: 'Toha. Chief of Otaheite. Oedidee. Middlesize. No.6';

6. *A girl of Tahiti with presents*, 31.8 × 19.7 cm, inscr. in ink: 'the present woman of Othehate. No.9';

7. *A dancing girl of Tahiti* 31.1 × 18.4 cm, inscr. in ink: 'Dancer. No.10';

8. *A dancer of Tahiti*, 31.1 × 20.0 cm, inscr. in ink: 'Dancer. Otahaite. No.11';

9. *A man of New Zealand*, 31.4 × 18.7 cm, inscr. in ink and in pencil: 'A Man of New Zealand. Tall. No.15';

10. a (so-called) *Tchutzki chief*, 30.4 × 18.4 cm, inscr. in ink: 'A Chief of the Tchutzki. Middlesize. No.28';

11. a (so-called) *Tchutzki woman*, 30.4 × 18.7 cm, inscr. in ink: 'A Tschutzki Woman. Short. No.30';

12. *A chief of Kamtchatka*, 31.4 × 18.7 cm, inscr. in ink: 'A Chief of Kamtchatka. Short. No.33';

13. *A man of Kamtchatka on snow shows*, 31.1 × 19.0 cm, inscr. in ink: 'A Kamtchadale. Short. No.34';

14. *A woman of Kamtchatka and her child*, 31.1 × 18.7 cm, inscr. in ink: 'A Kamtchadale Wom.ⁿ Short. No.35';

15. *A man of Nootka Sound*, 31.1 × 19.0 cm, inscr. in ink: 'Nootka or King. G. Sound. Middlesize. No.36';

16. *A man of Prince William Sound*, 31.1 × 18.7 cm, inscr. in ink: 'Man of Prince Williams Sound. Short. No.40';

17. *A woman of Prince William Sound*, 31.1 × 18.7 cm, inscr. in ink: 'A Woman Prince Will.ᵐ Sound. Middlesize. No.42'. – One other design is in the collection of Dr W. N. Gunson, Department of Pacific and Southeast Asian History, The Australian National University; this is:

18. the *prophet*, 23.8 × 18.5 cm, inscr. in pencil: 'prophets dress' in ink '46'. It was bought in London in the early 1960s.

Three more drawings recently appeared at Sotheby's, see Catalogue of *Topographical Paintings, Drawings, Prints and Bronzes* for 18 January 1978, lot 191, Pl.XXXIII:

19. *A Chief of New Zealand*, 30.0 × 18.0 cm, inscr. in ink: 'A Chief of New Zealand. Tall';

20. *A chief warrior of New Zealand*, 30.0 × 18.0 cm, inscr. in ink and pencil: 'A Chief Warrior, New Zealand. Tall';

21. *A Woman of New Zealand*, 30.0 × 18.8 cm, inscr. in ink: 'A Woman New Zealand. Middle Size'.

The author wishes to extend his thanks to Mr James Miller of Sotheby's for notifying him about the appearance of these drawings (numbers unknown), and for supplying photographs.

51 For the reproduction of three of the drawings in the National Library of Australia, see Smith (1960: Pls.66–68). The drawing owned by Dr Gunson was reproduced in the *Journal of the Polynesian Society*, Vol.71 (Wellington 1962: opp.209). For the drawings auctioned at Sotheby's see, Catalogue of 18 January 1978, Pl.XXXIII.

52 In Loutherbourg's sale catalogue, mention is made of 'a large Portfolio, with leaves, containing a variety of Sketches of Natives of the South Sea Islands, &c', but it is difficult to tell whether they are identical with our present costume designs, see Coxe (1812: 22, lot 193).

53 For a general discussion see Joppien (1972: 327–41), but without reference to the mad prophet and the three New Zealand figures of late discovery, which were not known at the time.

54 In toto the procession required about 80 people of 13 ethnic groups, including the Tahitian dancers. The following list gives the names of the participants in the procession according to O'Keeffe's libretto, with the numbers which show on the designs (in italics) and those which can be conjectured (in brackets). In some cases, however, the sequence of the conjectured numbers is problematic.

1   A dancing Girl of Otaheite. *10*;
        Six Men of Otaheite (as

Attendants preceding). *11*, (12)?

II One Chief of New Zealand; two Warriors ditto; One common Man, ditto; One Woman with a child, ditto. (13, 14), *15*, (16).

III One Chief of Tanna; Two Men of ditto; One Woman of ditto. (17), (18), (19).

IV One Chief of Marquesas; Two Men of ditto. (20), (21).

V One Chief of Friendly Islands; Four Men of ditto. (22), (23).

VI One Chief of Sandwich Islands; Seven Men of ditto (plain Helmets); One Chief of ditto (feathered Helmets); Seven Men of ditto (with ditto) (24), (25)?

VII One chief of Easter Island; Two Men of ditto. (26), (27).

VIII One Chief of Tchutzki Tartars; Four Men of ditto; One Woman of ditto. *28*, (29), *30*.

IX One Russian; Two Russian Women. (31), (32).

X One Chief of Kamtchatka: Four Men of ditto: One Woman and a Child, ditto. *33, 34, 35.*

XI Two Men of Nootka Sound; One Woman of ditto. *36*, (37).

XII Two Men of Oonalashka. One Woman of ditto. (38), (39).

XIII Two Men of Prince William's Sound. One Woman of ditto. *40*, (41), *42*.

XIV The Otaheitean Girl with Presents to the Captain. *9*.

55 A number of prototypes by Webber can be pointed out in various collections. For the *Girl of Tahiti with presents* see British Library, Add. MS 15513, fol.17 (Beaglehole 1967: Pt.1, Pl.25a); the *Dancing girl of Tahiti*, see BL Add. MS 17277, fol.19 (Beaglehole 1967: Pt.1, Pl.26); the *Dancer of Tahiti*, see BL Add. MS 15513, fol.9 (Beaglehole 1967; Pt.1, Pl.19); for the *Chief warrior of New Zealand* and the *Man of New Zealand* see two natives in the coloured aquatint of a *View in Queen Charlotte Sound, New Zealand* (Webber: 1808, Pl.1); a *Man of Kamtchatka on snow shoes*, for a reversed version of this man see the coloured aquatint of *The Narta, or Sledge for Burdens in Kamtchatka* (Webber: 1808, Pl.10); a *Man of Nootka Sound*, see Peabody Museum, Harvard University, 41-72/497, (Beaglehole 1967: Pt.1, Pl.37); a *Man of Prince William Sound*, for a head and shoulder portrait of this man see the Collection of Francis P. Farquhar, Berkeley, Cal. (Beaglehole 1967: Pt.1 Pl.45a); a *Woman of Prince William Sound*, see BL Add. MS 15514, fol.11 (Beaglehole 1967: Pt.1, Pl.44b).

56 The three Sotheby designs must be excluded from the following observations, since there was no chance to study the originals.

57 This drawing in particular suggests Loutherbourg's hand. It also reflects a distinct French influence in costume designing and as such can well be compared with Nicolas Boquet's design of a high priest in the Bibliothèque Nationale, Opéra, D.216 [I fol.18], see reproduction in the exhibition catalogue *2 siècles d'opéra français* (Paris 1972: Pl.XIII). A copy of the latter work was obtained through the kind services of M. Carlos van Hasselt, Paris.

58 Cook (1777: Pl.LXI).

59 Cook (1777: Pl.LV).

60 It would not be impossible that Loutherbourg himself owned dress elements of the required kind. His sale catalogue of 1812 lists 'A North American Pipe' and 'A North American Coat, made of the Skin of the Mouse Deer, curiously ornamented with Beads, and a Pair of Red Cloth Coverings for the Legs, worn by the Chiefs' (Coxe, 1812: 30). Perhaps a pictorial representation would have been a more likely source, but my study of engravings of eighteenth-century books related to North American Indians has brought no results. I believe that the Indian's gear resembles that worn by the Seneca tribe.

61 Coxe (1812: 14, lot 188), listed as 'Antient and Modern Dresses of different Nations, and old English Dresses, after Holbein, Vandyke, &c. with Historical Remarks, 2 vols'.

62 Jefferys (1772: Vol.2, Pls.XXII and LII).

63 On Jean-Baptiste Le Prince see Réau (1921: 147–65).

64 Chappe (1768: Vol.1, 333 as 'Tatares des Environs de Kazan'), and Chappe (1768:

Vol.1, 235 as 'Femme Samoyède et Enfant').
It is interesting to note in passing that the
Samoyede Woman was again copied in
Thomas Bankes' *New . . . Authentic and
Complete System of Universal Geography*,
London, 1784, opp.108.

65 Perhaps this was a homage paid by one artist
to another. The relationship between
Loutherbourg and Le Prince is not certainly
known. Both artists were, however,
members of the French Royal Academy and
had exhibited together in the *Salon* between
1765 and 1771. Le Prince is considered to
have invented the aquatint process in 1769,
and during the same year he exhibited 29
'estampes gravées à l'imitation du lavis par
un procède qui est particulier à cet Artiste'
at the *Salon*. It is peculiar that either during
this or the following year Loutherbourg
himself issued a series of aquatints (*Les
Maronites*) which both in technique and
subject matter are close to the productions
of Le Prince.

66 Folio volume 201 c.5, containing 299
drawings. Bought as a collection of loose
sheets from Colnaghi's, London, on 28
March 1868 (see *BM Print Room Register of
Purchases and Presentations* 12 October 1867
to 8 August 1868, Vol.xx). They are a
mixed collection of studies, many of which
correspond to the artist's paintings of *The
Battle of Valenciennes* (1793) and *Lord
Howe's Victory* (1794). Because of the
preparatory nature of the drawings and
because studies of battle pictures by
Loutherbourg were listed in the artist's sale
catalogue (Coxe 1812: 21–22) we may infer
that all drawings contained in the album
were once part of Loutherbourg's estate.

67 Binyon (1902: 77). In the *BM Print Room
Register* these drawings are listed in
indiscriminate order as nos. 74, 59, 278, 283,
58, 299, 202, 73, 272, 279, 276, 9.
Sometimes their titles are quite misleading
like 273 = *Head of a child*, or 283 = *Figure of
a beggar carrying a child over his shoulder*.
Obviously the *Register* did not recognize
these drawings as an interrelated group of
similar subject matter. This was understood
only when the drawings were pasted into the
album in the order which they have
maintained.

68 201 c.5, No.281 (Binyon 1902: 77, No.89b);
this watercolour represents a Cossack and is
a full-length figure study for Loutherbourg's
painting of the *Battle of Valenciennes*.

69 Kaeppler (1974: 68–92) Kaeppler (1978) as
well as Kaeppler (in the press).

70 Coxe (1812: 30); ethnographic items from
the South Seas and North America are listed
under lots 147–55, 158–60.

71 Loutherbourg seems to have collected
armour from an early date. Levallet-Haug
(1948: 114) mentions a source according to
which Loutherbourg received oriental
armour from the Empress Catherine of
Russia in about 1776. Day (1922: 58)
underlines the quality of Loutherbourg's
collection by pointing out that many of
Loutherbourg's pieces could be traced to
important armour collections of the
nineteenth century, such as the former
Meyrick Collection at Goodrich Court.
Samuel Rush Meyrick (London, 1830)
reproduces more than 50 weapons from the
Pacific and the Northwest Coast of America
on Pls.CXLIX and CL (Vol.2). These include
specimens similar to those in Loutherbourg's collection, but it can not be stated
with certainty whether they were the same.
In 1878 the famous Meyrick collection was
placed for sale at Mr Pratt's in Bond Street,
after the Government had declined to buy it
in its entirety. After 'the choicest objects
had passed into the hands of continental
collectors' the unsold portions were
eventually presented to the British Museum,
Department of British and Medieval
Antiquities, by Major-General Meyrick and
an inventory prepared. This inventory
which has been made available to me,
together with other documents concerning
Meyrick's gift, through the kindness of Mr
Jonathan King of the Museum of Mankind,
lists ethnographic objects on pp.305–9.
Included are a number of items, such as a
'Tahitian gorget . . . with feathers, sharkes
teeth and shells' (No.588), 3 Tahitian fish
hooks (Nos.597–599), or an 'Australian
wooden shield' (No.617) which have also
figured in Loutherbourg's collection, and
there is just a possibility that they were
identical.

72 In 1791 Webber bequeathed his entire
collection (or what was left of it?) to the
public library in Berne, Switzerland, where
his family originated. Today it is housed in
the Historisches Museum, see the catalogue
of his collection by Henking (1955–56:
325–89) and the discussion of Webber's
ethnographic material from the Northwest
Coast of America by Bandi (1956: 214–20).

73 In theory Loutherbourg could have bought
objects from any private collector of the
Third Voyage, for example from Lieutenant
James Burney, with whose family
Loutherbourg was acquainted and
professionally connected.

74 Lever was a distinguished collector of
ethnographica and natural history objects.
For a general account of his career see
W. L. Smith (1965), on his collection of
artefacts from Cook's voyages see Fabricius
(1784: 238–39), O'Reilly (1966: 11–23) and
Kaeppler (in the press); on his natural
history collections see Whitehead (1969:
167–68). When Lever received the Cook
collection of ethnographica from the Third
Voyage, the *Public Advertiser* (28 February
1781) reported on the addition of another
gallery to his museum 'on account of the late
considerable Aquisitions'. The paper makes
the following announcement: 'Sir Ashton
Lever has the Pleasure to inform the Public
that through the Patronage and Liberality of
Lord Sandwich, the particular Friendship of
Mr. Cook and the Generosity of the Officers
of the Voyage, particularly Captain King
and Captain Williamson, besides many
considerable Purchases he himself has made,
he is now in the Possession of the most
capital Part of the Curiosities brought over
by the Resolution and Discovery, in the last
voyage. These are now displayed for public
Inspection. One Room particularly contains
the magnificent Dresses, Helmets, Idols,
Ornaments, Instruments, Utensils etc. etc.
of those Islands never before discovered,
which proved so fatal to that able Navigator
Captain Cook . . .'. In 1786 Lever was
forced to give up his museum. It was
disposed of by lottery and won by a James
Parkinson, who ran it for another twenty
years and it was finally auctioned in 1806 in
7,879 lots. See also pp.175–6 below.

75 *European Magazine* (January 1782: 17); the
reviewer qualified Lever as a man 'who has
given his countrymen an opportunity of
surveying the works of nature and
contemplating the various beings that
inhabit the earth'. Thomas Pennant thought
that Lever's museum was 'a liberal fund of
inexhaustable knowledge in most branches
of natural history' (quoted from Kaeppler,
in the press: chapter 2, first page).

76 The *Public Advertiser* (21 February 1781)
referred to the Eidophusikon as showing
'various Imitations of Natural Phenomena,
represented by Moving Pictures . . .', and
Loutherbourg himself explained 'that by
adding progressive motion to accurate
resemblance, a series of incidents might be
reproduced which should display in the
most lively manner those captivating scenes
which inexhaustible Nature presents to our
view at different periods and in different
parts of the globe' (quoted Whitley 1928:
Vol.2, 352). The show first opened on 26
February 1781. Visited by leading artists of
the day, such as Gainsborough and
Reynolds, the Eidophusikon became a
popular attraction. For a discussion of its
scenic display see Allen (1966: 12–16) and
Joppien (1972: 342–66). A watercolour
drawing of its interior by Edward Francis
Burney is in the British Museum
(1963.7–16.1), for a note and reproduction
see Rosenfeld (1963:52–54). A description of
its interior decoration is provided by
Whitley (1928: Vol.1, 354–55).

77 Advertisements in the *Public Advertiser* (21,
22, 23, 27, February 1781) give its address
as 'the large House, fronting Leicester
Street, Leicester Square'. Dobson identifies
its situation as in Lisle Street (1912: 278).
Here the Eidophusikon had its first run until
the end of May 1781, followed by a short
spell from 10 December to 21 December
1781 (Dobson 1912: 278–79). Performances
during the following seasons were staged in
Cox's Museum, Spring Gardens (winter to
spring 1782) and in the Exhibition Rooms
over Exeter Change, Strand (spring 1784,
winter 1784 to mid-year 1785, and winter to
spring 1786).

78 For a list of scenery exhibited at the
Eidophusikon in 1781, 1782 and 1786 see

Dobson (1912: 278–80). A detailed review and description of each scene of the Eidophusikon during its second season is provided in the *European Magazine* (March 1782: 180–81), two months after the long and favourable account on Lever's Holophusikon had been published in the same paper.

79 It extended over 17 rooms. The ethnographical objects were displayed in room 14 ('dresses of various nations'), in 15 ('the Otaheite Room where the numerous dresses, ornaments, idols, domestic utensils etc. of the people in the newly discovered islands . . .'), in 16 ('in the Club Room are the war like weapons of the several nations of America . . .'), in 17 ('the Sandwich Island Room is a continuation of the subjects in the Otaheite Room, being full of curious Indian dresses, idols, ornaments, bows, etc. etc. etc. . . .'); see *European Magazine* (January 1782: 20–21). Kaeppler says that at the time of the lottery of Lever's museum in 1786 there were 'some 1859 objects in the Otaheite Room, Passage, Club Room and the Sandwich Islands Room' (in the press: chapter 3, first page).

80 Little is known about Sarah Stone as an artist except that she worked in Lever's museum, copying zoological and ethnographical specimens. The *Morning Post* (25 March 1784) and the *Public Advertiser* (6 May 1784) inform us that Lever exhibited 'transparent Drawings in Watercolours consisting of above one thousand different articles, executed by Miss Stone, a young lady . . .'. A portfolio of watercolour drawings from between 1781–85 mostly of zoological objects is in the British Museum (Natural History). A sketch-book (sketch-book No.1) by Sarah Stone, again mostly of zoological specimens and of ethnographic objects from Lever's museum, is in the Australian Museum, Sydney (Whitehead 1969: 191, fn.52). Two other sketch-books of ethnographic articles (sketch-books Nos.2 and 3) are kept in the Bernice P. Bishop Museum, Hawaii. They were published by Force/Force (1968). A more extensive publication in which their importance to ethnohistory is carefully examined has been prepared by Dr Adrienne Kaeppler of the Bishop Museum, Honolulu (in the press).

81 'With the aid of the sketch-books [Nos.2 and 3] it was possible to locate original specimens from the Leverian Museum in various European institutions'. (Kaeppler 1972: 198).

82 See for example the illustrations in Force/Force (1968: 113, 123, 124, 129).

83 Personal communication by Dr Adrienne Kaeppler, confirmed in letter of 16 October 1977. Inv. No. of the Cambridge club: 27.1382.

84 Measuring 31.1 × 18.4 cm, reproduced in Murray-Oliver (1975: Pl.32). I am grateful to Mr Anthony Murray-Oliver for his kind help and for allowing me to reproduce this work kept in the Alexander Turnbull Library.

85 The altar was probably used for Act 1, Scene 1. It is similar to the one depicted on the right in Webber's drawing of a *Human sacrifice at Tahiti*, British Library Add. MS 15513, fol.16 (Beaglehole 1967: Pt.1, Pl.24). The same drawing gives rather accurate models of the two drums shown in the sketch; these may have been used in the second of the Sandwich Islands scenes where natives are playing music. The feather image seen in profile in the centre of the sheet, was likewise copied from a Webber source. Its drawing is in the British Library Add. MS 15514, fol.27 and was reproduced in Cook/King (1784: Pl.LXVII). Of the idol depicted full-face no Webber drawing is known and it is possible that the drawing of it was made on the basis of an actual specimen. Similar feather images, said to represent the war god Kū are in the British Museum (VAN 231), in the Museum für Völkerkunde Berlin, and in Vienna. They measure 102, 55 and 60 cm, as opposed to the exaggerated height of 10 ft as indicated in the sketch. Very probably the idols had to be blown up for their representation on stage. A place for their exhibition may have been the scene *Inside of a Morai of the antient Aree-de-by's*, Act 1, Scene 2. The *London Chronicle* (20–22 December 1785) reports that also in the scene of the *Consecrated place in the Sandwich Islands*, a figure of an idol was set up.

86 See King (1977: 39, Pl.19).

87 The pipe tomahawk from Lever's Museum is recorded in Sarah Stone's first sketch-book in the Australian Museum, Sydney, p.103. Loutherbourg also owned 'a North American Pipe', see n.60.

88 The quiver, or rather an ethnographically more exact vision of it, was drawn by Sarah Stone (Force/Force 1968: 170). According to Dr Adrienne Kaeppler (personal communication) it was sold at the auction of the Leverian Museum in 1806 and has found its way into the University Museum of Archaeology and Ethnology, Cambridge, Inv. No.22.981. A highly accomplished and beautiful drawing of this, or a similar quiver by Webber, is in the British Library Add. MS 15514, fol.6.

89 British Library Department of Manuscripts Add. MS 23920, fols.77–79. (p.141 above.)

90 None of them is signed but it is quite safe to attribute these to Spöring. They do not match the style of any other artist or draughtsman on the First Voyage. For reproduction of a head and a stern ornament of a canoe see Beaglehole (1962: Vol.2, Pls.4a and 4b). Their authorship can be supported by comparison with the, stylistically very close, drawings of fish and crabs in the Rare Book Room of the British Museum (Natural History); they are included in volumes of zoological drawings by Sydney Parkinson: Vol.1, fols.45, 46, 47, 48, 55, 56; Vol.2, fol.23; Vol.3, fols.6, 7. Jonas Dryander, Banks's second librarian listed these under Spöring's name in his MS catalogue of animal drawings in Banks's library. For the examination of Spöring's drawings in the British Museum (Natural History) I am indebted to Dr Peter Whitehead who actively encouraged and assisted my research.

91 Besides the artefacts and zoological specimens already noted, Spöring drew landscapes, native structures and studies of tattooing patterns. His work on subjects other than natural history is spread over Add. MSS 15507, 15508, 23920 and 23921 in the British Library. There are two more drawings by him in the Mitchell Library, Sydney, (PXD 11, fols. IV and V), which I believe are not by Isaac Smith, as stated in the Cook-Bibliography (1970: 261).

Spöring's drawings, as far as can be judged, are from the Society Islands, from New Zealand and from Australia.

92 In 1827 Banks's library, including his drawings, was handed over to the Trustees of the British Museum. In 1832 the drawings were sent to the Print Room. From there those volumes which were not devoted to natural history were subsequently transferred to the Department of Manuscripts, in 1845, where Add. MSS 9345, 15507, 15508, 23920 and 23921 from Cook's First Voyage, and Add. MSS 15509–12 from Banks's voyage to the Hebrides, Orkneys and Iceland in 1772, are still kept today. Between 1881 and 1883 Banks's collection of natural history drawings was transferred from the British Museum (Bloomsbury) to the British Museum (Natural History) in South Kensington. A few volumes, such as 199$^+$ b.2 and 197$^+$ d.4, were retained in Bloomsbury by mistake.

93 Add. MS 23920, fol.77^b, inscr. by Spöring(?) 'The head of a canoe'.

94 The whole length of the canoe is stated in Spöring's(?) hand to be 68½ feet, the length of the prow 5 feet and 10 inches. These measurements correspond to those taken by Cook (Beaglehole 1955: 283). See also the entry in Banks's journal (Beaglehole 1962: Vol.2, 421).

95 A possible link between Loutherbourg and Banks could have been the Irish artist and scene painter John James Barralet who flourished in London between 1770 and 1779. Banks probably employed Barralet in the early 1770s, after his return from the voyage, to do watercolours from some of Sydney Parkinson's wash drawings. Three watercolours by Barralet after Tahitian and New Zealand views, signed by Barralet, are contained in Add. MS 15508 in the British Library, fols. 4, 19, 20; there is another signed watercolour by Barralet of a New Zealand canoe in the Dixson Library, Sydney, PXX 2, fol.15. Barralet and Loutherbourg were professionally connected when they both worked on a series of illustrations for *Tom Jones*, engraved by Picot and published by Burchell in 1782. For various accounts on Banks's collection

of artefacts from the South Seas, see Fabricius (1784: 81), Ryden (1963) and Lysaght (1971: 254).

96 For Webber's correspondence with Banks on the illustrations of Cook's voyage, see Dawson (1958: 862) and Joppien (1978a).

97 *London Chronicle* (20–22 December 1785).

98 Oil on canvas, 134.5 × 191.0 cm, Admiralty House, London, repr. in Beaglehole (1961: fig.26, detail), and Rienits (1968: 91).

99 Forster (1777: Vol.1, 148). A few pages before, Forster had compared the landscape around Dusky Bay with the 'rude sceneries in the style of Rosa' (124).

100 Forster (1777: Vol.1, 138).

101 Cook (1777: Vol.1, 75).

102 Ibid. As a matter of fact, the adze was an article which Cook had presented to the native. Forster mentions that adzes and nails were very popular with the natives and says of one particular man '. . . he never let a hatchet or spike-nail go out of his hands, after he had once taken hold of it.' (Forster 1777: Vol.1, 163). Perhaps he is the man whom Hodges drew.

103 I had considered the possibility that the native was a Maori, since he wears a narrow object fastened to his right ear. Forster (1777: Vol.1, 138) had noticed that the Maoris wore little pieces of albatross skin in their ears, and Hodges had illustrated that element in a portrait of a bearded Maori man now in the National Library of Australia (repr. Beaglehole 1961: fig.27a). However, my tentative identification was questioned by Peter Gathercole, of Cambridge, who was doubtful whether flax could be knotted at the breast and suggested tropical Polynesia for the sitter (letters 11 September 1975 and 3 June 1977).

104 See engraving in Cook (1777: Pl. XXXVII).

105 *Man of Easter Island* and *Woman of Easter Island*, in Cook (1777: Pls. XLVI and XXV). Corresponding crayon drawings by Hodges, measuring 54.0 × 36.8 cm and 55.2 × 37.5 cm, are in the National Library of Australia (N.L. 271/3 and N.L. 271/8). repr. in Beaglehole (1961: Fig.52a, b).

106 Cook (1777: Vol.1, 291) and Beaglehole (1961: 352).

107 They can be well compared with a collection of ten pen and wash drawings (laid in with tints of watercolour) of South Sea landscapes in the British Library Add. MS 15743.

108 Forster (1777: Vol.1, 425–26).

109 An almost identical boat, also manned by two rowers, can be seen in Watts' engraving after Hodges' *Boats of the Friendly Isles* (Cook 1777: Pl.XLII). For boats of Tonga see Hornell (1936: in particular 259 and Pl. on 275).

110 Forster (1777: Vol.1, 223–25). The scene is also mentioned by Cook (1777: Vol.1, 125–26), and by James Burney (1975: 57).

111 Discussed and reproduced (mirror-reversed) in Joppien (1976: 28–29, 33).

112 The acquisition of the so-called Pennant shell trumpet, its identification and ethnographical description is treated in an excellent and thorough paper by Gathercole (1976).

113 Coxe (1812: 19–22).

114 It is interesting to note that most of the drawings here discussed have lot numbers thinly pencilled upon them, such as No.271=64/1; No.272=9/4; No.273=9/2; No.274=8/1; No.275=8/2; No.276=8/3; No.277=?; No.278=37/1; No.279=64/2; No.280=?; No.282=?; No.283=9/3. Like the other drawings in Loutherbourg's album which have been numbered in this way they form sequential rows (8ff, 9ff, or 64ff). That both groups of drawings were numbered in the same way is evident from Loutherbourg's *Savage weapons* (numbered 37/1) and an emblematical *design with oriental arms* for Macklin's Bible (numbered 37/2); though both drawings have a very different content the fact that both show weapons was the reason for their arrangement in the same numerical order. Similarly, Spöring's *prow of a New Zealand canoe* (numbered 64/1) is followed in sequence by Hodges' drawing of *Maori men in their boat* (numbered 64/2). As neither Laurence Binyon in his *Catalogue*, nor the *BM Print Room Register* before him, had identified this scene, it is obvious that someone before 1868 knew the New Zealand subject matter of both drawings and arranged them accordingly. However, there is no way of telling when and by whom the drawings received their lot numbers.

115 'Rather to our misfortune, he [Hodges] was
not given to the figure and not very skilful at
it, so that his portraits are confined to the
head, or head and shoulder'. (Beaglehole
1961: CLVIII). In another paragraph
Beaglehole says: 'We should be happier had
he [Hodges] had a talent for the figure; for
we greatly lack any rendering of eighteenth-
century Pacific peoples unprejudiced by the
artist's natural idiom [. . .] The series of
head and shoulder portraits he did are no
substitute: the only conviction that some of
them carry, indeed, is the conviction that he
could not draw, and nothing could be more
really lamentable than some of the formal
groups put together for him in London . . .'.
(Beaglehole, 1961: XLII).

116 Forster, for example, speaks of a crowded
and happy scene in a hut at O-Aitepeha of
which Hodges took several drawings: 'Mr.
Hodges filled his portfolio with several
sketches which will convey to future times
the beauties of a scene, of which words give
but a faint idea'. (Forster, 1777: Vol.1, 292).
None of these drawings referred to have yet
come to light.

117 Lichtenberg (1971: Vol.2, 692) gives a short
account of his visit to Hodges' house on 25
November 1775. He saw, he says, drawings
of the inhabitants of Mallikolo and Tanna
who carried their genitals in a long, tube-
like band and had it fastened to their girdle.
Drawings of this kind by Hodges do not
seem to have survived.

118 A catalogue of all the drawings and
paintings produced during Captain Cook's
voyages which is at present being prepared
by Professor Bernard Smith of Melbourne,
and myself, reveals that the number of
known South Sea landscapes in oil and
watercolour by Hodges almost doubles his
anthropological material. There are about
forty ethnic drawings, the majority of which
represent bust portraits.

Bibliography

Alexander (1977): Michael Alexander, *Omai.
Noble Savage*. London.

Allen (1960): Ralph G. Allen, *The Stage
Spectacles of Philip James de Loutherbourg*.
Unpubl. Thesis (Yale University).

Allen (1962): 'De Loutherbourg and Captain
Cook', *Theatre Research*, IV, 3, pp.195–211.

Allen (1965): 'Topical Scenes for Pantomime',
Educational Theatre Journal, XVII, 4,
pp.289–300.

Allen (1966): 'Eidophusikon', *Theatre Design and
Technology*, 7, December, pp.12–16.

Angelo (1830): Henry Angelo, *Reminiscences*. 2
vols. London, 1828, 1830.

Bandi (1956): Hans-Georg Bandi, 'Einige
Gegenstände aus Alaska und British
Kolumbien, gesammelt von Johann Wäber
(John Webber), Bern/London, während der
dritten Forschungsreise von James Cook
1776–80', *Proceedings of the 32nd International
Congress of Americanists*, Copenhagen,
pp.214–20.

Beaglehole (1955): John C. Beaglehole, *The
Journals of Captain Cook . . . The Voyage of the
Endeavour 1768–1771*. Cambridge.

Beaglehole (1961): John C. Beaglehole, *The
Journals of Captain Cook . . . The Voyage of the
Resolution and Adventure 1772–1775*.
Cambridge.

Beaglehole (1962): John C. Beaglehole, *The
Endeavour Journal of Joseph Banks*. 2 vols.
Sydney.

Beaglehole (1967): John C. Beaglehole, *The
Journals of Captain Cook . . . The Voyage of the
Resolution and Discovery, 1776–80*. 2 pts.
Cambridge.

Binyon (1900, and 1902): Laurence Binyon,
*Catalogue of Drawings by British Artists and
Artists of Foreign Origin working in Great
Britain . . . in the British Museum*, 4 vols. 1898,
1900, 1902, 1907. London.

Boaden (1825): James Boaden, *The Memoirs of
the Life of John Philip Kemble*. 2 vols. London.

Boswell (1935): James Boswell, *Life of Johnson*.
Ed. by G. B. Hill, revised by L. F. Powell. 6
vols. Oxford 1934–50.

Burney (1832): Frances Burney (Madame D'Arblay), *Memoirs of Doctor Burney, arranged from his own manuscripts, from family papers, and from personal recollections by his daughter, Madame d'Arblay*. 3 vols. London.

Burney (1904): Frances Burney, *Diary and Letters of Madame D'Arblay (1778–1840)*. Ed. by Charlotte Barrett, introduced by Austin Dobson. 6 vols. London.

Burney (1907): Frances Burney, *The Early Diaries of Frances Burney, (1768–1778)*. Ed. by Annie Raine Ellis. 2 vols. London.

Burney (1975): James Burney, *With Captain Cook in the Antarctic and Pacific. The private Journal of James Burney* . . . ed. and with an introduction by Beverley Hooper. Canberra.

Chappe (1768): L'Abbé Chappe D'Auteroche, *Voyage en Sibérie*. 2 vols. Paris.

Clark (1941): Thomas Blake Clark, *Omai, First Polynesian Ambassador to England*. San Francisco.

Colman (1830): George Colman the younger, *Random records*. 2 vols. London.

Cook (1777): James Cook, *A Voyage towards the South Pole and Round the World* . . . 2 vols. London.

Cook/King (1784): James Cook and James King, *A Voyage to the Pacific Ocean . . . in the Years 1776, 1777, 1778, 1779 and 1780*. 3 vols. London.

Cook Bibliography (1970): *A Bibliography of Captain James Cook*. Mitchell Library, Sydney.

Coxe (1812): Peter Coxe, *A Catalogue of all the Valuable Drawings, Sketches, Sea-Views, and Studies of that Celebrated Artist James Philip de Loutherbourg*. London. The only copy I know of this catalogue is preserved in the Library of the Victoria & Albert Museum.

Dawson (1958): Warren R. Dawson (ed.), *The Banks Letters*. London.

Day (1922): F. H. Cripps Day, 'Meyrick's Collection of Armour', *Country Life*, 14. January, pp.58–59.

Dobson (1912): Austin Dobson, *At Prior Park and other Papers*. London.

Fabricius (1784): Joh. Chr. Fabricius, *Briefe aus London vermischten Inhalts*. Dessau und Leipzig.

Fairchild (1928): Hoxie Neale Fairchild, *The Noble Savage. A Study in Romantic Naturalism*. New York.

Force/Force (1968): Roland and Maryanne Force, *Art and Artifacts of the 18th Century. Objects in the Leverian Museum as painted by Sarah Stone*. Honolulu.

Forster (1777): George Forster, *A Voyage Round the World*. 2 vols. London.

Gardiner (1838): William Gardiner, *Music and Friends*. 2 vols. London.

Garrick (1963): David Garrick, *The Letters of David Garrick*, ed. by David M. Little and George M. Kahrl. 3 vols. Cambridge, Mass.

Gathercole (1976): Peter Gathercole, 'A Maori Shell Trumpet at Cambridge', *Problems in Economic and Social Archaeology*, edited by G. de G. Sieveking, I. H. Longworth and K. E. Wilson. London. pp.187–99.

Graves (1905): Algernon Graves, *The Royal Academy of Arts*, a complete dictionary of contributors and their work from its foundation in 1769 to 1904. 8 vols. London.

Hardie (1969): Martin Hardie, *Watercolour Painting in Britain*. Vol. 1, *The Eighteenth Century*, edited by Dudley Snelgrove. London.

Henking (1955–56): Karl H. Henking, 'Die Südsee- und Alaskasammlung Johann Wäber. Beschreibender Katalog', *Jahrbuch des Bernischen Historischen Museums in Bern*, XXXV and XXXVI (Berne); pp.325–89.

Hogan (1968): Charles Beecher Hogan, *The London Stage, 1660–1800*. Part 5 (1776–1800). 3 vols. Carbondale, Illinois.

Hornell (1936): A. C. Haddon and James Hornell, *Canoes of Oceania*. Vol. 1, *The canoes of Polynesia, Fiji and Micronesia*, by J. Hornell. Honolulu.

Huse (1936): William Huse, 'A Noble Savage on the Stage', *Modern Philology*, XXXIII, pp.303–16.

Jefferys (1772): Thomas Jefferys. *A Collection of the Dresses of Different Nations, Ancient and Modern, Particularly Old English Dresses . . . to which are added the habits of the principal characters on the English stage. 2 vols. London 1757, 1772.

Joppien (1972): Rüdiger Joppien, Die Szenenbilder Philippe Jacques de Loutherbourg. Eine Untersuchung zu ihrer Stellung zwischen Malerei und Theater. Printed diss. Cologne.

Joppien (1973): Rüdiger Joppien, *Philippe Jacques de Loutherbourg, R.A.* exhibition catalogue. London, Kenwood.

Joppien (1976): Rüdiger Joppien, 'Three Drawings by William Hodges, (1744–97)', *The La Trobe Library Journal*. Vol.5, No.18, October 1976, pp.25–33.

Joppien (1978a): Rüdiger Joppien, 'John Webber's South Sea Drawings for the Admiralty. A newly discovered catalogue among the papers of Sir Joseph Banks', *British Library Journal,*

Joppien (1978b): Rüdiger Joppien, 'The artistic bequest of Captain Cook's voyages', manuscript read at Cook Conference, Simon Fraser University, Burnaby BC, April 1978.

Kaeppler (1972): Adrienne Kaeppler, 'The Use of Documents in Identifying Ethnographic Specimens from the Voyages of Captain Cook', *Journal of Pacific History*, 7, pp.195–200.

Kaeppler (1974): Adrienne Kaeppler, 'Cook Voyage Provenance of the "Artificial Curiosities" of Bullock's Museum', *Man* (NS) 9 (1), pp. 68–92.

Kaeppler (1978): Adrienne Kaeppler, '*Artificial Curiosities*'. *An Exposition of Nature Manufactures Collected on the Three Pacific Voyages of Captain James Cook, R.N.* (Bishop Museum Special Publications, 65, Honolulu, 1978.

Kaeppler (in the press): Adrienne Kaeppler, *Captain James Cook, Sir Ashton Lever, and Miss Sarah Stone*. Incorporating *Art and Artifacts of the 18th Century* by Roland W. Force and Maryanne Force (to be published by the Bishop Museum Press, Honolulu, Hawaii).

King (1977): J. C. H. King, *Smoking Pipes of the North American Indian*. London.

Le Fanu (1960): William Le Fanu, *A Catalogue of the Portraits and Other Paintings, Drawings and Sculpture in the Royal College of Surgeons of England*. London.

Levallet-Haug (1948): Geneviève Levallet-Haug, 'Philippe Jacques Loutherbourg, 1740–1812', *Archives Alsaciennes*, XVI, pp.77–134.

Lichtenberg (1971): Georg Christoph Lichtenberg, *Schriften und Briefe*, ed. by Wolfgang Promies. 4 vols. München 1967–72.

Lysaght (1971): Averil Lysaght, *Joseph Banks in New Foundland and Labrador*. Berkeley and Los Angeles.

MacMillan (1939): Dougald MacMillan, *Catalogue of the Larpent Plays in the Huntington Library*. San Marino, Cal.

Manwaring (1931): G. E. Manwaring, *My Friend the Admiral. The Life, Letters, and Journals of Rear-Admiral James Burney* . . . London.

McCormick (1977): E. H. McCormick, *Omai*. Auckland University Press, Wellington, NZ.

Meyrick (1830): Samuel Rush Meyrick, *Engraved Illustrations of Antient Arms and Armour, from the collection of Llewelyn Meyrick . . . at Goodrich Court, Herefordshire, after the drawings and with the descriptions of Dr. Meyrick, by Joseph Skelton*. 2 vols. London.

Murray-Oliver (1975): Anthony Murray-Oliver, *Captain Cook's Hawaii*. Wellington, NZ.

O'Keeffe (1785): John O'Keeffe, *A Short Account of the New Pantomime Called Omai, or, a Trip Round the World . . . The Pantomime, and the Whole of the Scenery designed and invented by Mr. Loutherbourg. The Words written by Mr. O'Keeffe. And the Musick composed by Mr. Shields*(!). 2nd ed. London.

O'Keeffe (1826): John O'Keeffe, *Recollections of the Life of John O'Keeffe*. London.

O'Reilly (1966): Père Patrick O'Reilly, 'Le musée Ashton Lever de Londres et ses collections tahitiennes à la fin du XVIIIe siècle', *Journal de la Société des Océanistes*, XXII, December, pp.11–23.

Réau (1921): Louis Réau, 'L'exotisme russe dans l'oeuvre de Le Prince', *Gazette des Beaux-Arts*, (1921, I) pp.147–65.

Rienits (1968): Rex and Thea Rienits, *The Voyages of Captain Cook*. London.

Rosenfeld (1963): Sybil Rosenfeld, 'The Eidophusikon Illustrated', *Theatre Notebook*, XVIII, 2, pp.52–54.

Rosenfeld/Croft-Murray (1964–65): Sybil Rosenfeld and Edward Croft-Murray, 'A Checklist of Scene-Painters Working in Great Britain and Ireland in the Eighteenth Century (1), (2), (4)' *Theatre Notebook*, XIX, 1, pp.6–20; XIX, 2, pp.49–64; XIX, 4, pp.133–45.

Ryden (1963): Stig Ryden, *The Banks Collection. An Episode in 18th Century Anglo-Swedish Relations*. Stockholm.

Shield (1785): William Shield, *Omai, or, a Trip Round the World. A Pantomime Performed with the Greatest Applause at the Theatre Royal Covent Garden. Set to Music by W^m. Shield*. London. (Musical score, copy in the British Library, press-mark E.108.e.(2).

Shield (1785): William Shield, *The Airs in M^r. Loutherbourgh's Pantomine of Omai Composed and Adapted for the Piano Forte or Harpsichord by W. Shield*. London. (Musical score, copy in the British Library, press-mark: b.52(3).

Smith, B. (1960): Bernard Smith, *European Vision and the South Pacific 1768–1850*. Oxford.

Smith, E. (1911): Edward Smith, *Life of Sir Joseph Banks*. London.

Smith, W.J. (1965): W.J. Smith, *The Life and Activities of Sir Ashton Lever of Alkrington, 1729–1788*. Manchester.

Thomas (1944): Russell Thomas, 'Contemporary Taste in the Stage Decorations of London Theatres, 1700–1800', *Modern Philology*, XLII, 2, pp.65–78.

Thrale (1951): H.L. Thrale, *Thraliana. The Diary of Mrs. Hester Lynch Thrale*, ed. by Katherine C. Balderston. 2 vols. 2nd edition. Oxford.

Tinker (1922): C.B. Tinker, *Nature's Simple Plan*. Princeton.

Tinker (1938): C.B. Tinker, *Painter and Poet*. Cambridge, Mass.

Webber (1793): John Webber, *A Catalogue of the Genuine and Valuable Collection of Drawings and Prints . . . Late the Property of the Ingenious Mr. John Webber, R.A. . . .* which will be sold by auction by Mr. Christie . . . on Friday, June 14th, 1793, and following day. London. A copy of this catalogue is owned by Christie, Mansan and Woods Ltd.

Webber (1808): John Webber, *Views in the South Seas from Drawings by the Late James* (sic) *Webber, Draftsman on Board the Resolution, Captain James Cooke, from the Year 1776 to 1780*. London.

Webber (1821): *Siebenzehntes Neujahrsstück herausgegeben von der Künstler-Gesellschaft in Zürich auf das Jahr 1821. Enthaltend das Leben des Malers Johann Weber in Bern*. Zürich. pp.3–13.

Whitehead (1969): Peter P.J. Whitehead, 'Zoological Specimens from Captain Cook's Voyages', *Journal for the Society of Bibliographie for Natural History* 5 (3), pp.161–201.

Whitley (1928): William T. Whitley, *Artists and their Friends in England*. 2 vols. London.

At the Theatre Royal, Covent Garden,

This prefent FRIDAY, January 20, 1786,
Will be prefented (not Acted thefe SIX Years) the Revived COMEDY of

THE MISTAKE.

Carlos by Mr. LEWIS,
Lorenzo by Mr. FARREN,
Don Alvarez, Mr. WILSON, Don Felix, Mr. THOMPSON,
Lopez by Mr. EDWIN,
And, Sancho by Mr. QUICK,
Camillo by Mrs. BATES,
Jacintha, Mrs. WILLSON, Ifabella, Mrs. MORTON,
And Leonora by Mrs. T. KENNEDY.

To which will be added (for the 27th Time) a NEW PANTOMIME, called

OMAI:
Or, A Trip Round the World.

TOWHA, the Guardian Genius of OMAI's Anceftors, by Mrs. RIVERS,
OTOO, Father of OMAI, by Mr. DARLEY, OMAI by Mr. BLURTON,
HARLEQUIN, Servant to OMAI, by Mr. KENNEDY,
OEDIDDEE, Pretender to the Throne, by Mrs. KENNEDY,
OBEREA, an Enchantrefs, by Mrs. MARTYR,
Don STRUTTOLANDO, Rival to OMAI, by Mr. PALMER,
CLOWN, his Servant, by Mr. D'ELPINI, BRITANNIA by Mrs. INCHBALD,
LONDINA, the Confort deftined to OMAI, by Mifs CRANFIELD,
COLOMBINE, Maid to LONDINA, by Mifs ROWSON,
Native of TONGATABOO by Mr. WEWITZER,
Englifh Captain, Mr. BRETT, Juftice, Mr. DAVIES,
And An Englifh Sailor (with a SONG) by Mr. EDWIN.

With a PROCESSION

Exactly reprefenting the Dreffes, Weapons, and Manners, of the Inhabitants of Otaheite,
New Zealand, Tanna, Marquefas, the Friendly, Sandwich, and Eafter Iflands; Tfchutzki,
Siberia, Kamtfchatka, Nootka Sound, Onalafhka, Prince William's Sound, and the other
Countries vifited by Captain COOK.

The Pantomime, and the Whole of the Scenery, Machinery, Dreffes, &c. Defigned and
Invented by Mr. LOUTHERBOURG, and executed under his Superintendance and
Direction by Meffrs. RICHARDS, CARVER, and HODGINGS, Mr. CATTON, Jun.
Mr. TURNER, and a CELEBRATED ARTIST.

The MUSIC entirely NEW, compofed by Mr. SHIELD.

*** BOOKS containing a fhort Account of the Pantomime, as well as the Recitatives, Airs,
Duets, Trios, and Choruffes, and a Defcription of the Proceffion, to be had at the Theatre.

Nothing under FULL PRICE will be taken.

To-morrow, will be prefented the Comedy of ALL IN THE WRONG.

31 Play-bill for *Omai*, as performed on 20
January 1786. National Library of Australia
(NK 893).

119

OMIAH, the Indian from OTAHEITE, presented to their MAJESTIES at Kew, by Mr. Banks & Dr. Solander. July 17. 1774.

32 Omai presented to King George III.
Engraving. National Library of Australia
(NK 10666).

33 Sir Joshua Reynolds, *Portrait of Omai*. Pencil
drawing. National Library of Australia
(NK 9670).

'Omai, or a Trip round the World' 121

Otoo _King of_
Otahaite

Chief Mourner Otahaite

Obereyau Enchantress

Toha

A Chief of New Zealand.

A Chief Warrior New Zealand.

34 P. J. de Loutherbourg, *Otoo*. Costume design, watercolour. National Library of Australia.

35 P. J. de Loutherbourg, *Towha in the dress of the chief mourner*. Costume design, watercolour. National Library of Australia.

36 P. J. de Loutherbourg, *Oberea*. Costume design, watercolour. National Library of Australia.

37 P. J. de Loutherbourg, *Towha in martial dress*. Costume design, watercolour. National Library of Australia.

38 P. J. de Loutherbourg, *A chief of New Zealand*. Costume design, watercolour. Private Collection.

39 William Hodges, *Man of New Zealand*. Engraving by Michel, in Cook, *Voyage to the South Pole* (1777).

40 P. J. de Loutherbourg, *A chief warrior of New Zealand*. Costume design, watercolour. Private Collection.

A Man of New Zealand.

A Woman New Zealand.

A Chief of the Tchutzki

A Tchutzki Woman

124

A Chief of Kamtchatka

A Kamtchadale

A Woman of Kamtchatka

A Kamtchadale Wom.

41 P. J. de Loutherbourg, *A man of New Zealand*. Costume design, watercolour. National Library of Australia.

42 P. J. de Loutherbourg, *A woman of New Zealand*. Costume design, watercolour. Private Collection.

43 P. J. de Loutherbourg, *A chief of the Tchutzki*. Costume design, watercolour. National Library of Australia.

44 P. J. de Loutherbourg, *A Tchutzki woman*. Costume design, watercolour. National Library of Australia.

45 P. J. de Loutherbourg, *A chief of Kamtchatka*. Costume design, watercolour. National Library of Australia.

46 P. J. de Loutherbourg, *A man of Kamtchatka on snow shoes*. Costume design, watercolour. National Library of Australia.

47 P. J. de Loutherbourg, *A woman of Kamtchatka and her child*. Costume design, watercolour. National Library of Australia.

middle size

Nootka or
King G. Sound

Short.

Man of Prince William Sound
40.

middle size

A Woman Prince Will. Sound.

Dancer. Otaheite

126

Dancer.

The present woman of Ulhetatu

48 P. J. de Loutherbourg, *A man of Nootka Sound*. Costume design, watercolour. National Library of Australia.

49 P. J. de Loutherbourg, *A man of Prince William Sound*. Costume design, watercolour. National Library of Australia.

50 P. J. de Loutherbourg, *A woman of Prince William Sound*. Costume design, watercolour. National Library of Australia.

51 P. J. de Loutherbourg, *A dancer of Tahiti*. Costume design, watercolour. National Library of Australia.

52 P. J. de Loutherbourg, *A dancing girl of Tahiti*. Costume design, watercolour. National Library of Australia.

53 P. J. de Loutherbourg, *A girl of Tahiti with presents*. Costume design, watercolour. National Library of Australia.

54 P. J. de Loutherbourg, *A prophet*. Costume design, watercolour. Collection Dr W. N. Gunson, Department of Pacific and Southeast Asian History, Australian National University.

55 P. J. de Loutherbourg, Scene model for *Kensington Gardens* in *Omai*. Department of Prints & Drawings, Victoria & Albert Museum, London E.158–1937.

56 P. J. de Loutherbourg, Scene model for *Inside a Jourt* in *Omai*. Department of Prints & Drawings, Victoria & Albert Museum, London. E.157–1937.

128

57 P. J. de Loutherbourg or H. Hodgins (after John Webber), *A* heiau *in Hawaii*. Scene design for *Omai*, pen and watercolour. British Museum, Department of Prints and Drawings.

58 John Webber, *A* heiau *in Hawaii, or, a coastal landscape in the Sandwich Islands*. Scene design for *Omai*, oil on paper. Yale Center of British Art, Paul Mellon Collection.

59 W. Woollett after William Hodges, *The fleet of Otaheite assembled at Oparée*. Engraving, illustration to Cook, *Voyage to the South Pole* (1777).

60 P. J. de Loutherbourg, *The apotheosis of Captain Cook*. Pencil. British Museum, Department of Prints & Drawings, 201 c.5, No.252.

61 P. J. de Loutherbourg, *The apotheosis of Captain Cook*. Watercolour. Private Collection, England.

130

The APOTHEOSIS of CAPTAIN COOK.

From a Design of P. J. De Loutherbourg, R.A. The View of KARAKAKOOA BAY

Is from a Drawing by John Webber, R.A (the last he made) in the Collection of Mr G. Baker.

London, Pub.d Jan.y 20. 1794. by J. Thane, Spur Street, Leicester Square.

62 P. J. de Loutherbourg and J. Webber (after),
    The apotheosis of Captain Cook. Etching.
    British Museum, Department of Prints &
    Drawings.

Toha. Chief of Otaheite. oedidèe

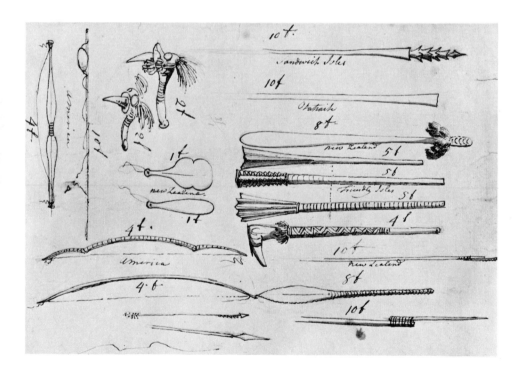

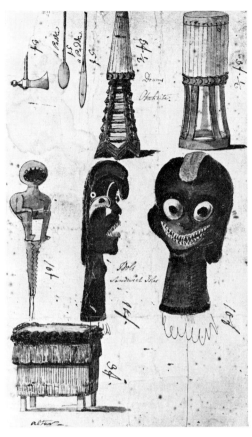

63 P. J. de Loutherbourg, *Towha-Oedidee*(?). Costume design, watercolour. National Library of Australia.

64 P. J. de Loutherbourg, *Head of a Polynesian*(?). Watercolour. British Museum, Department of Prints & Drawings, 201 c.5, No.280.

65 P. J. de Loutherbourg, *Study of weapons from the Pacific and the North-west Coast of America*. Pen. British Museum, Department of Prints & Drawings, 201 c.5, No.278.

66 P. J. de Loutherbourg (attr.), *Study of artifacts from the Pacific and North America*. Pen and watercolour. Alexander Turnbull Library, Wellington, New Zealand.

67 H. D. Spöring, *The prow of a New Zealand canoe*. Pencil. British Museum, Department of Prints & Drawings, 201 c.5, No.271.

 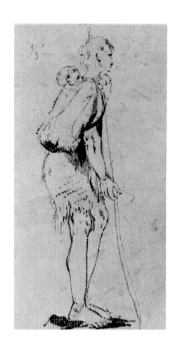 

68 William Hodges, *A man of New Zealand with an adze*. Red chalk over pencil. British Museum, Department of Prints & Drawings, 201 c.5, No.282.

69 William Hodges, *A woman of New Zealand with her child*. Red chalk over pencil. British Museum, Department of Prints & Drawings, 201 c.5, No.283.

70 William Hodges, *A native of Polynesia*. Pencil. British Museum, Department of Prints & Drawings, 201 c.5, No.276.

71 William Hodges, *Head of a woman of Sta. Christina*(?). Pencil. British Museum, Department of Prints & Drawings, 201 c.5, No.273.

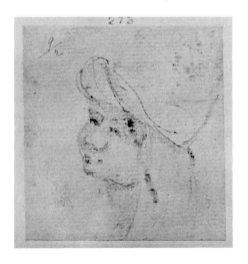

72 William Hodges, *Head of a man of Easter Island*. Pen and pencil. British Museum, Department of Prints & Drawings, 201 c.5, No.275.

73 William Hodges, *Head of a woman of Easter Island*. Pencil. British Museum, Department of Prints & Drawings, 201 c.5, No.274.

74 William Hodges, *Head of a woman of Easter Island*. Pencil. British Museum, Department of Prints & Drawings, 201 c.5, No.272.

75 William Hodges, *Natives of Tonga*(?) *in their canoe*. Indian ink. British Museum, Department of Prints & Drawings, 201 c.5, No.277.

76 William Hodges, *Natives of New Zealand in their boat*. Pen and ink. British Museum,

Department of Prints & Drawings, 201 c.5, No.279.

77 William Hodges, *Natives of New Zealand in their boat*. Pen, watercolour and wash. La Trobe Library (State Library of Victoria), Melbourne.

Ancient Pacific Voyaging: Cook's Views and the Development of Interpretation

BRIAN DURRANS

Department of Ethnography, British Museum (Museum of Mankind)

This paper focuses on three selected problems in the history of the interpretation of Pacific cultural origins, with particular reference to voyaging. First, the views of three explorers, Quiros, Roggeveen and Cook, are examined, Cook's neglect of traditional navigation is discussed and an interpretation suggested. Second, an attempt is made to relate to its wider intellectual context, the nineteenth-century convention of ascribing, without proof, considerable navigational skill to ancestral Polynesians.[1] Finally, some aspects of recent work on voyaging are critically considered in relation to the implicit theoretical assumptions which appear in much of the literature.

Certain dubious intellectual procedures underlie the history of the interpretation of Pacific cultural origins, and these recur in different forms, combinations and degrees of emphasis: the substitution of Polynesia and Polynesians for the Pacific and its population generally;[2] the identification of Polynesians, in varying degrees, on physical or cultural grounds with Europeans or 'Aryans'; the individualisation of societies and groups, involving a tendency to reduce social processes to personal motives; and the compression of sustained, complex activity sequences into critical moments or events.

The interpretations with which this paper is concerned are exclusively prompted by a scientific interest in Pacific origins and voyages. Although oral traditions of indigenous Pacific peoples often express an intellectual curiosity about origins, this is not their sole or main function. Together with evidence of distortions in oral tradition,[3] this prejudices their status as authentic interpretations. While by no means every island group boasts a migration myth,[4] some traditions have proved a rich source of information about the techniques by which early voyages could have been navigated.[5]

The historical context within which interpretations of Pacific cultural origins emerged cannot be examined here in detail, but a few general features are worth reviewing by way of background.

The first discoverers of the Pacific were not, of course, Europeans. By about A D 1000 the whole of Oceania was occupied, and most of it considerably earlier, by ancestors of the modern inhabitants.[6] It was not until 1780, with the completion of Cook's Third Voyage, that the main exploratory phase of European penetration of

1 Cultural divisions in Oceania (Drawn by Ann Searight).

the Pacific was brought to a close (map 1). In the two and a half centuries since Magellan first rounded Cape Horn, some sixteen major expeditions,[7] culminating in those of Cook, introduced the Oceanic world by instalments into the consciousness of Europe.

In its relationship with the Pacific, Europe's differentiation into separate nation-states is historically significant, for not all participated in the initial exploratory drive or in the following consolidation, and dominance among those that did shifted in relation to economic, political and ideological factors. A general analysis of the ideas arising from the conjunction of European thought and knowledge of the Pacific, would need to consider these historical variables, but for the present limited purposes, they can be ignored.

138

Consciousness of the Pacific was at every stage more extensive, and probably more varied, than literary evidence suggests. Images coloured by the imagination of one group, class or country, were incongruent with those of another whose experience and interests were different. The peoples of Europe had their own literary ephemera and oral traditions by which information and interpretation was disseminated. The surviving literary (and occasionally pictorial) evidence, on which the historian relies, cannot offer more than a partial view of this wider intellectual process. In tracing the development of ideas, such as the abstract Noble or Ignoble Savage, this may be a serious handicap since the political debates in which such ideas featured certainly concerned the interests and aroused the passions of wider sections of society than the philosophers or literate public alone.

The attitudes of Europeans when first confronted, in the flesh or by report, with the new-found peoples of the Pacific, were dominated by two kinds of question. First: Whence, when, how and why had they come to settle an ocean of such enormous extent? Second: What does their existence imply for us? A review of some interpretations of Pacific cultural origins[8] reveals a close connection between these two kinds of question, in that hypotheses about the first are also often covert answers to the second. This is scarcely surprising; when new peoples and societies are discovered, the impact is not restricted to anthropological hypotheses but extends also to political institutions, for the ideology legitimizing any political establishment is expressed in anthropological or sociological terms. New discoveries in the natural sciences have, by contrast, no necessary effect on political stability;[9] ideologies derive from the physical universe not their terms, but, if anything, merely supporting metaphors. The relationship between anthropological discovery and the subversion of convention is, however, a reciprocal one, for exploration is as much a consequence as a cause of dissatisfaction with the existing order; although if exploration is sponsored by interests discontented with existing options, such interests are usually best served by explorers who are not intemperately partisan. Particularly among seagoing explorers there is, in fact, a strong empirical bias. Successful voyages demand practical leaders. One consequence of this is a tendency towards the objective description of novelties encountered, rather than speculative interpretation of them. Navigation, cartography and ship management are sound disciplines.

Neither the opening of the Pacific to European involvement, nor the resultant use of Pacific-inspired images in speculative argument, was totally unprecedented in exploration or philosophy. What is striking about geographical exploration, from the Renaissance to the Enlightenment and beyond, is its continuity. The same applies to the disturbing influence of discovery on established ideas and institutions. Thus, Mercati's materialist interpretation of prehistoric tools excavated in Europe was partly inspired by reports and artefacts brought back from Asia and America by contemporary Renaissance voyagers.[10] Significantly still unpublished over a century after their author's death, these views expressed an anthropological rationalism which threatened religious dogma. The same is true in the case of Sir Walter Ralegh:

> 'The great intellectual stimulus of the sixteenth century had been its absorption of the existence of the New World, with all that this implied for relativity of standards. Ralegh brought to bear on the history of the ancient world a lively mind full of the marvels of the New World. He discussed the location of the earthly Paradise in the light of "those places which I myself have seen, near the line and under it". He decided that there was nothing beyond the normal course of nature in the Flood, comparing the torrential rainfall of the West Indies ... His recognition of climatic and geographical influences, of the pressure of population – all this had the effect of reducing (while not denying) the area of divine inspiration in history. He knew that Indian communities had "devised laws without any grounds had from the Scriptures, or from Aristotle's *Politics*, whereby they are governed"'.[11]

Ralegh is exceptional among notable travellers, in his overt association with revolutionary politics. In this sense he personifies the link between geographical discovery, philosophical criticism and political radicalism. The contiguity of the Renaissance and the European period of Pacific discovery is strikingly apparent in the coincidence, on 13 December 1642, of Galileo's death and Tasman's discovery of New Zealand.

The first images of Pacific peoples to take shape in European minds had antecedents in the stereotypes of other peoples recently discovered: in particular, the North American Indians. There were antecedents, too, in the styles of argument in which such images were invoked. For example, More's original *Utopia* (1516), apart from its formal similarity to Plato's *Republic*, was inspired by Vespucci's travels in the New World, where it is purportedly set. Although its prescriptions are unrelated to the recorded customs of other peoples, it is quasi-anthropological in its general impression. Literary descriptions of political Utopias in the seventeenth century have been described as 'almost a recognized branch of travel literature'.[12] Before the Pacific became known even to a handful of Europeans, therefore, the larger literate public was already thoroughly pre-disposed to draw political conclusions from the new anthropological information later provided by explorers and their associates. The various images and metaphors, associated by Europeans at different periods with the Pacific, were accordingly not brought back by voyagers as if they were artefacts or biological specimens, but rather were created by Europeans from facts preselected on the basis of subjective criteria. This applies to written descriptions and drawings

140

actually made in the field, as well as to reinterpreted versions which found a wider audience. Stereotypes of Pacific islanders vary, in the first instance, according to the opportunities for the use of available imagery offered to protagonists by the conditions of political debate. Only in the longer term, when accumulating evidence forces a revision of assumptions, or when a new political climate reduces their relevance, do the images at last conform more closely to reality.

While, abstractly considered, the intellectual climate of the sixteenth and seventeenth centuries tolerated or engendered a vogue for Utopias, the effects of particular versions cannot be deduced from abstractions but only from the concrete conditions in which they were deployed. This principle, which applies equally to the later notions of the Noble, Ignoble and Romantic Savage, can be illustrated by comparing the fate of two important Utopian visions. Harrington's *Oceana* (1656) used a classical idiom in a radical attack on Cromwell's new Puritan orthodoxy[13] and was more influential than rival Utopias expressed in religious terms. While Harrington may have deliberately chosen the classical idiom to accentuate his opposition to the Parliamentary establishment, the sharp reaction which he provoked from the neo-classicist Aristocracy leaves no doubt that it was the message, rather than the medium, of *Oceana* which carried most political weight. More's *Utopia* (1516), in contrast, was much less influential in its own time, and has been interpreted as expressing 'the futility of a moral aspiration that cannot make its account with brute fact',[14] the 'brute fact' in this case being nascent capitalism which needed attacks not on its methods but on the obstacles to its development. Yet considered in abstraction, *Oceana* appears parochial and *Utopia* inspired: in each case a contrast with its immediate historical role.

Sponsored, in the last analysis, by commercial interests, expeditions to the Pacific were led by trained pragmatists, whose inclination when confronted with intractable problems was towards religious, rather than purely classical, modes of explanation, or towards an empirical scepticism. A characteristic combination of slight classical allusion overshadowed by Biblical and empirical reasoning is found, for example, in the following views of the Dutch explorer Jacob Roggeveen, written in his *Journal* in June 1722:

'To make an end and conclusion of all the islands which we have discovered and found to be peopled, there remains merely the presenting of the following speculative question, which seems to me must be placed among those questions which exceed the understanding, and therefore are to be heard, but answered with silence. The question is then whether there is a sound reason to be thought of which could have any likelihood of revealing the means whereby these people arrived in the aforesaid islands, as the Paasch Island lies distant six to seven hundred miles and the others a thousand, eleven to twelve hundred miles from the main coasts of Chile and Peru, and these same islands are found to be separated from New Guinea and Nova Hollandia by an intervening space of more than a thousand, and others again of six, seven to eight hundred miles. Furthermore it must accordingly be agreed that these people must either have been created there or landed and brought by another means, and these thus preserved their race by procreation. Now when it is also noted how navigation was at the time when Jerusalem flourished in full power under the rule of King Solomòn and thereafter under the monarchy of the Romans and other peoples located in the Mediterranean Sea, one will be able to judge very distinctly with all [certainty] that this navigation was so imperfect for making settlements west of America that wanting to maintain this would resemble mockery rather than serious thought. Moreover, navigation increasing from century to century and becoming more efficient in its construction for withstanding the force of the sea, in these later times the lands of America were thus discovered, and then the South Sea, which bathes the western expanse of the American coasts of Chile and Peru. The Spaniards, who brought these lands under their dominion by arms, sailed along the said coasts with their ships for the discovery and possession of riches, but one does not find in any writings that they founded and erected colonies of Chilean or Peruvian Indians anywhere, but on the contrary all the journals of the past two centuries report that the said Spaniards, when they discovered any lands through their voyages in this sea, have written of them as of newly found land, and not of colonies, where the inhabitants, as an inevitable result, must have spoken their mother tongue, whether Chilean or Peruvian. Also it is impossible to comprehend the motivating reason whereby the colonizers would be encouraged to establish such a settlement, because the motive for founding this is either that one has an excess of subjects who inhabit a small region which is not rich enough to supply them with what is necessary for the support of life, when one (with or without force) takes into possession and occupation the nearest land and thus peoples that land as a conquest, or that one puts into operation this establishment for the pursuit of some hoped-for benefit, to conduct trade by voyaging. Since then the Spaniards or other peoples could not have been induced by these motives to set up colonies of Indians in these distant regions, which are outside the acquaintance of the known world, it is accordingly very easy to conclude that the Indians who inhabit these newly discovered islands are bred there naturally from generation to generation, and are descendants of Adam, although the ability of the human understanding is powerless to comprehend by what means they could have been transported. For of this nature are still many other substantial issues, which must only be believed, without any so-called expert demonstration having a place here, when this is opposed to and in conflict with the pronouncement of Holy Writ'.[15]

Cook himself[16] later conjectured on the same general problem, but in a thoroughly modern style:

> 'From what continent they originally emigrated, and by what steps they have spread through so vast a space, those who are curious in disquisitions of this nature, may perhaps not find it very difficult to conjecture. It has been already observed, that they bear strong marks of affinity to some of the Indian tribes, that inhabit the Ladrones and Caroline Islands; and the same affinity may again be traced amongst the Battas and the Malays. When these events happened, is not so easy to ascertain; it was probably not very lately, as they are extremely populous, and have no tradition of their own origin, but what is perfectly fabulous; whilst, on the other hand, the unadulterated state of their general language, and the simplicity which still prevails in their customs and manners, seem to indicate, that it could not have been at any very distant period.'

and

> 'Possibly, however, the presumption, arising from this resemblance, that all these islands were peopled by the same nation, or tribe, may be resisted, under the plausible pretence, that customs very similar prevail amongst very distant people, without inferring any other common source, besides the general principles of human nature, the same in all ages, and every part of the globe.... Those customs which have their foundation in wants that are common to the whole human species, and which are confined to the contrivance of means to relieve those wants, may well be supposed to bear a strong resemblance, without warranting the conclusion, that they who use them have common source.... But this seems not to be the case, with regard to those customs to which no general principle of human nature has given birth, and which have their establishment solely from the endless varieties of local whim, and national fashion. Of this latter kind, those customs obviously are, that belong both to the North, and to the South Pacific Islands, from which, we would infer, that they were originally one nation.... But if this observation should not have removed the doubts of the sceptical refiner, probably he will hardly venture to persist in denying the identity of race, contended for in the present instance, when he shall observe, that, to the proof drawn from affinity of customs, we have it in our power to add that most unexceptionable one, drawn from affinity of language ...'[17]

The omission from these views of Cook's of any discussion about how the islanders' ancestors could have colonized the Pacific is made good elsewhere in his writings. In these he is at one point impressed with extant inter-island voyaging, and at another with an example of an accidental drift voyage, each of which at the time of writing seems to have served as a model for a general hypothesis.[18]

For Quiros, the pilot on Mendaña's 1595 expedition, only short distances could be navigated without instruments, and navigation beyond the sight of land seemed to him impossible for the islanders. Accordingly, the only ways in which the islands could have been reached were by means of a great southern continent, *Terra Australis incognita*, as a springboard; by way of close-linked island chains, as stepping stones; by accidental drifting; or by 'a miracle'.[19] It is noteworthy that on a later voyage Quiros had evidence of ambitious deliberate voyaging from the Santa Cruz Islands in Melanesia, yet recorded little about the navigational techniques employed, and conspicuously failed, at least in his known writings, to confront his earlier hypotheses with this striking new experience.[20]

Quiros was not to know that neither the great southern continent nor the island chains of his imagination matched geographical realities; yet his interest in the problem of how the islands were first colonized at least generated falsifiable hypotheses: only after all apparently credible alternatives were disposed of would he concede divine intervention.

The views of Quiros, Roggeveen and, less obviously, Cook, show inconsistencies congruent with certain suspect assumptions. Quiros' failure to incorporate new evidence into his model for original settlement is inconsistent with his empirical bias, as is his apparent lack of interest in Santa Cruz navigational techniques, whatever difficulties there may have been in recording them. Possibly his refusal to accept navigation beyond sight of land and unaided by instruments expressed not only the assumed superiority of the navigator equipped with advanced technology, but also a limited identification of the islanders with Europeans themselves, who assuredly could not navigate on such conditions. Perhaps physical contrasts between such Polynesians as the Marquesans, and the Melanesians of the Santa Cruz Islands, favoured an identification or sympathy with the former but not with the latter. In any case, it is known that Quiros was very favourably impressed with the appearance of the Marquesans, one of whom, a child, seemed to him 'fair' and like an angel.[21] By contrast, while he did not report unfavourably on the Santa Cruz Islanders, neither did he explicitly admire their appearance, and narratives purportedly derived from Quiros carefully record such strikingly non-angelic features as dark or tawny pigmentation, frizzled hair and teeth stained red from chewing betel.[22] Whether or not differences of appearance between these Melanesians and the Polynesians encountered by Quiros influenced an identification with Europeans, they may have reduced the chance of linking the Melanesian evidence of ambitious voyaging with the colonization problem, conceived in Polynesian terms. Certainly the effect of excluding the Santa Cruz evidence was a reinforcement of a restrictively Polynesian model.

It may be relevant that in the Santa Cruz group voyages were undertaken as part of a network of regular trade;[23] almost certainly this was also the case around the beginning of the seventeenth century, when Quiros was there.[24] It is unlikely that Quiros would have had time, during his short sojourns, to discern the complexity of the trading/voyaging system, but the capacities of the Santa Cruz canoes, while adequate for their trading role, would have seemed conspicuously unequal to the heavy lading of a deliberate colonizing expedition. In the Marquesas, Quiros had already seen large war canoes with room for 30–40 rowers.[25] This experience alone could have made Santa Cruz canoes, which are, in fact, remarkably seaworthy with capacious platforms, seem insignificant by comparison. But more important, they would also have seemed insignificant in terms of a model of single-voyage colonization, as opposed to a system of regular inter-island traffic, such as existed within a considerable radius of the Santa Cruz and Reef Islands.

Roggeveen identifies Pacific islanders with Europeans only to the very limited extent that the navigational methods of the classical Mediterranean are first raised hypothetically before being dismissed as 'so imperfect' for colonizing Oceania. Later in his argument he identifies them with Peruvian or Chilean Indians. This in itself implies the substitution of a plausible east Polynesian model in place of a general model of Oceanic settlement, and is obviously a function of Roggeveen's itinerary, which took him to Easter Island. Once they are associated with Amerindians and refused kinship with the Romans, no autonomous movement of the islanders' ancestors is acceptable, and only by denying the Spanish motives for creating Indian colonies does Roggeveen finally exhaust his imagination.

For Cook, the existence of the same apparently arbitrary customs in widely separated islands of Polynesia corroborated the evidence of race and language in suggesting a shared cultural origin. Again, a Polynesian model substitutes for an Oceanic one: 'The problem of the Polynesian origin and diffusion would recur to him for as long as he lived'.[26] Vast though Polynesia is in area, the models of colonization which it suggested was restrictive. Cook apparently favoured sometimes deliberate and sometimes accidental voyaging, and while possibly counterposing the two,[27] did not explicitly or finally, in his writings, favour one or the other. He may have been closer to the modern view, which treats the two modes of voyaging as complementary in a more comprehensive model, than has been supposed.

Cook at least conceived of colonization proceeding by 'steps',[28] perhaps the germ of a more realistic processual model of cultural diffusion rather than the simplistically event-focused notion of so many equivalent, particular, virgin landfalls, whether deliberate or accidental. He was well aware of Polynesian traditions of colonizing fleets (even if Polynesian accounts of their own origins were 'perfectly fabulous'), of extant voyaging activities, and of large, seaworthy boats (Pls.78, 79, 80). In the Society Islands, during the First Voyage, he wrote as follows:

'In these Proes or Pahee's as the[y] call them from all the accounts we can learn, these people sail in those seas from Island to Island for several hundred Leagues, the Sun serving them for a compass by day and the Moon and Stars by night. When this comes to be prov'd[29] we Shall be no longer at a loss to know how the Islands lying in those Seas came to be people'd, for if the inhabitants of Ulietea have been at Islands laying 2 or 300 Leagues to the westward of them it cannot be doubted but that the inhabitants of those western Islands may have been at others as far to westward of them and so we may trace them from Island to Island quite to the East Indies.'[30]

This passage, with its deleted expression of confidence that traditional navigation methods would be proved effective, confirms that Cook knew as well as Quiros or Roggeveen that 'the degree of navigational accuracy attainable is the central question for any consideration of trans-oceanic contact and the key to understanding what was possible, probable or unlikely in the way of regular communication'.[31]

Yet despite his clear awareness of the problem, Cook recorded practically nothing about traditional navigation methods in Polynesia. Despite the presence of the Raiatean navigator Tupaia aboard the *Endeavour* during part of the First

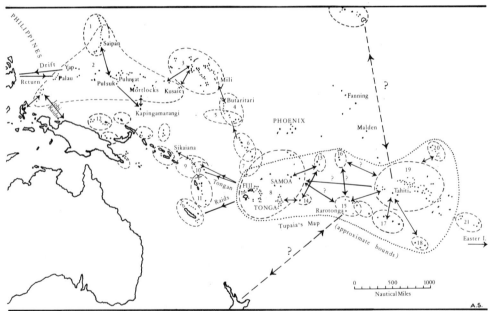

2 Close contact zones in the Pacific.
After D. Lewis, *We, the Navigators*, Map 2.
(See Key to numbers on p.159.) (Drawn by
Ann Searight).

146

Voyage,[32] 'no one seems to have asked him *how* he orientated himself, or what were his actual concepts and methods',[33] even though he constructed a map (see map 2). Lewis suggests some reasons for the neglect of traditional navigation techniques as an object of enquiry: explorers were generally interested in other things; preconceptions about the capabilities of native peoples made sophisticated technical skills inconceivable; and later Europeans were too preoccupied with their own livelihoods to enquire deeply into native culture.[34] It should be added, however, that for those exceptional individuals to whom these generalisations did not apply, difficulties would have in any case arisen from the reluctance of potential informants to reveal professional secrets; the ordinary problems of communication in an unfamiliar language; the basis of traditional navigation methods in a complex of assumptions and experiences alien to Europeans, and remote even from those of instrument-reliant European navigators; and, in many groups, the loss of some navigational theory with the decline of practice.

However, Polynesian cultural origins, far from being marginal to his interests, are described by Cook's best biographer as 'one of his chief problems';[35] and he was certainly well aware of both the technical competence of traditional canoe-builders and of the complexity of Polynesian social institutions. Doubtless any of the above-mentioned difficulties might have been encountered had Cook seriously enquired about navigational methods; and on three voyages and in many parts of the Pacific the opportunity of enquiring could have been taken up. But in his letters and journals there is evidence of neither the results nor the problems of such enquiry, and the conclusion is therefore inescapable that he neglected the very kind of information to which his grasp of the problem of cultural origins would apparently have attracted him.

It is suggested here that Cook's neglect of traditional Polynesian navigation methods makes sense in terms of three assumptions which can certainly or plausibly be ascribed to him. First, that even when deliberate, voyaging was hazardous. Thus, on Tongan voyages, Cook writes:

> 'In these Navigations the Sun is their guide by day and the Stars by night, when these are obscured they have recourse to the points from whence the Wind and waves of the Sea come upon the Vessel [Pl.81]. If during the obscuration both the wind and the waves shift (which seldom happens at any other time within the limets [*sic*] of the trade wind) they are then bewildered, frequently miss their intended port and are never heard of more.'[36]

Cook's earlier encounter with Tahitian castaways at Atiu in the Cook Islands,[37] must have been fresh in his mind while he was in Tonga.

Second, that short journeys, between islands not far apart, posed fewer problems than did long voyages to hypotheses favouring either accidental or deliberate voyaging. Increased chances of sight or sign of land reduce the problems of position fixing to those of augmented pilotage, and, other factors being equal, a short journey offers less scope than a long one for the intervention of adverse weather. The following views are from the journal of William Anderson, who was surgeon on the *Resolution* during the Second Voyage, until his death in 1778, and were probably known to, discussed with, and possibly shared by Cook himself:

> '[The Tongans] are undoubtedly of the same origin with the inhabitants of New Zeeland [*sic*] and the isles eastward, for though in some respects they differ in many others they also agree. Their first population happened no doubt in the same manner with the other islands of this vast ocean, and indeed from the great number of these already discover'd we can hardly be at a loss to form a judgement of this manner especially if it be allowd, which is not improbable, that they are much more numerous and at less distances from each other than is generally imagind. Necessity if not choice would soon force the surplus of people which must follow the population of a small isle to emigrate; and I believe a very short time would bring them to some other isle as yet uninhabited. Accident too as well as design has no doubt often had a share in peopling the different parts of the world, & this may be the case in all the places discoverd or visited in this voyage, though it might at first appear the people may be naturally the same. This is far from being the case, but we must attribute it to the different stock from which they sprung before their arrival in the south sea, or we must believe that at the creation every particular island was furnishd with its inhabitants in the same manner as with its peculiar plants and animals'.[38]

On 3 August 1778, when Anderson died, Cook records that 'He was a Sensible Young Man, an agreeable companion, well skilld in his profession, and had acquired much knowledge in other Sciences ...'.[39] Charles Clerke, in command of the *Discovery*, declared Anderson to have been a 'much esteemed Member of our little Society ...'.[40] What was true of the *Endeavour* on the First Voyage was presumably also true of the *Resolution* and *Discovery* on the Second: 'Doubtless the great cabin of the *Endeavour* witnessed a good deal of discussion, and it would be difficult to assign "priorities" in ideas'.[41] The argument that Anderson's views, quoted here, could also have been Cook's is considerably strengthened by the fact that these views, and those of Cook quoted previously, were both written during July 1777 in Tonga, when Cook's mind was evidently on this subject.

The close association of Anderson and Cook has also been emphasized by Andrew Sharp,[42] who claims not only that Anderson's reference to accidental journeys is a refutation of a deliberate colonization hypothesis, but also that Cook quotes Anderson to this effect. What Anderson really seems to be saying, both in the passage quoted by Sharp[43] and in that quoted here, is simply that, at the time he was writing, no voyages of prodigious length were made. It is central to the argument that, for Anderson, intervening islands could be inferred, so that a hypothesis of exclusively accidental dispersals is not only absent from his recorded views, but was also logically redundant.

Sharp recognizes that 'It cannot be said that Cook put forward his explanation [i.e., his hypothesis of accidental colonization, prompted by the Atiu experience] as a final conclusion. He and Anderson ... did not express a firm view that in earlier times deliberate long off-shore voyages did not occur'; but on the same page Sharp refers to Cook and Anderson 'giving their mature conclusions in a few pregnant paragraphs here and there in the journal of the third voyage'.[44]

In fact, there is no more evidence that these 'conclusions' are 'mature' than that they are 'final' or 'firm'. All this supports the interpretation offered here, that the way in which these views of Cook's or Anderson's were expressed, with no impression of the problem being fully discussed and loose ends tied up, invalidates the idea of a coherent development of thought on this subject between the First and Third Voyages. Only if this absence of intellectual development is itself recognized can a genuine attempt be made to interpret Cook's views on original voyaging in the context of his own assumptions.

Two main factors may have attracted Cook to the view that Polynesia was originally colonized by means of journeys over shorter inter-island distances than might at his time have been supposed to exist. In the first place, Cook's own apprenticeship in navigation, on the North Sea inshore collier run, was an education, in notoriously variable weather conditions, by rule of thumb rather than by book learning.[45] These are just the features which the older explorer might have recognized in the experience of Polynesian sailors on comparably short voyages. In the second place, no Polynesian voyaging which was extant in Cook's day rivalled the achievements of the great colonizing fleets of oral tradition. If, in Anderson's words, islands were 'much more numerous and at less distances from each other than is generally imagind', then Cook could have concluded that the whole of Polynesia was reached by voyages on the scale of those he knew were still undertaken. Like Quiros' island-chain hypothesis, Anderson's view was credible for only so long as knowledge of Pacific geography did not refute it. Cook's reflections in the Society Islands,[46] quoted above, show that he thought a chain of islands stretched from Polynesia to the East Indies, each adjacent pair no more than 200 or 300 leagues apart. Even using expanded target landfall techniques (map 3), the real distribution of islands still left considerably longer distances to be navigated, if Hawaii, Easter Island and New Zealand were to be reached.

This resurrection of Quiros' idea again seems designed to overcome the problem of navigating long voyages. Even so, with the obvious exceptions of the remote apices of the Polynesian triangle, and if significant temporal fluctuations in

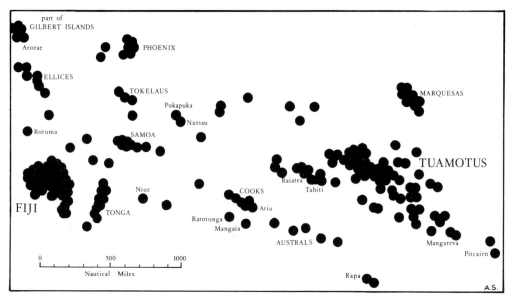

3 Island blocks formed by drawing a circle of 30 miles radius round each island. This represents the approximate distance within which land detection is possible by traditional techniques. After D. Lewis, *We the Navigators*, Fig.25. (Drawn by Ann Searight.)

communication are disregarded, most of Polynesia was indeed reduced by its inhabitants to a cluster of adjacent or overlapping contact zones, linked also with Melanesia and Micronesia (see Map 2).

The third assumption which helps make sense of Cook's neglect of traditional navigation is that accidental and deliberate voyaging both played a part in the settlement of Oceania. This is clearly stated in the quoted extract from Anderson's journal, and complements the idea of colonization by short journeys, since, because of the shorter travelling times required, these simultaneously make more credible both deliberate voyaging and the survival of accidental voyagers. There are two further reasons for supposing that Cook accepted a dual role for accidental and deliberate voyaging, unconnected with the question of whose opinions are expressed in Anderson's journal. In the first place, concern with traditional navigation is logically related to a desire to choose between these supposed alternatives. By this reasoning, developed navigation supports intentional voyaging, while poor navigation argues for accidental. His neglect of navigation therefore suggests that for Cook accident and intention were not polarized in this way. In the second place, the absence of polarization in writings, or of its resolution in favour of one or the other mode of voyaging, is additional circumstantial evidence in favour of the view that he regarded them as complementary rather than alternative.

150

If these assumptions are integrated: that voyaging was hazardous, that only short inter-island journeys were required for the settlement of Polynesia, and that both involuntary and intentional voyaging had a role to play, then the efficacy of traditional navigation methods becomes largely irrelevant. On these assumptions the original colonization of Polynesia did not depend on navigational skills so effective or elaborate that Cook could not reduce them to vague notions of steering by the sun, moon, stars, wind and currents, or account for the attainment of distant landfalls other than by drift voyaging or island hopping. The question of the method of navigation on deliberate long voyages could accordingly be shelved, together with serious investigation of navigational technique. If Cook, or the 'little Society' of his cabin, subscribed to this paradigm, even implicitly, then neglect of traditional navigation can be squared with an abiding interest in problems of original settlement without compromising his fundamental empiricism.

Once it became quite clear, as exploration proceeded, that island chains did not exist on the scale envisaged by Quiros, Anderson or Cook, and that colonizing remote islands therefore still posed problems, there remained logically only two possible alternatives to Quiros' miracle, Anderson's and Roggeveen's autochthonous creations, or the need to credit Polynesians with remarkable navigational abilities. One alternative, already considered, was accidental voyaging; the other was the idea of a sunken continent, of which extant islands are former mountain peaks to which the population was restricted by rising water levels.[47] The latter hypothesis was quickly discredited by geological evidence. But although unintentional voyaging never lacked support as at least a partial explanation of the means of original settlement,[48] the convention arose of taking for granted, without detailed evidence, navigational abilities sufficient for deliberate colonization of Oceania in its entirety. In the middle to late nineteenth century, the issue thus became simplified to the 'whence' of migration. But why should such a convention, flattering to the Polynesians, have emerged at all?

Already at the end of the eighteenth century the image of the Noble Savage, created largely from the reports of European explorers in the Pacific, was under attack from evangelical Protestantism;[49] and throughout the nineteenth and into the twentieth century an intellectual framework, embracing conceptions of the Noble, Ignoble and (in some respects) mediating Romantic Savage conditioned attitudes, in different ways, towards non-European peoples.[50] The Polynesian in particular was cast in an ambivalent role. If not the prototype, he became, through explorers, popularizers and philosophers, the quintessential Noble Savage.[51] On the other hand, various trends of thought, such as Biblical interpretation,[52] comparisons with India[53] and Mesopotamia,[54] and the close connection between the ideas of the Noble Savage and a Golden Age of classical antiquity (e.g. Pls.82, 83), combined with superficial physical resemblances to identify the Polynesians in some respects with Europeans. Brown was perhaps most explicit in identifying Polynesians with Caucasians on physical grounds.[55] The result of these two perspectives was not a single conspicuous hybrid like Tarzan, but rather a shifting image, projected from a framework of assumptions whose implicitness concealed their mutual incompatibility.[56]

The reasons assumed for the undertaking of voyages have a close bearing on the attribution of navigational skill to the ancestral Polynesians. Various factors seem to have prompted writers to infer dire imperatives. For instance, Hale thought voyages were either accidental or were undertaken, presumably without the aid of navigation, by victims of conflict.[57] In this case, the 'motive' reflects Hale's low opinion of the ability of ancestral Polynesians to navigate long deliberate voyages, although evidence of deliberate voyaging by exiles certainly exists.[58] Sittig also emphasized the involuntary nature of various long voyages recorded in European sources.[59] Smith inferred that 'great disturbances' in India induced the ancestors of the Polynesians to emigrate, and movement further eastward was a response to 'pressure' from other populations (recalling Anderson's argument that later emigration from intermediate islands was the consequence of local over-population).[60] But since Smith also accepted the convention that Polynesian ancestors were accomplished navigators, his reason for suggesting these 'motives' for migration probably reflects an ascription of European non-maritime prejudices to the ancestral population. According to these prejudices the sea is a dangerous obstacle to be overcome only in extreme necessity, rather than a medium to which a culture can become intimately adapted.

Whether or not the motives proposed by Smith or Hale are valid, they do represent attempted explanations at the social rather than the individual level. Perhaps they should be called 'causal factors' rather than 'motives'. The whole idea of 'motives', defined in terms of individual interests and then uncritically ascribed to groups or societies, betrays a shallow empiricism which is also ethnocentric in European writers. This is particularly obvious when such 'motives' as adventurousness are invoked (see below). Pictorial images are naturally suitable for conveying information about individuals rather than about societies, and voyaging, which was only one, if essential, element in original population dispersal mechanisms, is thus elevated in art above its correlates; voyaging craft are isolated (Pl.84 is a notable exception); crews are personalized; and their stances Europeanized with dramatic gestures (Pls.85, 86 – compare Pl.87), characteristic of a Western view.

While compulsion, in various forms, can be maintained as a motive either for accidental or deliberate voyaging, i.e., with or without navigational skill, the motive of exploration or love of adventure is much more closely tied to volition and navigational expertise.

152

The nineteenth-century convention of conceding navigational ability to ancestral Polynesians, in the absence of justifying evidence, therefore seems to relate to two main factors. First, a complex of assumptions, deeply entrenched in European thought, made it possible to attribute sophisticated technical skills to people who in other contexts were regarded as close to Nature, desperately in need of redemption, or, in the second half of the nineteenth century, as of relatively low social evolutionary status. Second, the 'motive' of adventure or exploration, which was in fact a projection of two contemporary European attitudes – a pioneering spirit and non-maritime prejudice, became much more credible if some degree of skill was conceded above that strictly necessary for short-distance augmented pilotage. Even those favouring an accidental voyaging hypothesis for the initial settlement of distant islands, could scarcely deny a navigational ability sufficient for journeys within closely clustered island groups. As a reason for voyaging, adventurousness was particularly compelling in terms of either or both of the images with which the Polynesian was ambiguously associated, and the outcome contributed significantly to what Finney calls 'the heroic vision of Polynesian migration'.[61] These images screened their parent assumptions, whose implicitness helps explain not only their persistence, but also their wide influence.

Comparison of the nautical prowess of Polynesians with European models is particularly tenacious, extending well into the first half of the twentieth century. The parallels are generally romantic and loaded with misleading implications. For books aimed at a wide readership, publishers devise arresting titles, but in Malinowski's *Argonauts of the Western Pacific* (London, 1922) and Buck's *Vikings of the Sunrise* (New York, 1938) the romantic ring of the titles is also echoed in the contents. Malinowski's book largely concerns only one of a group of Melanesian societies off eastern New Guinea, yet its title alludes to classical mythology and substitutes the romantic 'Pacific' for the obscure 'Melanesia'. Publisher's licence, perhaps; but it is clear from his emphasis on the inside view of voyaging and trading, consistent with the participant-observation fieldwork which he helped pioneer, that Malinowski recognized among his informants the personal interests which feature in literary and popular conceptions of personalized motives in the age of ancient Greek or Viking voyages. Despite the narrow geographical focus of Malinowski's book, the imagery of its popular title also reflects the implicit attitudes of scholars towards the wider phenomena of early Pacific voyaging. Comparable attitudes are also evident in Buck's book.

Apart from hypotheses of migratory 'waves', each of a distinct racial character, which emerged in the late nineteenth century under the influence of evolutionary racial classification,[62] there was also a consistent trend of empirical research which greatly enlarged the data base for future interpretations.[63] The development of scientific interpretations of Pacific cultural origins, which might be traced from the beginning of the twentieth century when evidence from archaeology and physical anthropology first came to be used seriously, is usefully reviewed by Howard[64] in terms of the growth of empirical knowledge through successive hypotheses. The period since his article was written has witnessed many important new insights into Oceanic prehistory, some of which affect the interpretation of voyaging and original settlement.

It has been argued above that aspects of serious nineteenth-century interpretations of Pacific cultural origins were significantly influenced by widely current images and implicit assumptions. The development of research has since provided new data on the basis of which to revise, replace or sustain earlier hypotheses. Nevertheless, 'Polynesian archaeology has always been fundamentally influenced by both romantic and scholarly interest in Polynesian origins and migrations',[65] and this is true also, to a greater or lesser extent, of other subdisciplines of Pacific anthropology.

Some contemporary work seems to demonstrate the legacy of earlier, deeply rooted assumptions. For instance, as Davidson says, 'There has ... been a great emphasis on identifying the date and origin of the *first* settlement of any island or group'.[66] If, as she claims, this emphasis is a consequence of the influence of interest in origins and migrations, it is also a consequence of the particular form which this interest has taken. While Cook, with his idea of cultural diffusion, may have foreshadowed a processual model, most writers have treated the problem of origins and migrations exclusively as a matter of first arrivals (Pl.88). This is in line with several kinds of simplification and distortion of the real problem. Thus, while the issue was considered in Polynesian terms, the suggestiveness, for example, of extant Melanesian maritime trade systems was reduced. While first arrivals remain the focus of interest, the social processes which generate voyages, and the extended timescale on which communication is organized, simultaneously lose relevance. Preoccupation with initial colonization, compressed into a pioneer event, expresses the legacy of the nineteenth-century romantic Polynesian image, together with an ethnocentric individualism. To a certain extent, this legacy re-emerges in the broad design of voyaging and navigational research in recent years. At the same time, striking new evidence underlines the viability of a processual model for primary settlement.

For example, in Melanesia, archaeological evidence of early trade in pottery and obsidian,[67] and analyses of extant or recent local trade systems,[68] suggest original population dispersal mechanisms operating simultaneously at social, political and economic levels. One particular prehistoric trade system, lasting over half a millennium in the Reef and Santa Cruz Islands, involved journeys of between 1000 and 2000 km – far greater distances than in any recent or contemporary system.[69] Within the historical period, 'temporal fluctuations in ranges of contact'[70] have

154

obscured the potential former extent of such systems, but archaeological evidence now increasingly supports an interpretation of sociocultural processes responsible for settlement by the extension of pre-existing adaptive strategies.

As Lewis says, 'both motives and categories (of voyaging) were mixed and overlapping and, moreover, did not exactly correspond to the European terms we have perforce used to describe them. The maintenance of clan and kinship relations and obligations do not, for instance, fit into a European social mould';[71] and it should be added that the long familiarity of the islanders with their present particular environments (sea as well as land), and their exposure to European influence, have certainly generated attitudes which their ancestors did not share. The factors which induced the ancestors to travel may not therefore be the same as those which animate their modern descendants. The autonomous development of Pacific societies, from the occupation of their present environments to the arrival of Europeans, in any case probably reshaped the cultural mechanisms which had been responsible for original settlement. Later, outside influences further accelerated and distorted cultural change, so that quite apart from the methodological error of attaching individualistic 'motives' to social systems, even the traditional communication networks, which were alluded to by some early European explorers, are not necessarily comparable with those which operated during original settlement. For these reasons, historical or contemporary observation, though essential as a source of models or perspectives for interpreting archaeological evidence, is no substitute for archaeological evidence itself.

It is useful, for example, to know the performance characteristics of certain kinds of boats, possibly comparable with those used by early sailors, under experimental voyaging conditions;[72] to know the details of navigational techniques, discovered by participant observation (Pl.89), until recently scarcely known to scholarship;[73] to understand the conceptual organization and mode of transmission (Pl.90) of navigational knowledge;[74] and to have a comprehensive statistical analysis of the possibilities of Polynesian settlement by drift voyaging.[75] Collectively these studies narrow the scope of legitimate speculation, suggesting promising directions for archaeological and ethnographic enquiry.[76]

Voyaging and navigational experiments, by their very nature, tend, however, to perpetuate the preoccupation with first arrivals, isolated journeys and individualized motives. For example, there is now a clear convention that twin-hulled canoes were used for Polynesian colonization: the craft used to reach distant landfalls like Hawaii, New Zealand and Easter Island 'were almost certainly large double canoes. Polynesians apparently favoured these twin-hulled canoes for long-range voyaging over single-hull outrigger canoes because of their greater stability and carrying capacity'.[77] Lewis emphasizes the considerable carrying capacity of certain outrigger canoe types.[78] The reasoning in favour of double canoes as the colonizing vehicles used to reach the distant apices of the Polynesian triangle is not in question, but logically a great deal of Oceania could have been effectively colonized, and integrated by regular traffic, using smaller, less robust vessels, perhaps comparable with Micronesian single outrigger types. But the main point is that if a model of isolated one-way voyaging is credible for very distant landfalls, it need not, and probably does not, apply for shorter journeys. Hence, the modern convention that twin-hulled craft were the key colonizing vehicles in Polynesia probably reflects an unjustified extension to the rest of Polynesia of a model of distant colonization by isolated expeditions.

Within the scope of this paper it has been possible to briefly consider only a few aspects of the interpretative history of Pacific origins and voyages. There has long been a space in the library for a comprehensive analytical history of European thought about Pacific peoples and their origins, developing existing treatments of selected themes[79] towards a sociological history of ideas. While it is clear that even the most narrowly empirical research is conditioned by implicit assumptions, it is also obvious that the historical genesis of such assumptions in the field of Pacific origins is only imperfectly understood. This field of enquiry could usefully develop greater theoretical self-consciousness, as well continuing the tradition of Cook's own exemplary empiricism.

Notes

1 Distinctively Polynesian culture probably emerged only in Polynesia itself, and the immigrant ancestors of the Polynesians were therefore not themselves Polynesians. Nevertheless 'ancestral Polynesians' is perhaps justifiable stylistically, provided this corrective is borne in mind.

2 E.g., as recognised in Michael Levison, R. Gerard Ward and John W. Webb, *The Settlement of Polynesia: A Computer Simulation*. Minneapolis, 1973, p.3.

3 See Dorothy B. Barrère, 'Cosmogonic Genealogies of Hawaii', *Journal of the Polynesian Society*, 70 (1961), pp.419–28; 'Revisions and Adulterations in Polynesian Creation Myths', in Highland *et al.* (eds.), *Polynesian Culture History*. Honolulu, 1967, pp. 103–19.

4 E.g., Ragnar Numelin, *The Wandering Spirit.*
A Study of Human Migration. London, 1937.

5 David Lewis, *We, the Navigators*. Canberra, 1972.

6 Peter Bellwood, 'The Prehistory of Oceania', *Current Anthropology*, 16 (1975), pp.9–28; William Howells, *The Pacific Islanders*. London, 1973.

7 J. C. Beaglehole, *The Exploration of the Pacific*. London, 3rd edition, 1966; Andrew Sharp, *The Discovery of the Pacific Islands*. Oxford, 1960.

8 Alan Howard, 'Polynesian Origins and Migrations. A Review of Two Centuries of Speculation and Theory', in Highland *et al.*, *Culture History*; see also G. R. Lewthwaite, 'Geographical Knowledge of the Pacific Peoples', in H. R. Friis (ed.), *The Pacific Basin: A History of its Geographical Exploration*. New York, 1967.

9 Christopher Hampson, *The Enlightenment*. Harmondsworth, 1968, p.25.

10 A. Cheynier, *Jouannet – grand-père de la préhistoire*. Paris, 1936.

11 Christopher Hill, *Intellectual Origins of the English Revolution*. Oxford, 1965, p.189.

12 Elizabeth Rawson, *The Spartan Tradition in European Thought*. Oxford, 1969, p.180

13 Rawson, *Spartan Tradition*, pp.193–4; see also Zera S. Fink, *The Classical Republicans: An Essay in the Recovery of a Pattern of Thought in Seventeenth Century England*. Evanston, Ill., 1945.

14 George H. Sabine, *A History of Political Theory*. Hinsdale, Ill., 4th edition, 1973, p.406.

15 Andrew Sharp (ed.), *The Journal of Jacob Roggeveen*. Oxford, 1970, pp.153–4.

16 Or possibly Banks (J. C. Beaglehole (ed.), *The Journals of Captain James Cook on His Voyages of Discovery*, Vol.1, Cambridge, 1955, p.cxci, footnote 1). Though if these are indeed Cook's own views, their author was elsewhere capable of cautious Biblical allusion, as when suggesting Society Islanders might have been exempt from the divinely-imposed curse of work (e.g., Bernard Smith, *European Vision and the South Pacific 1768–1850*. Oxford, 1960, p.247).

17 Quoted by Howard, in Highland *et al.*, *Culture History*, p.46.

18 Beaglehole, *Exploration*, p.154; J. C. Beaglehole (ed.) *The Journals of . . . Cook . . .* Vol. 11, Cambridge, 1967, part one, pp.86–7. The relative importance of these views within the context of Cook's thought is discussed below.

19 A. Dalrymple, *An Historical Collection of Seven Voyages and Discoveries in the South Pacific Ocean*. London, 1770–1, Vol.1, p.98; Elsdon Best, *Polynesian Voyagers. The Maori as a Deep-Sea Navigator, Explorer and Colonizer*. Wellington, 1954 (1923), p.35.

20 C. Markham (ed.), *The Voyages of Pedro Fernandez de Quiros*. London, 1904, Vol.1, pp.227–8; 490.

21 Beaglehole, *Exploration*, p.66.

22 Sharp, *Roggeveen*, p.53.

23 W. Davenport, 'Notes on Santa Cruz Voyaging', *Journal of the Polynesian Society*, 73 (1964), pp.134–42.

24 Lewis, *Navigators*, p.28, footnote.

25 A. C. Haddon and James Hornell, *Canoes of Oceania*. Honolulu, 1936–8. Vol.1, p.31.

26 J. C. Beaglehole, *The Life of Captain James Cook*. London, 1974, p.224.

27 If Anderson's views quoted below are also Cook's (see discussion below), polarization of Cook's two opinions would be unjustified. See also Lewis, *Navigators*, p.19.

28 E.g., Howard, in Highland *et al.*, *Culture History*, p.46.

29 Beaglehole remarks in a footnote that at this point Cook writes then deletes '(which I have now not the least doubt of)'.

30 Beaglehole, *Journals*, I, p.154.

31 Lewis, *Navigators*, p.17.

32 Beaglehole, *Journals*, I, p.117, footnote.

33 Lewis, *Navigators*, p.17.

34 Ibid., p.18.

35 Beaglehole, *Life*, p.374.

36 Beaglehole, *Journals*, II, p.164. Cook was familiar with bad weather in the Pacific, but was careful not to exaggerate its dangers, even when considering accidental voyaging as in this passage. In contrast see Andrew Sharp, *Ancient Voyagers in the Pacific*. Harmondsworth, 1957.

37 Beaglehole, *Journals*, II, pp.86–7.

38 Ibid, p.960.

39 Ibid., p.406.

40 Ibid., p.406, footnote 1.

41 Beaglehole, *Journals*, I, p. cxci, footnote.

42 Sharp, *Ancient Voyagers in the Pacific*, pp.18, 29. His position is maintained in *Ancient Voyagers in Polynesia*. London, 1964.

43 Sharp, *Ancient Voyagers in the Pacific*, pp.21–2.

44 Ibid., p.29.

45 Beaglehole, *Life*, p.12.

46 Beaglehole, *Journals*, I, p.154.

47 J. A. Moerenhout, *Voyages aux Iles du Grand Ocean*. Paris, 1837.

48 E.g., Horatio Hale, 'Ethnography and Philology', *United States Exploring Expedition*. Philadelphia, 1846, Vol.VI; J. L. Armand de Quatrefages, *Les Polynesians et Leurs Migrations*. Paris, 1866.

49 See Smith, *European Vision*, pp.243–7.

50 Ibid., pp.6–7; Brian V. Street, *The Savage in Literature. Representations of 'primitive' society in English fiction 1858–1920*. London, 1975, pp.5–8

51 Hoxie Neale Fairchild, *The Noble Savage. A Study in Romantic Naturalism*. New York, 1928, p.104; Smith, *European Vision*, p.65; see also Pl.5.

52 E.g., Samuel Marsden, *The Letters and Journals of Samuel Marsden*, J. R. Elder (ed.). Dunedin, 1932 (Marsden writing 1814–38).

53 E.g., John Fraser, 'The Malayo-Polynesian Theory', *Journal of the Polynesian Society*, 4

(1895), pp.241–55; S. Percy Smith, *Hawaiki: The Original Home of the Maori*. London, 1910.

54 Abraham Fornander, *An Account of the Polynesian Race*. London, 1878, Vol.1.

55 J. Macmillan Brown, *Maori and Polynesian: Their Origin, History and Culture*. London, 1907.

56 Cf. Street, *Savage in Literature*, p.8.

57 Hale, *United States Exploring Expedition*.

58 E.g., D. Porter, *Journal of a Cruise made to the Pacific Ocean . . .* New York, 2nd edition, 1822, p.51.

59 Otto Sittig, 'Compulsory Migrations in the Pacific Ocean', *Smithsonian Institution Annual Report*, Washington, 1896, pp. 519–59.

60 Smith, *Hawaiki*.

61 Ben R. Finney, 'New, Non-Armchair Research', in Ben R. Finney (compiler), *Pacific Navigation and Voyaging*. Wellington, 1976, p.5.

62 Howard, in Highland *et al.*, *Culture History*, p.57; Street, *Savage in Literature*.

63 Smith, *European Vision*.

64 Howard, in Highland *et al.*, *Culture History*.

65 Janet M. Davidson, 'Western Polynesia and Fiji: prehistoric contact, diffusion and differentiation in adjacent archipelagoes', *World Archaeology*, 9, 1 (1977), p.82.

66 Ibid.

67 E.g., R. C. Green, 'Sites with Lapita Pottery: Importing and Voyaging', *Mankind*, 9 (1974), pp.253–9.

68 E.g., Jim Allen, 'Sea Traffic, Trade and Expanding Horizons', in J. Allen, J. Golson and R. Jones (eds.), *Sunda and Sahul. Prehistoric Studies in Southeast Asia, Melanesia and Australia*. London, 1977, pp.387–417; H. C. Brookfield with Doreen Hart, *Melanesia. A Geographical Interpretation of an Island World*. London, 1971, pp.314–34; G. Harding, *Voyagers of the Vitiaz Straits: a study of a New Guinea trade system*. Seattle, 1967.

69 Green, *Mankind*, 9 (1974), p.256.

70 Lewis, *Navigators*, p.292.

71 Ibid, p.277.

72 E.g., Steven M. Horvath and Ben R. Finney, 'Paddling Experiments and the Question of Polynesian Voyaging', *American Anthropologist*, 71 (1969), pp.271–6; Edwin

Doran Jr., 'Wa, Vinta, and Trimaran', *Journal of the Polynesian Society*, 81 (1972), pp.144–59; Ben R. Finney, 'Voyaging Canoes and the Settlement of Polynesia', *Science*, 196 (1977), pp.1277–85; see also Alexander Spoehr, 'The Double Outrigger Sailing Canoe of Zamboanga and the Sulu Archipelago, Southern Philippines', *Occasional Papers of the Bernice P. Bishop Museum*, 24 (1971), pp.115–26.

73   E.g., Lewis, *Navigators*; K. Åkerblom, *Astronomy and Navigation in Polynesia and Micronesia*. Stockholm, 1968.

74   E.g., Thomas Gladwin, *East Is a Big Bird. Navigation and Logic on Puluwat Atoll.* Cambridge, Mass., 1970.

75   Levison *et al.*, *Settlement*; cf. Sittig, *Smithsonian Report* (1896); Sharp, *Ancient Voyagers in the Pacific.*

76   E.g., Finney, *Pacific Navigation*, p.11.

77   Finney, *Science* 196 (1977), p.1277.

78   Lewis, *Navigators*, pp.273–7.

79   E.g., Smith, *European Vision.*

Close contact zones in the Pacific (Map 2, p.146)

Key to numbers

1	Marianas	12	Ninigo
2	Carolines	13	Pukapuka
3	Marshalls	14	Niue
4	Gilberts	15	Cooks
5	Banaba	16	Manahiki-Rakahanga
6	Tuvalu (Ellices)	17	Tubuai
7	Rotuma-Ellice	18	Rapa
8	Tonga	19	Tahiti-Tuamotu
9	Santa Cruz	20	Marquesas
10	Tikopia	21	Mangareva
11	New Hebrides		

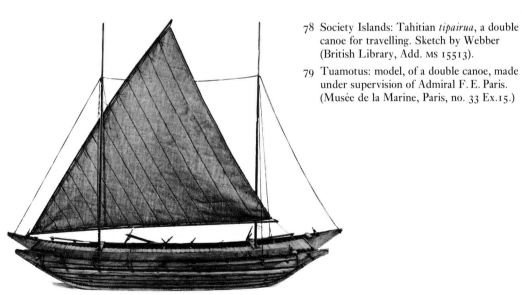

78 Society Islands: Tahitian *tipairua*, a double canoe for travelling. Sketch by Webber (British Library, Add. MS 15513).

79 Tuamotus: model, of a double canoe, made under supervision of Admiral F. E. Paris. (Musée de la Marine, Paris, no. 33 Ex.15.)

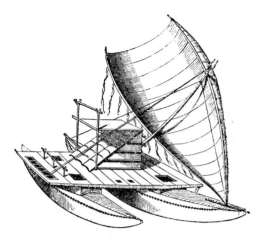

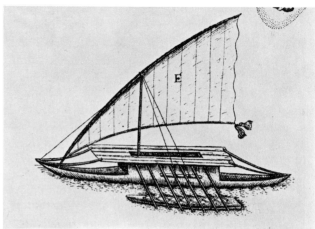

80 Fiji: *ndrua*, double canoe. (Thomas Williams, *Fiji and the Fijians* ... London, 1860, p.86)

81 Tonga: ancient voyaging canoe seen by Tasman at Namuka, Tonga, in 1643. (Abel Janszoon Tasman, *Tasman's Journal of his discovery of Van Diemens Land and New Zealand in 1642* ..., Amsterdam, 1898.)

82 Romanticised crew of Tongan *tongiaki* double canoe, by unknown engraver on basis of drawing by Labillardière. (Le Cen. Labillardière, *Atlas pour servir à la relation du voyage à la recherche de la Pérouse* ..., Paris, n.d., Pl.28.)

162

83 The Classical idiom: 'The landing at
Middleburgh [Eua], one of the Friendly
Islands [Tonga]', engraved by J. K. Shirwin
after Hodges. (James Cook, *A Voyage towards
the South Pole*, London, 2nd edn., 1777, Pl.iv.)

84 *The arrival in New Zealand of the Maori Fleet
from Hawaiki.* Painting by Kenneth Watkins.
Courtesy of Auckland City Art Gallery.

Ancient Pacific Voyaging 163

85 The heroic pose: sketch from P. Buck, *Vikings of the Sunrise*, 1938, p.12. By permission of J. B. Lippincott Company.

86 The heroic pose: 'Moikeha sails out against the wind', illustration of a mythological episode (Drawn by Ann Searight from Johannes C. Anderson, *Myths and Legends of the Polynesians*, London, 1928, facing p.54.)

87 Navigator on his bench, modern Puluwat,
   Caroline Islands. (T. Gladwin, *East is a Big
   Bird*, 1970, p.100). Courtesy of Dr Thomas
   Gladwin and the President and Fellows of
   Harvard College.

88 The first landfall: sketch of the first Easter
   Islanders from Buck, *Vikings of the Sunrise*,
   p.222. By permission of J. B. Lippincott
   Company.

Ancient Pacific Voyaging 165

89 Out of the armchair: traditional navigation expert David Lewis at 10 knots, off Ninigo, north of New Guinea (Lewis, *We, The Navigators*, 1972, Pl. VII). Courtesy of Dr David Lewis and the Australian National University Press.

90 Navigator teaching new apprentices the star compass using pebbles, modern Puluwat, Caroline Islands. (Gladwin, *East is a Big Bird*, p.129). Courtesy of Mr Peter Silverman and the President and Fellows of Harvard College.

Tracing the History of
Hawaiian Cook Voyage Artefacts
in the Museum of Mankind

ADRIENNE L. KAEPPLER

Bernice Pauahi Bishop Museum, Honolulu, Hawaii

It is one of the unfortunate accidents in the history of museums that although the British Museum probably has the most extensive collection of objects from the voyages of Captain Cook existing anywhere, much of it cannot be identified.[1] The collection has not been dispersed, destroyed, or lost, as might have happened in other museums. Indeed, most of it probably reposes in the well-organized coffers of the storage areas of the Museum of Mankind. The problem is not missing objects, but missing documentation. An understanding of this lack of documentation and other problems arising from the Cook voyage collection at the British Museum will be explored here, namely: how can we use the documentation that does exist for objects from Cook's voyages; how this documentation has been used and misused; possible reasons for the rather cavalier attitude toward this important material – surely one of the most important collections in the Ethnography Department of the British Museum – and why, in fact, the collection is not better than it is.

One of the problems of the British Museum, and one that must be examined when dealing with the history of Cook voyage artefacts, is the association of the National Collection with the eighteenth-century Establishment, and particularly with Sir Joseph Banks. This association generated or intensified problems arising from prestige rather than science, which had far-reaching ramifications for Cook voyage collections – and not only for those in the British Museum. A related problem is the rather unenlightened attitude of the administration and early caretakers responsible for the 'stepchild' ethnography collections. The history of the department has been detailed by Braunholtz,[2] and it would be superfluous to repeat it here. Suffice it to say that the responsibility of that 'noble cabinet' toward the artefacts of the 'noble savage' might be considered less than noble.[3] Historically, British attitudes toward such 'uncivilized' nations as were discovered by Cook 'in that vast unknown tract' of the Pacific Ocean has always been rather Rousseauesque. Unlike the great civilizations of Greece, Rome, India, China, or Japan, which, it was conceded, made 'works of art', Pacific Islanders were considered more like amorous children to whom one traded mainly beads or cloth for the 'trifles' they gave in return. It is to the credit of Cook and many who travelled with him, however, that he described the people he encountered dispassionately and compared their works, often favourably, with European counterparts. But it is unfortunate that a like attitude was not continued when the materials reached that 'noble cabinet', and were confined to 'the rag-and-bone Department', a contemptuous nickname recorded by Braunholtz.[4] Such attitudes were not confined to the British Museum, of course, for Cook voyage collections in other museums in Britain and elsewhere had an even more chequered history. Enrico Giglioli describes the 'barbarous treatment' in the Florence Museum of their Cook voyage collection, and similar objects elsewhere have simply been allowed to disintegrate. Surprisingly, however, many Cook voyage pieces have survived virtually intact, in spite of the treatment given them by their owners.

Much of the early neglect of Cook voyage objects themselves and their lack of documentation derives from the eighteenth-century emphasis on the importance of 'natural curiosities', with only secondary consideration, if any, extended to 'artificial curiosities', as ethnographic artefacts were called in the eighteenth century. Wallis, for example, on HMS *Dolphin* did not even want to obtain such objects, and while he was in Tahiti in 1767, he attempted to give back Queen Oberea's gift of bark cloth 'as it was of very little use to us and certainly a great loss to them'.[5] The British Museum, although truly excited about their newly acquired collections of natural curiosities from Cook's voyages, relegated the artificial curiosities to near obscurity.

The collection of ethnographic artefacts – terms which did not even exist at the time – was only incidental to Cook's voyages. Geographic exploration, testing of navigational instruments, astronomical observations, and the scientific gathering, cataloguing and systematizing of 'nature's storehouse' were the important aims of the voyages – all of which were accomplished in the most sophisticated manner. Scientific investigations were carried out, records kept, and drawings detailing scenery and natural history specimens made. Even the artificial curiosities were not forgotten, although their collectors did not know quite what to do with them. Sydney Parkinson on the First Voyage, William Hodges and George Forster on the Second Voyage, and John Webber on the Third Voyage made drawings of numerous ethnographic specimens, both of those *in situ* and those that were collected during the voyages. These drawings testify to the types of artefacts that existed at the time. Often the drawings depict specific objects that can be identified. But what were the collectors to do with the objects when they returned home? The objects were not systematically collected or described, as plants, for example, were. Collection information was not recorded. Most often they were simply assigned a provenance of 'Otaheite', a catch-all term for the South Seas. On their return to England only a few objects could be assimilated into cabinets of curiosities of the rich and the dilettanti – or given to one's patrons, friends, and guests along with entertaining stories.

Many objects eventually found their separate ways to the British Museum, but, because they were not considered very important and they had to compete for curators' time within the Department of Antiquities, of which ethnographic specimens were then a part, little attention was paid to them. From the First and Second Voyages, at least parts of the collections of Cook, Banks, Furneaux, and Clerke were given either directly or through the Lords of the Admiralty to the British Museum. These are the individuals who would be expected to give collections to the National Museum – the prestigious in rank or science. But how about the other officers, men, and supernumeraries who were not among the chosen few to be recognized by those at the National collection? The Forsters, who probably made the best collection during the Second Voyage, after a falling out with the Admiralty and the scientific élite, gave a large part of their collection to the University of Oxford. The curators at the British Museum were apparently not interested in soliciting objects or buying them from the crew. This was left to private collectors such as George Humphrey, who went to the ships as soon as they docked and bought whatever he could. Humphrey amassed two large collections, one that he sold at auction, and a second that he sold to the University of Göttingen, Germany, in 1782. This collection, obtained at the urging of Blumenbach, is now the largest identifiable and best preserved Cook voyage collection extant.

The British Museum did not even catalogue the objects that came in as gifts. Entries in the British Museum register show that objects were given from all three of Cook's Pacific voyages – but there the hard evidence ends. Apparently what was important was the giver, not the object. Seldom is there any indication of how many objects were given, or what they were. Fortunately, Banks had drawings of objects from the First and Second voyages made by his draughtsmen John Frederick Miller and John Cleveley, and some of the objects in the British Museum can be identified by comparison with these drawings. Further, a few labels pasted on specimens apparently identify Cook voyage pieces. Even so, we must look elsewhere for concrete documentation. Forster, in his journal,[6] for example, states that the Tahitian mourning dress in the British Museum was given by Cook – while no records in the British Museum can be found which give this information. Forster also notes that he gave to the British Museum the unique Easter Island carved hand,[7] but he is not given credit anywhere for this or any other gift.

When the objects were placed on exhibition in the British Museum, the donors – and especially Joseph Banks – were noted, but apparently the objects were given no labels. In comparing the British Museum to the private museum of Sir Ashton Lever, a German preacher in 1785 made the following remark:

'What I like about it [the Leverian Museum] is, that one can walk around for hours without the need of a guide, because every case contains the name of the article on a small printed label stuck to the glass. I am surprised that the British Museum with all its natural rarities does not follow this example at least with major objects. It would be a great help to the guides and a great service to the public.'[8]

If the treatment by the British Museum of the artificial curiosities from the first two voyages was cavalier, that given to objects from the Third Voyage is even more surprising. On 10 November 1780, an entry in the British Museum register reads:

'A collection of artificial curiosities from the South Sea Islands, the West Coast of North America and Kamchatka; lately brought home in His Majesty's ships "Resolution" and "Discovery": from Joseph Banks, Esq.'.

A second entry for the same day reads:

'Several natural and artificial curiosities from the South Seas: from John Gore, Esq. Commander of the "Resolution," James King, Esq. Commander of the "Discovery," James Burney, Lieut. Phillips, Lieut. Roberts, Mr. William Peckover and Mr. Robert Anderson gunners, and Mr. Thomas Waling, quartermaster'.

And on November 24th, 1780, is entered:

'Several artificial curiosities from the South Sea, from Captain Williamson, Mr. John Webber, Mr. Cleveley, Mr. William Collett and Mr. Alexander Hogg'.

Again, these individuals might have been expected to give 'several' curiosities, officers and supernumeraries as most of them were. But James King, for example gave most of his collection to Trinity College, Dublin, and to Ashton Lever's collection; Williamson gave objects (including a magnificent green feather cloak from Hawaii) to the Leverian collection; and Webber retained much of his collection until he later gave it to his ancestral city Berne, Switzerland, and perhaps he also gave some objects to Philippe Jacques de Loutherbourg. But Joseph Banks – who was not even on the voyage – is credited not with several objects, but a 'collection'. Who did he get it from? Why are they not credited? Could it be Cook's collection perhaps? No, that is too easy. Cook's collection went mainly to Sir Ashton Lever, through the good offices of Daines Barrington,[9] because Barrington apparently thought it would be better taken care of by Lever. Evidently the British Museum did not even object, because Barrington accomplished this *coup* with only two letters. Banks's gift to the British Museum must have come mainly from Captain Clerke, who died on the voyage and left his curiosities to Banks in his will. But Clerke is nowhere mentioned. And what objects did the various individuals give? Unfortunately, we do not know. Evidently they were not catalogued at all until much later, apparently by Edge-Partington. At one time there may have been lists or at least a set of labels that gave collection or accession information, but no such lists can be found today.

There are two series of objects that one might expect to be composed of specimens from Cook's voyages. One series, known as the 'Cook Collection' is distinguished by labels pasted on the objects. In this 'Cook Collection' series the highest number that is noted on a label is 73, but there are only 12 objects that have such numbered labels. In addition, there are a number of pieces that have similar labels and are designated 'Cook Collection' but the labels do not include numbers. The objects with this series of old labels ('Cook Collection' either with or without a number) are probably authentic Cook voyage pieces – but not necessarily collected by Cook. For example, in this series is the Tahitian mourning costume ('Cook Collection No.3' [TAH 78]) that Cook gave to the British Museum after the Second Voyage. There is also a New Zealand cloak ('Cook Collection No.1' [NZ 137]), the *taniko* border of which is similar to the cloak that Banks wears in his portrait by Benjamin West.[10] Also in this series is a Hawaiian feather standard (*kāhili*) which may have been collected by Captain Clerke on Kauai in 1779 (see below); that is, it was not collected by Cook himself.

A second series of objects is designated 'Banks Collection'. Most of the objects so noted which can be found with such a label or number, are from the Northwest Coast of America. In spite of circumstantial evidence which suggests that these pieces might be from Cook's voyages, it is equally likely that they came from Menzies, botanist on Vancouver's voyage.[11]

Imagine, then, the difficulty and frustration encountered in trying to identify Hawaiian objects in the British Museum that might have come from Cook's voyage, especially when the most obvious piece – a Hawaiian feather image that is with little doubt the one depicted by Webber from Cook's Third Voyage – is catalogued as having come from the voyage of Vancouver, acquired from the descendants of Hewett, surgeon's mate on Vancouver's voyage. In the 'Cook

Collection' series only two Hawaiian pieces are included with assigned numbers: a feather standard, 'Cook Collection No.23' (Pl.95), and a boar tusk bracelet, 'Cook Collection No.26' (Pl.91). One other piece has a matching label but without a number, a gourd water container (Pl.92).

In 1961 a list of Cook voyage artefacts in the British Museum was made at the request of Ernest Dodge, who was compiling an inventory of Pacific Islands specimens from the voyages of Cook.[12] The list for Hawaii included some thirty-two pieces. If one checks the evidence for the attributions for these objects, however, only six have convincing documentation. These include the three listed above (feather standard, boar tusk bracelet, and gourd water container), two pieces of bark cloth, and a spear. Not very impressive for the National Collection. Also included in the list were two pieces from the 'Banks Collection' series – feather helmet and a feather *lei* (ornament for neck or hair). We will give these two latter pieces the benefit of the doubt, for the moment, because it is possible that they came to Banks from Clerke, but the evidence can only be considered circumstantial. Clerke certainly would have been a likely recipient for a helmet and *lei* and none are included in the 'Cook Collection' series. Further, even the rest of the list that cannot be documented as having an association with Cook's Third Voyage, is not very impressive – fragments of bark cloth, cord, basket, another gourd water container, a dagger, a gourd rattle, but no feather cloaks, no feather images, no wooden images, no bowls with human images, no shark tooth weapons, or other objects characteristic of Hawaiian Cook voyage collections.

On this 1961 list is a barbed wooden spear (1946.Oc.1.1) (Pl.93). It bears the note, 'Thrown into the boat when Captain Cook was murdered, brought to England by Thomas Bean, whose wife was nurse to Thomas Green, and gave it to her master'. From the Beasley collection, but not on the 1961 list, is a Hawaiian hook ornament of shell and turtle shell (1944. Oc.2.715) (Pl.94) which has an old label that reads, 'This fishhook was brought from the South Seas by Mr. Alex Dewar, who accompanied Capt. Cook as clerk to the ship, on two voyages and witnessed his death at Owhyee, 14 Feb. 1779'. Since both of these individuals were on the voyage, there is no reason to doubt this information.

In short, if we depend on British Museum documentation, six, or at the most eight, pieces from Hawaii can be attributed to Cook's voyage. Could it be that only a few relatively minor pieces are really all the Hawaiian objects included in the 'collection' given by Banks and the 'several' given by others in November of 1780? The collection given by Banks probably included the things he inherited from Captain Clerke and from William Anderson, surgeon on the *Resolution* who died on the Northwest Coast of America between Cook's visits to Hawaii in 1778 and 1779. It is possible that the more important objects of Anderson's collection, including twelve pieces of Hawaiian featherwork, were among the gift of curiosities given to Major Behm at Kamchatka,[13] and perhaps only an unimpressive residue was inherited by Banks. Although Captain Clerke had not been well during much of his time in Hawaii, in the detailed journals kept aboard ship a number of occasions are described in which Clerke was a recipient of ethnographic objects and two of these encounters may identify two objects in the British Museum collection. The feather standard (*kāhili*), 'Cook Collection No.23' (Pl.95) may be the one described in Clerke's journal on Kauai on 4 March 1779:

> 'Her daughter had a curious Fan or Fly flapper compos'd of a bunch of Feathers made to adhere to a Human Bone as a Handle; the feathers were very fine & the Handle curiously wrought with Tortoise shell, which made it a pretty piece of furniture'.[14]

That this is the object in the British Museum is quite likely because a 'mate' to this *kāhili* (Pl.96) is described by David Samwell, who traded a wash basin and a sheet for it in March 1779, and sold it in his 1781 auction. Although it is possible that Clerke and Samwell are describing the same *kāhili*, there is no reason that there would not be two similar ones. The Samwell *kāhili* can be traced step by step to its present location in the National Museum, Wellington, New Zealand,[15] and if Clerke also obtained one, it surely would have gone to Banks, which the label seems to indicate.

The second object (which also has a mate described and collected by Samwell and traceable step by step to a private collection) is a bowl in the British Museum with human images (HAW 46). This bowl is not in the 'Cook Collection' series that is identified either by a number or label – but a label may simply have been lost. Such a bowl is described as being presented to Captain Clerke in February 1778:

> 'Captain Clerke made him [Chief "Tamahano"] some suitable presents and in return he gave him a large Cava bowl that was supported by two car[v]ed men, neither ill designed nor executed'.[16]

And the astronomer Bayly writes:

> 'I kissed him According to their custom, & he presented me with a curious Yava bowl as captain, but I undeceived him & told him that Capt Clerke was the Aree de hoi or King of the Ship, & consequently gave him the bowl'.[17]

These two superb bowls (Pls.97 and 98) are so similar that it seems safe to conjecture that they might have been made by the same craftsman. They represent one of the high points of Hawaiian artistry at the time of first European contact.

There were surely some other things from Hawaii in Clerke's collection, for example, some bone fishhooks described in his journal:

'Her Majesty made me a present of some fish hooks which she assur'd me were made of the Bones of Terre'oboo's father, who was killed in a descent he made upon Wou'a'hoo where his party were routed'.[18]

But which fishhooks are they? On another occasion one of the chiefs 'returned & brought a red & yellow feather cloak with him which he put on C. Cl. [Capt. Clerke] and then tyed a piece of cloth round his waist'.[19] But which objects are they? And what other things are there that were not specifically mentioned? Apparently Captain Clerke was not terribly interested in collecting 'artificial curiosities', for on one occasion one of the Chiefs 'brought with him a fine Drum as a present to the Capt[n] [Clerke] who did not accept of it'.[19a] As far as Clerke's collections go, there are more questions than answers. One possible answer is that part of Banks's gift was, in fact, withdrawn. According to the entomologist Johann Fabricius, much of Banks's gift of artificial curiosities languished without proper care and eventually he gave permission to some of his friends to remove objects from the British Museum for themselves. Fabricius records this transaction in a letter from London.[20]

'The British Museum is one of the public institutions where there are several superintendents but of whom none devotes himself with true zeal to that institution, with the result that many things remain neglected. A case in point are the objects which Banks had acquired from Cook's last voyage, dresses, weapons, instruments, and which according to his noble thinking he had sent to the Museum, in order that the museum could choose from them what they thought best. There they remained for about two years, without anybody taking any notice about them, until finally Sir Joseph, – not uninfluenced by our arguments – gave permission to me and two other friends to bring everything back from the Museum to his house and to divide it among ourselves. You may well imagine that I received no small quantity of different objects of different fabrication, mats, spears, bludgeons, nets, angle hooks and other things, with which I was very pleased. I shall certainly have some trouble in transporting everything of this precious freight back to the continent, however, quite a bit of what I take back shall serve for the pleasant entertainment of my friends'.

Fortunately that is not all we can say about Hawaiian objects from Cook's voyage in the British Museum. If we look elsewhere for documentary evidence, it can be demonstrated that the British Museum does in fact have a number of quite spectacular Hawaiian objects from Cook's voyage. Two sketchbooks of water-colour drawings by Miss Sarah Stone, which were completed c.1783, depict a number of objects now in the British Museum. The 1783 date is important because after Cook's visits no ships called in the Hawaiian Islands until 1786, and did not

174

return to Europe for some years. The drawings depict objects that were then in the private museum of Sir Ashton Lever – a collection that was dispersed in 1806.

As mentioned above, a large Third Voyage collection, including much of Cook's own collection, was acquired by Ashton Lever through the good offices of Daines Barrington and Mrs Cook. Objects were also given to Lever by Captain King and Lieutenant Williamson, and a number of objects were purchased by Lever at the sale of David Samwell. Indeed, in a public announcement on 31 January 1781,[21] Lever states, probably with a good deal of truth, that 'he is now in possession of the most capital part of the curiosities brought by the Resolution and Discovery in the last voyage'.

Originally at Alkrington Hall, Manchester, Ashton Lever's collection, which he called the Holophusicon (or Holophusikon) to signify that it embraced all of nature, was moved to Leicester Square, London, in 1775. The undertaking proved too great for Lever and in 1783 he petitioned Parliament that his collection be added to that of the British Museum rather than be broken up and sold at auction. He would take only a fraction of its worth, which had been valued before a Parliamentary Committee at £53,000. This same committee also emphasized the discredit to the country should Lever's Museum be dispersed because it was considered by scientists to be the most important collection, not only in England, but in Europe. The petition went unheeded and Lever was forced to dispose of his collection by lottery in 1786. The lottery was won by a dentist, James Parkinson, who moved it to the 'Rotunda' at Blackfriars Bridge.

Parkinson, too, had financial difficulties and again the collection was offered to the nation.

> Lord Grenville referred it to Lord Henry Petty, who approved the proposal and the conditions offered by Parkinson. ... But Ministers declined responsibility and referred it to Sir Joseph Banks who disapproved purchasing it. Parkinson says Sir Joseph hated Sir Ashton Lever and therefore hates the collection'.[22]

This disapproval by Joseph Banks is confirmed by H. Syer Cuming (whose father purchased largely at the Leverian sale):

> 'Sir Joseph Banks had a bitter spite against Sir Ashton Lever and when the latter's Museum was offered to the Nation Sir Joseph declared that there was nothing in it worth the purchase and the ill temper of one Man deprived the Country of the finest general Collection which had up to that time ever been formed in England'.[23]

Because of Joseph Banks the British Museum not only failed to acquire the collection but failed even to send a representative to the auction, because 'there was nothing in it worth the purchase'. Perhaps the antagonism of Banks toward Lever can be traced to Banks's desire to obtain at least some of the 'official' collection from Cook's Third Voyage and to his wish not to share his own glory as benefactor of the British Museum with one whom he regarded as socially and scientifically inferior. Banks was well known and acknowledged for his gifts to the British Museum; for example, Robert Jameson visiting the Museum in 1793 noted that 'the most valuable articles in this room were presented to the Museum by the illustrious Sir J. Banks'.[24]

Having failed to interest the British Museum, and not wishing to sell the Museum in its entirety to a foreign nation, Parkinson decided to sell the collection at an auction beginning 5 May 1806. There were some 7,800 lots which were dispersed over sixty-five days. The largest collection of Cook voyage ethnographic material was purchased at the Leverian sale by Leopold von Fichtel for the Kaiser of Austria and these ethnographic specimens are now in the Museum für Völkerkunde, Vienna. Although specimens were purchased on behalf of the Royal College of Surgeons, the Hunterian Museum, Glasgow, William Bullock's Liverpool Museum (which eventually moved to London), Danovan's London Museum, Richard Cuming's private collection (now the Cuming Museum, Southwark, London), Sir John Soane's collection, and Lord Stanley, the 13th Earl of Derby, nothing was bought by the British Museum. Moreover, later, when Joseph Banks apparently became the recipient of a Hawaiian feather cloak from the Leverian collection, he gave it, not to the British Museum, but to the private museum of William Bullock. This, the most valuable of all Hawaiian feathered cloaks, because it was given by Kalani'opu'u, High Chief of the Island of Hawaii, to Captain Cook on his 'state visit' to Cook's ships, is now in the National Museum, Wellington.

Fortunately, other important Hawaiian objects were purchased by other English collectors – and some of these found their separate ways to the British Museum by strange, devious, and unknown means. None of the Hawaiian pieces, however, were marked as associated with Cook's voyage, and only one was marked as having been in the Leverian Museum. The identification of these important objects and their attribution to Cook's voyage has involved several years of ethnological sleuthing and all of the questions have not yet been resolved. A few of the devious routes from the Leverian Museum to the British Museum will be summarized here.

The one Hawaiian piece that is marked as having been in the Leverian is a feathered image (LMS 221) (Pl.99). When this image went from the London Missionary Society to the British Museum in 1890 it was marked 'LMS 1, An idol representing a huge helmeted head covered with red feathers from the Sandwich Islands. Formerly in the Leverian Museum'. This information is confirmed by the *Catalogue of the Missionary Museum* where it is entered as 'An idol representing a huge helmeted head covered with red feathers, from the Sandwich Islands. Formerly in the Leverian Museum'.[25] Who purchased it at the Leverian auction is unknown and unfortunately it is not among the feathered images depicted by Sarah Stone in 1783. Among the feathered images from the Leverian Museum whose genealogy is so far untraced, are two which could possibly refer to the image in question. One was sold at the Leverian auction as lot 213, 'Idol, curiously constructed of feathers, etc. Sandwich Islands'. It was purchased by 'Newman' for 15s 6d. The second was lot 6158, 'An uncommonly large and perfect scarlet and yellow feather idol, with pearly eyes, Sandwich Isles'. It was purchased by 'Brent' for £1.6s. Unfortunately the collections of neither Newman nor Brent can be traced. A Mr T. S. Newman of Crown Street, London, is associated with the London Missionary Society, and he is a possibility. The description of Brent's purchase as 'uncommonly large and perfect', however, would be an exact description of the London Missionary Society image, which, at 104 cm, is the largest of the known Cook voyage feather images, and only two cm larger than another large feather image from the Leverian Museum which was sold as 'a remarkably large feather idol'. In any case, there is no reason to doubt that the London Missionary Society feathered image, now in the British Museum, came from the Leverian Museum and is with little question an authentic Cook voyage piece. The individual involved in its transference from the Leverian Museum to the London Missionary Society is, however, unknown.

A second large feathered image in the British Museum (Pl. 100) has confused researchers for years. This image, catalogued as VAN 231, is accessioned in the so-called 'Vancouver collection' because it was obtained in 1891 from the descendants of W. George Goodman Hewett, surgeon's first mate on HMS *Cambridge* under Captain Vancouver. That it was actually collected by Hewett in Hawaii during Vancouver's visit has apparently not been seriously questioned, although the similarity of this image to the image depicted by Webber has been recognized. The similarity was noted, for example, by Captain A. W. F. Fuller, bibliophile, collector, and former owner of two of the Sarah Stone sketchbooks which are now in Bishop Museum.[26] Captain Fuller noted in the sketchbook, 'I think there is little doubt that this larger head is the one shown in Cook's third voyage, *Atlas*, Plate 67, Figure 4, and is also the one in the British Museum, although the open part beneath the eye is only indicated here by black shading'.

With the Hewett/Vancouver collection is a manuscript list of the specimens made by Hewett, apparently on the voyage or shortly thereafter. No feather image is, however, listed. The only possibility is the last item in the Hawaiian series which reads 'otu Idol', apparently as an afterthought. This entry is followed by an empty space and then begins the list of objects from the Northwest Coast of America. In the Leverian sale catalogue, there are eight lots that include feathered images. One of these, lot 5662, 'A remarkably large feather idol, from ditto [Sandwich Islands]' was purchased by Hewett for 10s 6d.

Tracing the route of this image, then, can be satisfactorily accomplished with precise documentation. The image was probably given to Cook on one of the ceremonial occasions when he was honoured as an incarnation of the Hawaiian god Lono, god of peace and agriculture.[27] After the return of the ships to England the image went into the Museum of Sir Ashton Lever in Leicester Square. Won in the lottery by Parkinson, it was moved to the 'Rotunda' and purchased by Hewett at the 1806 dispersal of the collection. It was sold by the Hewett descendants in 1891 to A. W. Franks, of the Department of Antiquities, and catalogued in the British Museum for the last eighty-eight years as from the 'Vancouver collection'.

It was depicted by Webber, probably during the voyage, and engraved for the official account (Pl.101). The engraving actually shows the opposite side of the image[28] which accounts for the difference in the treatment of the eye; while in the Leverian Museum the image was sketched and coloured by Sarah Stone who, with a bit of artistic licence, did not clearly depict the hole under the eyes but drew the same side of the image as that drawn by Webber.[29] The image was also illustrated by Philippe Jacques de Loutherbourg (Pl.102), probably when he was preparing the stage scenery for the pantomime, *Omai or A Trip Round the World*.[30] The question of whether Loutherbourg worked from Webber's drawing or from the actual image while in the Leverian Museum is an intriguing one. I suggest that Loutherbourg's drawing of the image was done from the engraving because the complete eye with seed pupil is on the wrong side of the face. Although it is possible that both eyes were complete at the time, it seems too much of a coincidence for both Webber and Sarah Stone, who are each known to have drawn from the actual image, to have chosen the left side. The two drums and altar in the Loutherbourg (?) drawing also appear to have been taken from the engraving of Webber's original of the Tahitian *marae*, because there are no drums with this same carved configuration of the drum base traceable to Cook's voyages. The other feathered image in the Loutherbourg drawing, does not appear to depict any known specific image. I am not aware of other drawings of feathered images by Webber and it is possible that Loutherbourg's second example may be a composite of several images, such as the seven in the Leverian Museum.

At the Leverian sale the only other lot purchased by Hewett which included Hawaiian objects was lot 6398, 'Black, scarlet, and yellow feather helmet, a small feather cloak, and a feather ornament'. Three feathered helmets are accessioned in the 'Vancouver collection' and one of them was drawn by Sarah Stone (Pl.103).[31] The Stone drawing of this helmet shows that red feathered strips were once attached to the side of the crest while a red, black, and yellow *lei* was attached along the edge. Although feathered strips and *lei* are no longer attached to the British

178

Museum specimen, similar feathered strips are included in the 'Vancouver collection' (VAN 253a, b; VAN 258). Each of the two red feathered strips is about twice as long as the strip shown in the drawing and it appears that a strip began at one side of the crest, was looped around one of the corded feather elements of the crest and then doubled back to its starting point. In the Hewett manuscript list No.40 is 'Feather Helmet' with '2' added at the end of the line. Hewett probably collected VAN 235 which he listed as No.40, bought the second helmet at the Leverian sale, and simply annotated his manuscript with a '2'. Another 'Helmet', listed as No.85, is probably VAN 237.

No.57 of the manuscript list is 'cloaks' and the 'Vancouver collection' includes three, VAN 232, 233, and 234. It is likely that the feathered cape purchased as part of lot 6398 of the Leverian sale, 'a small feather cloak', is VAN 234, which is not only the smallest of the three, but is of a trapezoidal type so far traceable only to Cook's voyage (Pl. 104). Finally, the 'feather ornament' of lot 6398 is probably one of the forty feather necklaces of entry 100 of the Hewett manuscript. One of the feathered *lei* in the 'Vancouver collection' looks very much like one of the Sarah Stone drawings.[32]

An entirely different route to the British Museum from the Leverian Museum was taken by a rather large collection bought at the Leverian sale in the name of 'Higgins', often 'Mrs. Higgins'. All of the pieces which can be shown to be a purchase of Higgins, either by comparison of an object with a Sarah Stone drawing or by a detailed description, have no accession information in the British Museum, but are simply catalogued in the early geographical/numerical series. That some of Higgins's purchases are now objects in the British Museum is, however, indisputable. The Nootka Sound carving of a woman and child, for example, was not only drawn by Sarah Stone,[33] but is matched by a description of a sale lot. Lot 2531, 'Resemblance of a woman and child, carved in wood, Otaheite'[34] was purchased by Higgins. It is catalogued in the British Museum as NWC 62. Among the Hawaiian pieces that must have come from the purchases of Higgins are lot 849, 'A very curious feathered idol, ornamented with hair, Sandwich Islands'. In the British Museum collection a feathered image with human hair, HAW 78, (Pl.105), is also depicted in the Sarah Stone sketchbooks.[35]

Higgins also purchased Leverian lot 4342, 'Scarlet and yellow feather cloak, black and scarlet ditto, two necklaces, and a dagger, Sandwich Islands'. A black and scarlet feathered cape now in the British Museum is distinctive enough and close enough to the drawing by Sarah Stone[36] to make it relatively sure that it is the specimen (although a second cape in the collection is also similar). Not only does this piece have no historical information, it has no number either (Pl.106). Another Hawaiian object, possibly from Higgins's purchases, may have been part of lot 4373, 'A beautiful feather gorget from the Friendly Islands'. As Tonga did not make feather gorgets, this may refer to one of the Hawaiian feathered 'aprons' in the British Museum, also unnumbered (Pls. 107 and 108), or the feathered helmet band numbered HAW 116 (Pl.109). Both of these artefact types are very rare and known only from Cook voyage collections. Unfortunately the evidence is not clear enough to relate them to specific sale lots and thus to confirm that they are the objects from the Leverian sale. Several other lots purchased by Higgins included Hawaiian objects, but without drawings we cannot be sure to which objects (if any) in the British Museum collection they refer.

Mrs Higgins was Theresa Longuet of Bath, who married John Higgins in 1804 and lived at Turvey Abbey in Bedfordshire. According to family tradition, John Higgins formed a wide-ranging collection including some specimens from Cook's voyages. John and Theresa's son Charles married Helen Burgon in 1853. Helen was the daughter of Thomas Burgon, who at one time worked in the Department of Antiquities of the British Museum.[37] In 1842 he sold a collection of Greek antiquities to the British Museum (records in the Director's office), but this is all we know for sure. According to the *Dictionary of National Biography* Charles Longuet-Higgins built a *village* museum, and John Burgon (an affinal relative) says that Charles was interested in the formation of *local* museums.[38]

In an address given to the Bedfordshire Architectural and Archaeological Society in 1865, Charles Longuet-Higgins states:

'. . . that it is a great mistake to attempt, in ordinary towns and villages to form a general museum. . . . A collection infinitely better may be seen, displayed with all the advantages which skill and arrangement can bestow, within a distance so moderate that a person really desirous of inspecting any branch of natural history or antiquities would do well to betake himself at once to the place where the best information on the subject which he seeks is to be obtained'.[39]

Instead of a general museum, Higgins advocates the formation of local museums which would include objects only from within 'seven miles in a direct line from the parish church'.[40] No doubt he is referring to the British Museum 'within a distance so moderate'. Was he justifying having given much of his own collection, inherited from his parents, to the British Museum? It was probably between 1853, when Charles married Helen Burgon, and 1865, when he gave the above address, that the collection went to the British Museum through his father-in-law. Any references to such transactions in the British Museum are, however, yet to be found.

Another group of artefacts accessioned into the Christy collection as 2006, 2007, 2008, 2009, and 2010 must also have been from the Leverian Museum. There is no historical information associated with them, but the Sarah Stone sketchbooks and the 1790 *Companion*, guide to the Leverian Museum, offer corroborating evidence.

A neck ornament composed of six tiny ivory hook ornaments strung on human hair (Pl.110, top) appears to be an ornament sketched by Sarah Stone.[41] However, because there are at least two similar ornaments – one also in the British Museum with four hooks (HAW 117 with no accession information) and one in Cambridge with three hooks – the latter traceable to the Leverian Museum – it is difficult to say with certainty whether the British Museum specimen is the one depicted. One of the hooks, however, has a '4' label on it (top left hook of Pl.110). This is a Leverian Museum label that refers to its place in the exhibition, as set out in the *Companion*. These hook necklaces were referred to as 'breast gorgets', and in the Sandwich Room in glass case IV on shelf 11 is described: '4. This is an ornament in the form of the handle of a cup, made of wood, bone, ivory, or shell, polished, which is hung about the neck by fine threads of twisted hair, sometimes doubled an hundred fold'.[42] The British Museum/Christy number of this necklace is 2008 and coincidentally number 2007, an implement of three shark teeth strung on cord (Pl.111), appears on the same page of Sarah Stone drawings as the necklace.[43] If the next numbers in the series are checked it is found that 2006 is another similar implement with two shark teeth (Pl.112); 2009 is two small hook ornaments – one of black coral and one of bone (Pl.113); and 2010 is two rare ivory hook ornaments of a variant form (Pl.114), undoubtedly the two hooks depicted by Sarah Stone.[44] The series of numbers, the drawing of four of the pieces by Stone in 1783, and the label that keyed the hook necklace to the *Companion*, can only indicate that the objects came as a series to the British Museum from a purchaser at the Leverian sale.

Slightly further in the Christy list is another rare form of shark tooth implement (Pl.115 top), only one other similar implement being known.[45] Numbered 2043, it is exactly like one drawn by Sarah Stone,[46] and has an inked '8' on one side. Checking the *Companion* we find: '8 Instruments made of various kinds of wood, bone, &c. set with sharks teeth'.[47] This shark tooth implement along with two others, 2044 and 2045, one composed of a handle of bone and one shark tooth, the other of two shark teeth in a wood handle, must surely also be part of the earlier series. They could all have come, in fact, from the series of lots bought by Higgins at the Leverian sale, such as lot 1565: 'Instrument set with shark's teeth and a gorget, from ditto [Sandwich Islands]', but such descriptions are not specific enough to assign specific objects to specific lots. Further correspondences between British Museum specimens, Sarah Stone drawings, and the purchases of Higgins suggest that the two unnumbered ivory turtles (Pl.116), at least four necklaces (Pls.117 and 118) (HAW 122 and Q77. Oc.2, 3, 4), and the calcareous limestone game stone (Pl.119), are all Cook voyage specimens from the Leverian Museum. Admittedly the evidence is circumstantial, but the correspondences are too close to be simply the result of chance.

A magnificent Hawaiian sculpture in the British Museum (Pl.120) which has no accession information (HAW 74) has an even more complex and hypothetical association with Cook's voyages – in this case based on style and logic. The carving conventions and style of this image in the British Museum leave little doubt in my mind that it was carved by the same craftsman as an image now in the Delgado Museum in New Orleans. The New Orleans image was sketched by Sarah Stone in the Leverian Museum,[48] and probably belonged to Cook. Elsewhere,[49] I have hypothesized that these two images may have come from the fence at Hikiau *heiau* (a Hawaiian outdoor religious structure) which Cook's men removed for firewood along with some of the wooden images.[50] The firewood was divided between the two ships and if one image went to Captain Cook on the *Resolution* it is probable that its mate went to Captain Clerke on the *Discovery*. Since Captain Clerke's curiosities went to Banks, and Banks gave his collection to the British Museum, this image could well have followed this route.

A bowl with human images (HAW 48) in the British Museum (Pl.122) can also be related by style to Cook's voyage. A Hawaiian bowl/ladle illustrated by Stone,[51] and now in the Museum für Völkerkunde, Vienna (Pl.123), is carved with such stylistic likeness to the British Museum bowl – in the finishing of the bowl itself and in the similarity of the images – that they seem to bear the stamp of an individual style. Unlike the other instances mentioned above, however, where specific occasions were suggested for collection of objects by two different individuals, for these two bowls I have no suggestions to offer. That the Vienna bowl is a Cook piece there is no doubt, but because of lack of accession information, the British Museum bowl can only be related to it by style.

A final association of an object with Cook's voyage will be made on the basis of the similarity of a gourd rattle ('*ulī'ulī*) to drawings by Webber. It appears that most of Webber's artefact drawings were made from objects collected by Cook; what we might call the 'official collection'. As seen above, Cook's own collection went mainly to Ashton Lever's private museum. That Lever had one of these gourd rattles in his collection there is no doubt, for one was drawn by Sarah Stone.[52] Webber, however, appears to have represented two such rattles. The rattle drawn by Stone seems to be the same as the one drawn by Webber for the engraving of Hawaiian artefacts for the official account of the voyage. The Stone rattle (seen from two views) has a decorated gourd, while the Webber drawing, that appears in the engraving, also has decoration on the gourd. Another gourd rattle, now in the British Museum (HAW 93) (Pl.124), is exactly like one depicted in another drawing by Webber in two views (British Library Add. MS 15, 514.28) (Pl.125). This latter gourd rattle appears to be the one that Webber has drawn in his field sketch of three views of a Hawaiian man with a gourd rattle (now in Bishop Museum) and in a later more finished drawing that was engraved (Pl.126).

182

I suggest that Webber, having made the sketches of the man 'dancing', obtained the gourd rattle so that he could delineate it more precisely. This, then, may be the object (or one of the objects) among the 'several' given by Webber and others to the British Museum on 24 November 1780.

We conclude that an inventory of objects collected on Cook's voyages in the British Museum cannot be made by studying documentation in the British Museum itself. Associated documentation is, for the most part, non-existent and often simply incorrect. An attempt to make order out of chaos is unrewarding and each object that can finally be credibly associated with Cook's voyages requires its own individual ethnological sleuthing. Only after detailed examination of other documentable Cook voyage pieces in other far-flung collections, can one begin to try to attempt to separate out Cook voyage pieces in the British Museum – unless by some fortunate accident of history we find some document that has so far eluded even the most tenacious of researchers.

Notes

1 Research on Cook voyage artefacts in the British Museum and elsewhere was carried out between 1969 and 1977 supported by the Wenner-Gren Foundation for Anthropological Research, the National Endowment for the Arts and the American Philosophical Society to whom I wish to express my warmest appreciation. I also wish to thank the many people who assisted me in my work on Cook voyage collections, especially B. A. L. Cranstone, Dorota Starzecka, and Jonathan King from the Museum of Mankind, and Peter Gathercole and Peter Whitehead for helpful comments and discussions. Most important, I wish to thank the late Captain A. W. F. Fuller and Mrs Estelle Fuller for the generous gift to Bishop Museum of the two sketchbooks of watercolours by Sarah Stone which made much of this research possible.

2 H. J. Braunholtz, 'Ethnography Since Sloane' in *Sir Hans Sloane and Ethnography*. London, 1970.

3 E. Miller, *That Noble Cabinet*. London, 1973.

4 Braunholtz, 'Ethnography', p.45.

5 G. Robertson, *The Discovery of Tahiti*. London, 1948, p.166.

6 G. Forster, *A Voyage Round the World in His Brittanic Majesty's Sloop Resolution Commanded by Capt. James Cook*. London, 1777, Vol.2, p.72.

7 Forster, *Voyage Round the World*. Vol.1, p.581.

8 D. G. Wendeborn, *The Position of the State, the Religion, the Education and the Arts in Great Britain Towards the End of the 18th Century*. Berlin, 1785, p.2. Typescript translation in Middleton Library, Manchester.

9 Daines Barrington was a lawyer and antiquary who was on the Council of the Royal Society and a friend of Lord Sandwich.

10 The cloak in the portrait, however, is decorated with dog hair, which NZ 137 is not.

11 The objects in the 'Banks Collection' are catalogued in the NWC numerical series. This entire series from NWC 1–117 has always been interpreted to mean that they came from Cook's voyage, see, for example, E. Gunther, *Indian Life on the North West Coast of North America*. Chicago, 1972.

12 Dodge's preliminary Inventory was published in R. Duff (ed.), *No Sort of Iron: Culture of Cook's Polynesians*. Auckland, 1969, p.88.

13 A. L. Kaeppler, *Cook Voyage Artifacts*. Honolulu, 1978.

14 J. C. Beaglehole, *The Journals of Captain James Cook*. Cambridge, 1967, p.577.

15 A. L. Kaeppler, 'An Eighteenth Century Káhili from Kaua'i', *Archaeology on Kaua'i*, 4.2 (1975), pp.3–9.

16 Cook in Beaglehole, *Journals*, p.281.

17 Beaglehole, *Journals*, p.281.

18 Clerke in Beaglehole, *Journals*, p.577.

19 Samwell in Beaglehole, *Journals*, p.1165.

19a Ibid., p.1227.

20 J. C. Fabricius, *Briefe aus London vermischten Inhalts*. Dissau and Leipzig, 1784. I am indebted to Rüdiger Joppien for bringing this to my attention, and for the translation.

21 Newspaper clipping in the Perceval Bequest, Fitzwilliam Museum, Cambridge.

22 J. Greig (ed.), *Farington Diary* (1924), Vol.3, p.273.

23 Letter from H. Syer Cuming to Spencer G. Perceval in the Perceval Bequest, Fitzwilliam Museum.

24 J. Sweet, 'Robert Jameson in London, 1793', *Annals of Science* 19.2 (1963), p.100.

25 *Catalogue of the Missionary Museum*, [London?, 1890?], p.14.

26 A gift of Mrs Estelle Fuller.

27 A. L. Kaeppler, 'The significance of Cook's third voyage . . .', Vancouver, 1978.

28 Engravings show a mirror image of the original drawings. The original drawings of this feather image showing it in reverse can be found in the British Library Add. MS 15,514.27.

29 See R. W. and M. Force, *Art and Artifacts of the Eighteenth Century. Objects in the Leverian Museum as painted by Sarah Stone*. Honolulu, 1968, p.23.

30 Although this watercolour is not credited to Loutherbourg, I feel confident that it was done by him because of the similarity to this and several other drawings which can be traced to Loutherbourg. See Jöppien

pp.81–102 for further information and
drawings on this eighteenth-century stage
production.

31 See also Force and Force, *Art and Artifacts*,
p.33 top.

32 Ibid., p.65 middle.

33 Ibid., p.101.

34 'Otaheite' here is simply a catchall word
meaning that its specific area of origin is
unknown. Many objects from Cook's
voyages are simply ascribed a provenance of
'Otaheite'.

35 Force and Force, *Arts and Artifacts*, p.25.

36 Ibid., p.59.

37 *Dictionary of National Biography*. London,
1917, p.818.

38 *Dictionary of National Biography*. London,
1888, p.405.

39 C. Longuet-Higgins, 'A Few Plain Remarks
on Local Museums', *Bedfordshire
Architectural and Archaeological Society*,
8(2), (1865), p.323.

40 Ibid., p.325.

41 Force and Force, *Art and Artifacts*, p.87.

42 *A Companion to the Museum*, (Late Sir
Aston Lever's). London, 1790. p.14. Several
other labels on former Leverian Museum
specimens also exist on artefacts now in the
University Museum of Archaeology and
Ethnology, Cambridge, and the Museum für
Völkerkunde, Vienna.

43 Force and Force, *Art and Artifacts*, p.87.

44 Ibid., p.83.

45 In the Oldman Collection (310) in
Canterbury Museum, Christehurch, New
Zealand.

46 Force and Force, *Art and Artifacts* p.86 top.

47 *Companion*, (1790), p.14.

48 Force and Force, *Art and Artifacts*, p.97.

49 A. L. Kaeppler, 'The significance of Cook's
Third Voyage for the study of Hawaiian Art
and Society'. Paper presented at the
symposium 'Captain Cook and his times',
Vancouver, April 1978.

50 Beaglehole, *Journals*, 1, p.516.

51 Force and Force, *Art and Artifacts*, p.99.

52 Ibid., pp.79, 81.

Bibliography

Beaglehole, J. C. *The Journals of Captain James
Cook*. Cambridge University Press for the
Hakluyt Society, 1967.

Braunholtz, H. J. 'Ethnography since Sloane', in
Sir Hans Sloane and Ethnography. London,
1970.

Burgon, John Williams. *Lives of Twelve Good
Men*. London, 1888.

Dodge, E. S. 'The Cook Ethnographical
Collections', in Duff, R. (ed.) *No Sort of Iron:
Culture of Cook's Polynesians*. Auckland, 1969.

Force, Roland W. and Maryanne. *Art and
Artifacts of the 18th Century. Objects in the
Leverian Museum as painted by Sarah Stone*.
Honolulu, 1968. To be issued in revised form
as *Captain James Cook, Sir Ashton Lever, and
Miss Sarah Stone* by Adrienne L. Kaeppler.

Forster, George. *A voyage round the World in His
Britannic Majesty's Sloop Resolution
Commanded by Capt. James Cook . . .* London,
1777.

Greig, J. (ed.) *Farington Diary*. London, 1924.

Gunther, E. *Indian Life on the Northwest Coast of
North America: As Seen by the Early Explorers
and Fur Traders During the Last Decades of the
Eighteenth Century*. Chicago, 1972.

Kaeppler, Adrienne L. 'An Eighteenth Century
Kāhili from Kaua'i', *Archaeology on Kaua'i* 4.2
(1975), pp.3–9.

Kaeppler, A. L. '*Artificial Curiosities': Being an
Exposition of Native Manufactures Collected on
the three Pacific Voyages of Captain James
Cook, R.N.* (Bishop Museum Special
Publication 65). Honolulu, 1978.

Kaeppler, A. L. *Cook Voyage Artifacts in
Leningrad, Berne and Florence Museums*,
(Bishop Museum Special Publication, 66).
Honolulu, 1978.

Kaeppler, A. L. 'The significance of Cook's third
voyage for the study of Hawaiian Art and
Society'. Paper presented to the Cook
Conference, Vancouver, 1978.

Leverian Museum. *A Companion to the Museum*.
London, 1790.

London Missionary Society *Catalogue of the
Missionary Museum*. [London(?), 1890(?)]

Longuet-Higgins, Charles. 'A Few Plain Remarks on Local Museums', *Bedfordshire Architectural and Archaeological Society*, 8(2), (1865), pp.321–29.

Miller, Edward. *That Noble Cabinet*. London, 1973.

Robertson, George. *The Discovery of Tahiti: A Journal of the Second Voyage of H.M.S. Dolphin ... 1766 ... 1768.* (Hakluyt Society, Ser.2, No.98.) London, 1948.

Sweet, Jessie. 'Robert Jameson in London, 1793'. *Annals of Science*, 19.2, (1963), pp.81–116.

Wendeborn, D. Gebhard. 'The Position of the State, the Religion, the Education and the Arts in Great Britain Towards the End of the 18th Century'. (Typescript translation in Middleton Library, Manchester, from German original published in Berlin, 1785.)

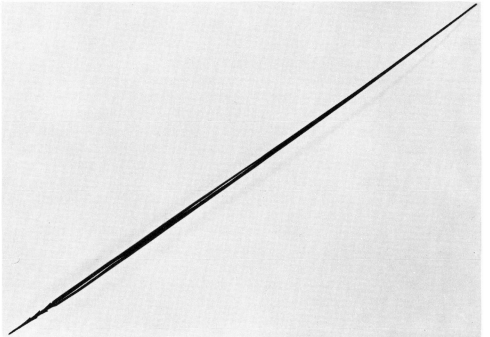

91 Bracelet of boar tusks strung on cord (HAW 156).

92 Decorated gourd water container (HAW 51).

93 Barbed wooden spear (1946.Oc.1.1).

94 Hook ornament of shell and turtle shell
(1944.Oc.2.715).

95 Feathered standard with handle of human
bone and turtle shell discs (HAW 167).

96 Feathered standard with handle of human
bone and turtle shell discs. National Museum
of New Zealand, Wellington (FE 329).

188

97 Wooden bowl with human images (HAW 46).

98 Wooden bowl with human images
(Anonymous private collection).

99 Feathered image (LMS 221).

100 Feathered image (VAN 231).

101 Engraving of a feathered image after John Webber. British Library Add. MS 23,921.79.

102 Drawing probably by Philippe Jacques de Loutherbourg. Alexander Turnbull Library, Wellington, New Zealand.

190

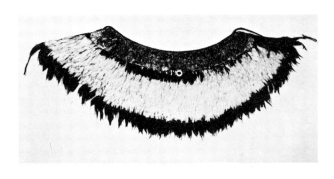

103 Feathered helmet with feathered strips that
were probably once attached (VAN 236 and
VAN 258, 253).

104 Feathered cape (VAN 234).

105 Feathered image with hair (HAW 78).

106 Feathered cape (NN).

Hawaiian Artefacts 191

107 Feathered apron (NN).

108 Feathered apron (NN).

109 Feathered helmet band (HAW 116).

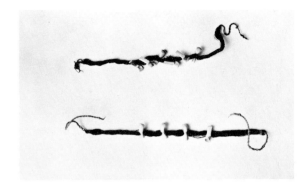

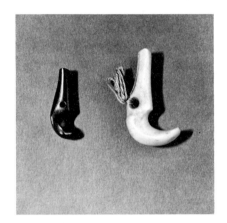

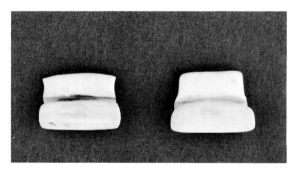

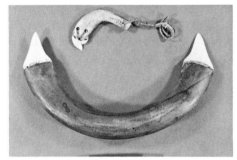

110 Two necklaces with ivory hook ornaments
(top 2008, bottom HAW 117).

111 Implement of three shark teeth on fibre
(2007).

112 Implement of two shark teeth on fibre
(2006).

113 Two hook ornaments of shell and black coral
(2009a and b)

114 Two hook ornaments of variant form (2010).

115 Two shark tooth implements (2043, 2045).

Hawaiian Artefacts   **193**

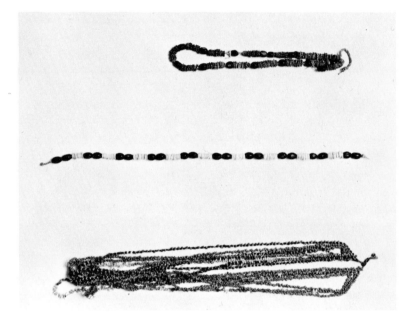

116 Two ivory and bone turtles (NN).

117 Necklace of shell hook ornament on strings
of tiny shells (HAW 122).

118 Three necklaces of shells and seeds
(Q77.Oc.2, 3, 4).

119 Game stone (HAW 83).

194

120 Wooden image (HAW 74).

121 Wooden image. Isaac Delgado Museum, New Orleans Museum of Art.

122 Bowl with human images (HAW 48).

123 Bowl with human image. Museum für
Völkerkunde, Vienna (175).

124 Rattle of gourd and feathers (HAW 93).

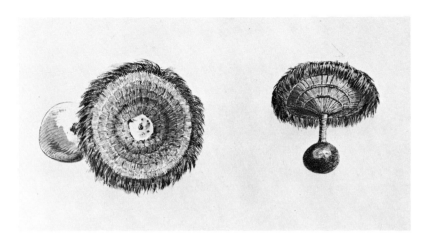

125 Two views of a gourd rattle. Drawing by
John Webber. British Library Add. MS
15,514.28.

126 *A Man of the Sandwich Islands Dancing.*
Engraving after John Webber. British
Library Add. MS 23,921.76.

Hawaiian Artefacts 197

Art and Ethnographica from the Solomon Islands in the Museum of Mankind

DEBORAH B. WAITE

University of Hawaii

A prominent collection of artefacts in the Ethnography Department of the British Museum comes from the Solomon Islands, one of the principal groups of Melanesian Islands in the Western Pacific (see map). Major islands and island groups in the Solomons include, from north-west to south-east: Buka and Bougainville (now politically part of the country of Papua New Guinea), Choiseul, the New Georgia islands (e.g. Roviana), Ysabel, the Florida islands, Malaita, Guadalcanal, and San Cristobal. The eastern islands of Ulawa, Uki, Santa Ana, and Santa Catalina, though small in size, have long been of major importance in the production of art and other artefacts. Marginal islands populated by Polynesian-speaking peoples, such as Rennell, Bellona, Ongtong Java, and Sikiana, as well as the Santa Cruz islands which lie south of Santa Ana and Santa Catalina, are somewhat removed, culturally, from the major group that constitutes the Solomon Islands.

The Solomon Islands collection in the British Museum has a variegated history that is not always easy to unravel. Available data from the museum accession files indicates that the first artefacts from the Solomon Islands to be acquired by the British Museum came into the museum in the 1860s as part of the Christy Collection. Henry Christy was a collector of archaeological implements and ethnographica who lived in London during the first half of the nineteenth century. His collection was given to the British Museum following his death in 1865; the collection was considerably augmented by gifts from other donors in the years thereafter.[1]

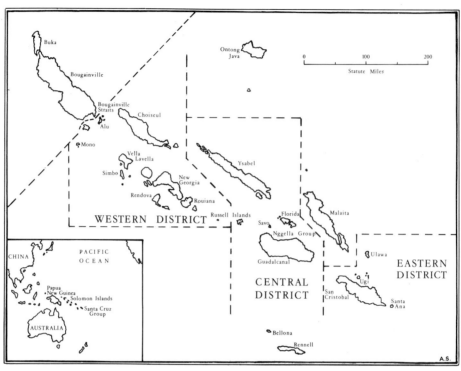

The Solomon Islands (Drawing by Ann Searight)

It is impossible to know just how many of the early Christy pieces from the Solomon Islands actually may have belonged to Christy himself. A catalogue of Christy's private collection published in 1862 lists eighty-six items from Australia and Oceania. Among these was item 82: 'a very interesting knife or saw from the Solomon Islands made of a pearl oyster and about four and one-half inches long'.[2] This shell scraper, now St 887 in the British Museum collection, appears to be the only item in the catalogue attributed to the Solomon Islands. It is possible that there are other unrecognised artefacts from the Solomons in the collection.

Numerous artefacts from the Solomon Islands found their way into the Christy Collection between 1865 and 1868. This is indicated in the contents of a second catalogue written in 1868 by Augustus W. Franks, one of the four trustees of the Christy Estate. The collection, then part of the British Museum holdings, had been set up temporarily in Christy's home at 108 Victoria Street, London. According to the catalogue, Room 111 in the Victoria Street home was reserved for objects from Melanesia and Polynesia. Four cases contained Melanesian material:

'Objects mostly still in use among the black races of the Pacific, including specimens from New Guinea, New Caledonia, New Hebrides, and the Solomon

200

Islands ... Among the more remarkable are black carvings in wood inlaid with mother-of-pearl, paddles with singular devices, bows and arrows of different types, a staff with a perforated stone at one end, javelins with obsidian heads, clubs elegantly ornamented with plaited work, adzes with shell and stone blades, a basalt chisel from the Fiji Islands, petticoats of vegetable fibre, and pillows made of bamboo.

Over the case are wooden vessels principally from the Solomon Islands, and on the walls a few clubs and paddles of unusual forms'.[3]

By 1868 the original Christy Collection had been enlarged through the gifts of sixty-five donors listed in the 1868 catalogue. Of these, only four – William Blackmore, Robert Day, A. W. Franks, and E. A. Roy – have been recorded as donors of objects from the Solomon Islands. Sixteen artefacts from the Solomon Islands are documented in the museum accession files as having been presented by Roy, Franks, and Day between 1865 and 1868. Blackmore's gift of seven objects from the Solomons (7620–27) was not presented to the museum until 1872. Other early acquisitions from the Solomons with no recorded year of acquisition or donor may well correspond to some of the 'black carvings in wood inlaid with mother-of-pearl' mentioned in the 1868 catalogue. (This is a common decorative technique in the Solomon Islands.) Proof is, however, next to impossible.

Extensive acquisitions of artefacts obtained in the Solomon Islands during the last half of the nineteenth century constitute the bulk of the Solomon Islands holdings in the British Museum. Many of these objects came into the museum in the nineteenth century; other pieces acquired in the Solomons at that time arrived in the museum at a much later date. Outstanding donations from this period came from three missionaries who were stationed in the Solomon Islands with the Melanesian Mission: The Rev[d] R. H. Codrington, who was with the Mission from 1867 to 1886, The Rev[d] Richard B. Comins (1877–1890s), and the Rev[d] Alfred B. Penny (1877–1885). Other major groups of material were acquired by Henry B. Guppy, who travelled through the eastern Solomon Islands and the Bougainville Straits as a surgeon with the surveying ship HMS *Lark* in 1882; Charles F. Wood, a visitor to San Cristobal and other Solomon islands in the late 1860s and early 1870s; and Rear-Admiral Davis of HMS *Royalist*, a British Royal Navy ship which led a 'punitive' expedition against headhunters of the New Georgia islands in 1891–93.

Especially notable among the large groups of artefacts acquired during this period are the approximately sixty objects presented to the museum in 1870 by Julius L. Brenchley, a resident of Maidstone, Kent. In the summer of 1865, Brenchley travelled through the central and eastern Solomon Islands on HMS *Curacoa* as a guest of the ship's captain, Commodore Sir William Wiseman.[4] The

Brenchley collection, also represented extensively at the Maidstone Museum, comprises wood carvings, shields, and other objects from Ysabel, Guadalcanal, Florida, San Cristobal, Ulawa, and Uki islands.

The most extensive collection of material acquired in the Solomons by one individual came from Charles M. Woodford, the first District Commissioner of the British Solomon Islands Protectorate formed in 1893. Woodford made his first two trips to the Solomon Islands in 1888 for the purpose of collecting botanical specimens. His subsequent residence as District Commissioner made possible the acquisition of large quantities of ethnographica. Approximately 296 objects collected by Woodford are now in the British Museum.

A number of these early collectors wrote about their experiences in the Solomon Islands. Brenchley, Codrington, Penny, Guppy, Wood, and Woodford published works which describe aspects of nineteenth-century life in various parts of the Solomons – a task of reporting that was limited to some extent by language barriers, time limitations, and a not unexpected degree of prejudice owing to the Western origins and professional occupations of the writers. Nevertheless, the records provide valuable insights into the life styles of the period and occasionally describe the usage of artefacts similar to those collected. Only Brenchley, Penny, and Codrington actually mention specific objects that are now in the British Museum. As a rule, the writings of nineteenth- and early-twentieth century collectors of artefacts from the Solomons rarely divulge information as to how and under what circumstances these acquisitions took place.

Augustus W. Franks did not travel to the Solomon Islands, yet he should be numbered among the major contributors to the collection of artefacts from this area. Franks was one of the four trustees of the original Christy Estate and wrote the 1868 catalogue of the Christy Collection. As Keeper during the remainder of the nineteenth century of the Department of British and Medieval Antiquities, which at that time included Ethnography, he augmented the collection through exchanges with other museums in Great Britain, as well as purchases from private collectors and dealers. The Solomon Islands material obtained by Franks includes artefacts originally acquired by Admiral Davis, Woodford, and others.

Artefacts from the Solomon Islands presented to the museum since 1900 comprise a vast assortment of acquisitions from many donors. Among those of note are collections made by Gerald C. Wheeler (donated 1927), The Revd Walter Ivens (donated 1940), Harry G. Beasley (donated 1944), and J. D. Bradley (donated 1956).

Wheeler, a former Director of Science at the London School of Economics, undertook anthropological research in 1908–9 on the islands of Mono and Alu in the Bougainville Straits. He collected approximately two hundred artefacts, many of them wooden images, canoe carvings, and dance ornaments. Field documentation as to the place of origin, artist, and function of most of the carvings enhances the historical value of the Wheeler collection.

Ivens was stationed with the Melanesian Mission on Ulawa and in Sa'a, Malaita between 1896 and 1909. He returned to Sa'a and Ulawa in 1924 for anthropological and linguistic research. Twenty-two artefacts collected by Ivens represent some of the outstanding wooden carvings from this region.[5]

An important group of ethnographica from Rennell and Bellona islands was acquired in 1953 by J. D. Bradley, at that time an entomologist with the British Museum (Natural History). The collection is sizable (approximately 142 objects), and, like the Wheeler Collection, has especial significance due to the fact that local names and functions of most of the objects were obtained by Bradley at the time of collection.

Lastly, the Harry G. Beasley Collection of Solomon Islands material represents perhaps the largest group donated by one person (about 414 objects), although the artefacts were not collected in the islands by Beasley himself. The Beasley material includes large groups of wooden combs and shell kapkap ornaments from Bougainville, wooden images from Santa Cruz, and many other items obtained by Beasley through traders, missionaries, and other sources.

In order to explore the depths of the Solomon Islands collection to a limited degree, certain artefacts in the collection should be examined in some detail. A typological/functional grouping of the objects is probably the most effective one for presenting the material within what was once its cultural context. The mammoth scope of the collection demands a certain amount of selectivity. For this reason, the marginal islands (Santa Cruz, Rennell, Bellona, etc.) will be excluded from detailed consideration. Among the various categories of artefacts, a major emphasis will be placed on carvings or sculpture of which there are so many early examples of quality.

Canoes

Canoes from all parts of the Solomon Islands have aroused the admiration of visitors to the islands since the sixteenth century. In 1568, Alvaro de Mendaña, a Spaniard who sailed from Peru to become the first 'discoverer' of the Solomon Islands, wrote in his journal that:

> 'Their canoes are very well made and very light; they are shaped like a crescent, the largest holding about thirty persons. They are so swift that, although our ships under sail started two leagues ahead of them, with a good wind and all the sails set, they caught up within the hour. Their speed in rowing is marvelous ...'[6]

Most canoes from the Solomon Islands were built of planks carefully shaped with an adze so as to fit tightly, one next to another, and lashed together with fibre looped through holes in adjoining planks. Seams between adjoining planks were made watertight with a glue made from the parinarium nut. In the words of an eighteenth-century observer:

'The canoes of these islanders . . . are not formed of a trunk of a tree made hollow by stone implements or fire (i.e. dugout canoes) . . . but are made of pieces put together. In the small canoes the planks are not more than a third of an inch in thickness, and in working them they form on the inside a kind of loop, which at intervals are tied strongly with rattan to ribs of wood; nor are the planks held together by any other means; the joints are stopped with a black mastic, tolerably hard, which renders these frail vessels impenetrable to the water. The prow and stern are raised very high . . . and in general they are ornamented with pieces of mother-of-pearl forming different designs and applied with mastic.'

So wrote the French trader, Jean François de Surville, of canoes from Ysabel Island in 1769.[7]

The British Museum collection of ethnographic material from the Solomon Islands contains five canoes in addition to several canoe models; one of the canoes (Pl.127) was constructed on Vella La Vella Island in the Western District (1927. 10–22.1). The tall upturned prow is elaborately decorated in a manner characteristic of the large forty- to fifty-foot war canoes (*tomako*) from this part of the Solomons. Circular pieces of nautilus shell are inlaid in rows along the sides of the bow and prow peak. Further decoration is provided by shells tied along the front of the canoe and a row of triangular shells fastened to the inner rim of the prow (Pl.128). The triangular shells resemble in shape larger triangular pieces of tridacna clam shell once fastened in clusters to sticks placed in or near huts containing the skulls of deceased social group leaders (Pl.148); the shell-covered sticks, called *serenbule*, were also placed in the bows of war canoes taken out on headhunting raids. The wooden figurehead lashed to the bow of the canoe constitutes another standard ornament of headhunting canoes from Vella La Vella and surrounding islands.

This particular canoe was constructed around 1910, some years after the practice of headhunting was outlawed by the British Protectorate government, but it is a characteristic example of the type of vessel that participated on headhunting raids.[8]

Canoe Ornaments

Canoes from all parts of the Solomon Islands were ornamented with intricate patterns of shell inlay as well as attached wooden carvings. Such elaborate decoration has always traditionally been reserved for large canoes that served important public functions, as for example, headhunting in islands of the Western District (e.g. New Georgia Islands). In the Eastern District islands of San Cristobal, Santa Ana, Santa Catalina, Uki, and Ulawa, canoes used on ritual bonito fishing expeditions undertaken during puberty initiation festivals for young boys were profusely ornamented with shell-inlaid designs of birds and fish as well as birds and fish carvings.

In view of the acute social importance of the decorated canoe, it is not surprising that canoe carvings would form a major group of artefacts in any collection of art from the Solomon Islands. The British Museum possesses approximately forty-seven canoe ornaments from the Solomons. Of these, the majority come from the Western – Central Districts (New Georgia islands, Vella La Vella, Choiseul, and Ysabel). Twenty-two of these carvings are canoe prow figureheads.

PROW FIGUREHEADS

Carved wooden figureheads (Pls.128–130) were once lashed to the bows of headhunting canoes in the New Georgia islands, Choiseul, Vella La Vella, and Ysabel. Generally, they did not appear on canoes from islands to the southeast, although the Rev[d] R. H. Codrington recorded and made a drawing of a figurehead attached to a canoe constructed at Boli, Florida.[9] The origins of canoe prow figureheads cannot be ascertained, but their existence can be documented as early as the middle of the eighteenth century in the journals of Louis A. de Bougainville, the French soldier/navigator whose ship cruised through the waters of the Western District islands in the summer of 1768. In describing two canoes that he allegedly captured at Choiseul Bay, Bougainville noted that:

> 'On the forepart of one of these canoes was the head of a man carved; the eyes were of mother-of-pearl, the ears of tortoise shell, the lips were stained of a very bright scarlet, and the whole had the appearance of a mask with a very long beard.'[10]

The figureheads usually depict the head and arms of an anthropomorphic being. Only a very few represent complete figures. The three examples shown (Pls.128, 129 and 130) illustrate stylistic traits common to figureheads from the Western District as well as differential features accountable to the styles of individual artists working at various periods of time. All three figureheads have large heads supported on upraised hands. A conspicuous feature is the forward extension of the lower face, in which that part of the head beneath the brow is drawn out into space to an exaggerated degree. Curving bands of nautilus shell inlay appear on the brow, cheeks, and jaw of each figurehead; the shell-inlaid patterns reproduce designs once painted on the faces of warriors from this region.

Possibly one of the oldest figureheads in the British Museum is also one of the most recent acquisitions (1968, Oc.3.1) (Pl.129). In 1968 the figurehead was presented to the museum by L. T. Hope of Essex, together with the information that it was collected between 1830–40 by the donor's maternal grandfather surnamed Smith. Smith had reputedly been a missionary with the London Missionary Society and was a colleague of the LMS missionary John Williams. The donor later related that Smith had worked on Raiatea in the Society Islands and had been given the carving by a chief Taumatoa.

London Missionary Society records indicate that a Revd James Smith was stationed on Raiatea from 1830 to 1834, and he appears to be the only missionary surnamed Smith on Raiatea at this period. Letters of James Smith written to LMS headquarters in London indicate that he was indeed closely associated with John Williams, and that he met two chiefs Taumatoa.[11] The letters do not mention the acquisition of wooden images of any sort.

This, then is the fragmentary evidence which suggests that a canoe figurehead of a characteristic Solomon Islands type may, conceivably, have fallen into the hands of an early trader or other navigator and made its way to Polynesia from whence it was brought to England by the Revd James Smith. Or, perhaps even more likely, Smith could have obtained the carving in Sydney where he stopped on his return trip to London in 1834. In either case, the figurehead must have been carved prior to 1834, the date of Smith's return to England – and perhaps considerably earlier in view of its former existence for an unknown period in the Solomon Islands. The figurehead might, thus, represent one of the oldest carvings from the Solomon Islands to reach Europe.

Another figurehead (1661A) which may be almost as old as the previous example is one of five figureheads which bear numbers assigned to objects in the Christy Collection (1660, 1661A, 1662, 1282, 1659) (Pl.130). Particularly distinctive features of this figurehead include the smooth-surfaced vertically-oriented brow and even planes of the face which expands in width at the jawline. The sharp-edged browline, sensitively rendered long nose, and narrow ovoid mouth contrast markedly with the broad dilated nostrils, full lips, and separate brow treatment of the figurehead donated by Hope (Pl.129).

This figurehead was formerly attached to the heads of two standing images (1661) carved in a radically different style (Pl.131). The trio bore a label, 'Two

206

Marquesan slaves bearing the head of a great chief'. The three carvings were separated in the museum but can easily be reassembled, for projections from the heads of the two standing figures fit exactly into areas between the shoulders and elbows of the figurehead. Bases of the standing images also interlock (Pl.132). All three carvings have been attributed on stylistic grounds to Roviana by C. M. Woodford. Why they were joined together remains a mystery.

It has been said that canoe figureheads depicted or embodied the essence of spirits empowered to ward off other spirits that might cause storms and heavy seas which would capsize the canoes, whereupon the malevolent spirits would devour the helpless crew.[12] This function, repeatedly related to travellers in the Western District, appears an awesome one not reflected in the comparatively small size of the figureheads (eighteen to twenty-three cm high) when viewed in position lashed to the bows of canoes just above the waterline (cf. Pl.127). The fact that the images largely represent detached heads, as opposed to full figures, would seem to relate directly to the use of these decorated canoes on headhunting raids; this visual reflection of symbolic function seems never to have been noted in the literature.

OTHER CANOE ORNAMENTS

The remaining canoe carvings (Pls.133–135) in the British Museum collection of material from the Solomon Islands originate largely from the Western and Central Districts and consist of anthropomorphic or bird carvings attached to the canoe prow or stern. War canoes from the Roviana area were traditionally adorned with a carving of two half-figures (head and arms) usually placed on the tip of the canoe prow directly above the canoe prow figurehead (Pl.133). The half-figures were, in fact, small paired duplicates of the canoe figurehead and were always represented facing in opposite directions. The images, called *beku* or *kesoko*, were said to represent the storm-causing water spirits that the prow figureheads supposedly warded off.[13] Information describing the relationship between these two carvings is sparse, but an attempt to represent opposing forces in sculptural form as a means of symbolic protection seems implicit in the positioning of the carvings on the prow. A *beku/kesoko* carving (Pl.133; 1914–311), was presented to the museum by A. M. Hocart, who collected the piece in 1908 while doing anthropological research on Simbo and Roviana islands.

Five canoe carvings attributed to Roviana, Savo, and Rennell Islands (1957, Oc.4.22, 23, 25; 1954, Oc.2, 1792; 1927–83) constitute a single typological group in the British Museum Solomon Islands collection. The carvings range in length from fifty-one to seventy-five centimetres. Each consists of a single piece of wood: the bottom half a solid triangle, the upper part carved into a standing three-dimensional figure surrounded by a rectangular frame (Pl. 134). The figure stands or sits with arms extended laterally to touch the frame. In the example illustrated here, the figure holds a miniature head in each hand. Prominent among carved low-relief designs on the frame is the triangular form also observed in the shells attached to the inner rim of the prows of headhunting canoes (cf. Pl. 128). The predominance of these designs, together with the small heads held by the one figure, suggest a headhunting symbolism.

All five canoe carvings, despite their different attributed provenances, bear the marks of a figure style characteristic of imagery from the New Georgia (Roviana) Islands. Of particular note, as evidenced in the illustrated example (Pl. 134), are the tall heads with extended lower faces, open tooth-filled mouths, and large circular ear ornaments. Incised bands of facial decoration correspond to shell-inlaid patterns on the faces of canoe prow figureheads from this region. The carving illustrated here bears an especially strong resemblance to the two images attributed to Roviana that once were attached to a canoe prow figurehead (Pl. 131).

A reference in J. Edge-Partington's *An Album of the Weapons, Tools, Ornaments ... of the Natives of the Pacific Islands* (1898) pertaining to a carving of this type says that the carvings were affixed to the sterns of canoes, but that when the canoes were not in use, the carvings were removed and hung up in the house (type of house unspecified).[14] This appears to represent the major recorded clue regarding the use of these canoe carvings. Five canoe carvings from islands in the Bougainville Straits (south of Bougainville Island) appear in the Solomon Islands collection of the British Museum. Three of the carvings were obtained from Mono and Alu islands by Gerald C. Wheeler (1927. 10–3, 26, 43, 46). Another (1909–41) was obtained by Woodford. The fifth carving in the group (1944 Oc.2, 1790), from the Beasley Collection, may be attributed to this region on stylistic grounds. Canoe carvings from the Bougainville Straits islands, like those from the area of Roviana, are anthropomorphic, and many have two heads facing in opposite directions.

Canoe carving (1927. 10–3, 46; Pl. 135) illustrates characteristic features of the highly distinctive imagery from this island group. The carving, $25\frac{1}{2}$ cms high, comprises an anthropomorphic head and arms which rest on four large scrolls (*fafotu*). The motif of a large head resting on the detached shoulders and arms of a bodiless image relates morphologically to canoe prow figureheads from the New Georgia (Roviana) area (cf. Pls. 127–130). Visually, however, the Mono-Alu carving displays striking differences: notably, the large hollow cup-shaped form atop the head representing hair; faceted planes of the face; the red, black, and white colour scheme of the carving; and the absence of shell-inlaid decoration so characteristic of carvings from the Roviana region.

According to Wheeler, this carving was made by a man named Mukolo of Faleta village, Alu Island. It was one of two such carvings that originally had been placed at the bow and stern of a thirty-man canoe which had been 'broken up' by the time Wheeler arrived in the islands. This carving was intended for the canoe stern; its maker, Makolo, was one of the co-owners of the canoe. The other owner, Piloto, had made the bow carving. Formerly, feathers and fur from the opossum and flying fox were attached to the carving which was referred to as a *beku* or 'carved wooden image' (cf. the use of the term *beku* for canoe images placed in a comparable position on Roviana canoes – Pl.133).[15]

Canoe Paddles

Canoe paddles were an indispensable item in the Solomon Islands, and, like the canoes, many were decorated. Paddles from the north-western and south-eastern islands have long pointed blades; those from the central islands (e.g., Roviana, Vella La Vella, and Ysabel) have broad leaf-shaped blades pointed at the tip as well as a crescent-shaped or 'crutch' handle (Pl.136). Carved and painted low-relief designs rendered on the blades of the paddles generally reflected the iconographic motifs characteristic of other art forms peculiar to each region.[15a]

Fish Floats

Carved wooden floats (Pls.137–139) used for line and net fishing in the islands of the Western and Eastern Districts of the Solomons constitute a significant category of Solomon Islands sculpture. The British Museum possesses a group of nineteen fish floats, all of nineteenth-century vintage and possessing reliable historical documentation. The Rev[d] Richard B. Comins, Julius Brenchley, the Rev[d] R. H. Codrington, and C. M. Woodford were responsible for the bulk of the collection. Five of the floats come from the Roviana area in the Western District; the remainder were obtained from Eastern District islands of Malaita, San Cristobal, and Ulawa.

In islands of the Eastern District, wooden floats (70 cms long) have traditionally been used to catch flying fish. The floats consist of a long stick carved at the top into the form of a bird, fish, or other image. A stone weight encased in a net is fastened to the bottom of the float; the line with bait attached is tied round a projecting spur located just below the carved image.[16]

Walter Ivens observed on Ulawa and Malaita that a number of these line floats were tied together and set some distance from shore in a line leading out to sea. Each float terminated in a carved image which was visible to fishermen in nearby boats. When a fish took the bait, the float (and image) were jerked under water.

According to Ivens each float image was named, and these correspond to locally-known birds, fish, and spirits associated with the sea.[17] The British Museum contains floats of each category; they are painted black, and one, collected by Comins on Ulawa and donated in 1883, is beautifully decorated with shell inlay (Pl. 137).

A float obtained on Ulawa in 1865 by Brenchley (Pl. 138) represents a standing anthropomorphic figure whose head terminates in a scroll. A fish fin (partly broken) caps the head. The tense, compact little image, *c*.25 cms in height, also displays a curious projecting spinal column and pronounced rib cage. The figure stands on a crescentic form that resembles a miniature canoe. All of these iconographic features are characteristic of spirits of the sea, *ataro ni matawa*, on Ulawa, Malaita, San Cristobal, and adjacent islands. These creatures were thought to inhabit the sea and air; they were propitiated with food offerings by voyagers and fishermen for, if provoked or displeased, it was their practice, allegedly, to upset canoes or shoot their miniature arrows into fishermen.[18] Sea spirits appear in carved form as fish floats, architectural ornaments, and on other art forms.

Carved wooden floats, 12–15cms in length, were once attached to fish and turtle nets in the Western District, particularly in the New Georgia Islands (Pl. 139). Turtle nets of the late nineteenth century were described by Lieutenant B. T. Somerville, a crew member of the Royal Navy surveying ship HMS *Penguin* stationed in the Marovo Lagoon area of Roviana island in 1892–93. The turtle nets that Somerville observed were:

> 'weighted with stones which have a hole bored through them, and the floats are joints of bamboo or lumps of wood with a "debbleum" kneeling or squatting on them. Occasionally, they assume a conventional form which is called *pepele* or "butterfly"'.[19]

A. M. Hocart, writing of his 1908 research on Simbo and Roviana islands in the New Georgia island group, noted that:

> 'The big fishing nets are called *vangara*. They have floats and weights and require a large number of people to hold them. The late chief of Simbo had one made, the men of Narovo (district) assisting. There is at present no such net in Narovo'.[20]

Net floats in museum collections consist largely of bird images, birds with anthropomorphic heads (e.g. the float illustrated in Pl. 139; presented in 1887), and the reverse – anthropomorphs with bird heads. Spirits associated with the nets and propitiated with food offerings to ensure success in fishing have been linked with birds or took the form of birds, a likely explanation for the preponderance of bird and bird/anthropomorphs on net floats.[21]

Architectural Sculpture

Among islands in the Eastern District of the Solomons (San Cristobal, Santa Ana, Santa Catalina, Ulawa, and Uki), the village canoe house and custom house have always constituted major foci of artistic expression. The buildings were long and rectangular with gable roofs. The upper parts of the supportive posts were (and still are) carved to represent anthropomorphic spirits accompanied by fish and frigate birds, the creatures of sea and air that have always played an important role in the earthly and spiritual life of Eastern Solomon islanders.[22] Carved wooden gable ornaments and large decorated wooden tie beams that span the interiors of some of the more elaborately decorated structures constitute other standard ornamented features (Pls.140, 141).

The British Museum contains a single post figure allegedly obtained from Ulawa by Admiral Davis, who led the punitive expedition against headhunters from the New Georgia Islands in 1892–93 (Pl.140). The standing image (1894–189) was carved in the round at the upper end of a post; a fraction of the uncarved post remains as the base of the present figure. The image bears stylistic traits characteristic of anthropomorphic imagery from the eastern Solomon Islands: an erect posture with arms drawn back at the elbows, exaggeratedly large legs with slightly bent knees, and a long rectangular face. The straight brow ridge, square mouth, and sharply planed jaw are endemic to many images from this region. The figure terminates in a triangular form with curved upper surface shaped to hold a horizontal house beam.

A carved figure said to be a 'door ornament' from San Cristobal was also obtained by Admiral Davis on the *Royalist* expedition. The anthropomorphic figure has a fish head with upward curving tail fin. Hands are shellfish claws, and fish tail fins substitute for feet. These features, notable in other images from the eastern Solomon Islands (cf. Pl.138), identify the figure as a spirit of the sea. The image reveals no visible means of attachment to a door or gable; the fragile nature of the pointed tail-fin feet would, however, seem to require that the figure be attached to something – probably the gable of a house or a post of a canoe or custom house.

Shark Caskets

A rare feature in museum collections are *airi*, shark caskets (Pl.142) made on the island of Santa Ana to hold the skulls of deceased people of importance. Admiral Davis obtained one of these caskets on Santa Ana in 1893–4 (Pl.142; 1904. 6–21.13).

Writing of Santa Ana eighty years later, Sidney Mead recorded that:

'Once all the proper (funeral) ceremonials had been carried out and the skull placed into a shark casket, the dead ancestor was transformed into a "living" and powerful spirit. He was worshipped by his relatives and they ate his special food in small individual bowls. Ancestors whose skulls were placed either in *tarigau* (a container made of vines) or were left exposed on a raised platform inside the custom house were not fully transformed because the full cycle of ceremonials was not undertaken. Thus, they lacked both the social and religious power of skulls placed in shark caskets ... It was only at Santa Ana that these traditional containers were still to be seen during the period of fieldwork'.[23]

Documentation going back to the late nineteenth century reveals the use of fish caskets on Malaita, San Cristobal, and Ulawa. The bonito and swordfish were preferred for caskets on these islands.[24]

Freestanding Anthropomorphic Images

Anthropomorphic images that are freestanding, that is, not carved for attachment to canoes, house gables, or other objects have long been produced in the Solomon Islands (Pls.143, 144). The number of these images is relatively small when compared with the quantity of figures rendered in low-relief or three-dimensionally on other artefacts; information regarding their function is sparse.

WOODEN IMAGES

There are twenty-one freestanding wooden figures from the Solomon Islands in the British Museum. Two that number among the first carvings from the Solomons to come into the museum appear to have originated from the area of Roviana, a regional stylistic attribution entered into the accession files by C. M. Woodford. One of these figures, formerly in the collection of R. F. Whitfield, was presented to the museum in 1877 (+436D) (Pl.143). The other (5163) was purchased nine years earlier in 1868 by A. W. Franks in Hamburg, Germany (Pl.144). Nothing more is known about the history of these figures.

The two figures exhibit some degree of similarity indicative of a common regional derivation. Heads are defined as smooth-surfaced volumes with a marked vertical orientation; they lack the abrupt jaw extension so characteristic of many images from the Roviana area (e.g. Pl.131). Nonetheless, the deep serration of the large shell-inlaid eyes, the narrow noses, and tight ovoid lips rendered in low-relief

bear a noticeable resemblance to corresponding features of other Roviana –
attributed images produced during the early to mid-nineteenth century (cf.
Pls.135, 154). (There are obvious gaps in documented knowledge of the
distribution and provenance of carving styles in this region for the period in
question.) Bodies of the figures differ considerably in posture and surface
treatment; it is above all in the faces that the two images concur visually.

STONE IMAGES

Anthropomorphic images carved in stone are far less common than wooden images
in museum collections of art from the Solomon Islands. Of the seven stone images
in the British Museum Solomons collection, one of especial value is a small
(11·5 cms high) egg-shaped stone head that was acquired in the Florida Islands by
The Revd Alfred Penny of the Melanesian Mission (Pl.145). Little has altered the
natural appearance of the stone save for rudimentary facial features and a faint
band of designs on the back of the head. The stone (1920.3–13.1) is said to have
represented the *tindalo* (spirit) Kulanikama. Penny describes a *tindalo* image
similar to this one in his book *Ten Years in Melanesia* (London, 1888) as:

> 'a stone, the size and shape of a lemon, carved into the rude resemblance of a
> human face. Kelekona (a chief of Gaeta island in the Floridas) told me that
> before he started upon any expedition by land or sea it was his custom to go to
> the grove in which this effigy was stored and pray to it, asking for protection in
> danger and "mana" in fighting. No one but himself had seen it for twenty years,
> or knew its place of concealment. His father before his death gave it to him, and
> he now gave it to me'.[25]

In the traditional religion of the Florida Islands, carvings of stone, wood, and shell
represented and bore the names of *tindalos*, spirits of the dead. The number of
tindalos was apparently almost infinite. They were allegedly classified into groups
which exercised powers in war, agriculture, sea travel, fishing, health, and love-
making. There were, in addition, private *tindalos* owned by chiefs, warriors, and
others of importance. Supposedly the power of the images was reflected in the
power of their owners and vice versa. *Tindalo* images, kept hidden in caves or
special houses, included clam shell armlets and breast ornaments, wooden clubs,
and stone images. From all available evidence, the stone *tindalo* image given by
Penny to the British Museum would appear to be the *tindalo* owned by Kalekona.
It was Kalekona who, in 1883, led his people in putting an end to their old religion
in order to adopt Christianity.[26] At this time, the secret hiding places of the images
were revealed, and many images were destroyed or given away.

Clam Shell Openwork Carvings

Thick flat slabs of tridacna gigas clam shell (Pls.146, 147), carved into an open fretwork of designs, were once placed in burial caves, skull huts, or other shrines of the deceased on islands in the Western District (e.g. Choiseul, Vella La Vella, Rendova, Simbo, and Roviana). The British Museum possesses seventeen openwork plaques (*mbarava*). The first came into the museum in 1887 (3528) (Pl.146). It represents only a fragment of the original carving and was acquired in 1867 by its former owner, Enrico Giglioli, on Guadalcanal. Additional plaques in the collection were obtained by C. M. Woodford and other visitors to the Solomon Islands between 1888 and *c.*1920.

All who wrote of their first encounter with tridacna plaques in the islands were led to believe that the plaques were very old and that their production pre-dated the lives of their informants. A Choiseul islander, writing in 1976, revealed that his people in eastern Choiseul believed that the plaques were made by the gods, though he suggests that they may have been produced by the first inhabitants of Choiseul.[27]

Two distinct types of design structure operate within the tridacna plaques. One comprises a gridwork design scheme in which anthropomorphic figures or faces, rings, and spirals are arranged in superimposed rows (Pl.146). Frequently, individual motifs are separated by vertical bars. Plaques of the gridwork type have been collected from (or attributed to) Roviana, Vella La Vella, Rendova, and Choiseul. A second group of plaques displays large frontal anthropomorphic figures arranged in groups or superimposed rows (Pl.147). The frontal standing figures may be flanked by a pair of seated figures rendered in profile. A certain amount of zoning occurs in this group of plaques, but the dense gridwork of motifs rendered in a uniformly small scale on plaques of the first type is much less evident. Images of a canoe and hornbill bird occasionally appear on plaques of the second group, (e.g. 1915–21; Basel Museum für Völkerkunde, Vb7517, and Fiji Museum, Suva, 53). Plaques of the second type have been collected from Choiseul and Roviana.

The symbolism of the motifs on the plaques is somewhat elusive. The frontal figures represented standing in a crouching position on some of the plaques have been interpreted (in the absence of field documentation) as dancing figures.[28] One resident of Choiseul who was questioned about these figures surmised that the figures represented the members of the descent group owning the burial shrine near which the plaque was found.[29]

Rings rendered in large and small size on all of the plaques may well allude to the tridacna shell rings formerly used as currency, worn as ornaments, attached to skull huts, and, on occasion, fastened to the skulls themselves.[30] In each of these

214

contexts, the shell rings symbolized the wealth and prestige of their owner. They, thus, constituted a not inappropriate motif for reproduction on the openwork plaques which functioned as burial monuments for the deceased. In eastern Choiseul, offerings of food were presented to the openwork plaques at the beginning of the new year or when new skulls were placed in a shrine.[31]

Some conclusions and speculations can, thus, be made about the tridacna clam shell plaques, but other matters such as their production: when they were made, at what time within an individual's life, and by whom; must remain ambiguous.

Eating Utensils

BOWLS

In the eastern Solomon Islands from Florida to Santa Ana, carved wooden bowls used mainly to hold food at public feasts have always constituted a major category of sculpture (Pls.149, 152). The bowls were (and are) carved in various sizes ranging from small bowls for individuals to bowls nine to twelve feet in length – large enough to serve a huge gathering of people. Forty-six wooden bowls from the eastern islands belong to the British Museum. The majority fall into the category of small to medium-sized bowls used by a single person, and most are carved to represent creatures from the sea and air which characterize the iconography of all art forms from this region.

Most of the bowls are oval in shape with rounded or pointed ends fashioned into a variety of sculptural forms. On Ulawa, according to Walter Ivens:

> 'the smaller bowls are known by the style of the handles which are cut to imitate various objects, sea birds, crickets, squids, etc., and these give the names to the bowls'.[32]

Prominent in the British Museum collection are bird bowls of an oval shape that terminate in a bird head at one end and a scroll-shaped tail at the other. Two of the bird bowls illustrated here were collected by Brenchley from San Cristobal (Pl.149; 6356) and Ulawa (Pl.150; 6534). Charles F. Wood obtained a bird bowl (Pl.151; 7631) from San Cristobal in or before 1872. Miniature fish carved at the tips of the bird beaks (Pls.149, 151) represent a frequent motif on bird bowls from the eastern Solomons and probably reflect the symbolic (and actual) association between birds and fish that permeate the traditional mythology and life of these islanders.

The bowl collected by Wood (Pl.151) displays a tiny anthropomorphic figure crouched against the side of the bowl directly beneath the fish held in the bird beak.

It is likely that the small figure was originally intended to represent one of the spirits of the sea once widely venerated in association with various other sea creatures. Sea spirits, frequently recognizable by their crouching posture and, in some instances, appended scrolls and fish features (cf. Pls.138, 141), are often depicted in pairs on bowls from the eastern Solomons; the appearance of a single spirit image on a bird bowl, as in this nineteenth-century example, is relatively uncommon.

One of the oldest and most unusual food bowls in the early collections was obtained in 1865 by Brenchley and is said to come from San Cristobal (6357; Pl.152). Carved openwork designs extend from both sides of the bowl. Each section of openwork carving is framed by a zig-zag form and terminates at the bottom in a small anthropomorphic figure represented facing downward. The bent knees, sharp muzzle-like lines of the head, and scrolls extending from the buttocks of these tiny images identify them as spirits of the sea. Close examination shows that the undulating forms rising from the heads of these images resemble snakes. The superimposed rhomboid forms that make up the main body of the design resemble fish, and the ends of the bowl itself, almost obscured by the prominence of the openwork designs beneath, may be seen to depict in outline the heads of two birds facing in opposite directions. The filigree design thus incorporates in a highly unusual and intricate manner the bird-fish-sea spirit (and sea snake?) iconographic complex appropriate to this region.

LIME BOXES AND LIME STICKS

The custom of betel nut chewing is widespread in the Solomon Islands and elsewhere in the western Pacific. The nuts or leaves of the betel pepper (piper beetle) are chewed together with small bits of powdered lime made by burning shells or coral or by grinding limestone. The lime, traditionally, is kept in containers made from bamboo, gourds, wood, or coconuts (Pls.153, 154).

Limesticks or spatulas of wood or bone were utilized to take the lime from the containers. The sticks often were intricately carved to represent various beings prominent in local mythology. A bone limestick (Pl.153) was collected by Walter Ivens from the Sa'a, Malaita-Ulawa region (1940.Oc.3, 18). The slim, pointed limestick, 43 cms long, terminates in a carved image of the shark anthropomorph, Karemanua – a spirit widely depicted in art from San Cristobal, Ulawa, and Santa Ana. Karemanua, allegedly, was once a human being who was partly transformed into a shark while swimming with his brother off the coast of Santa Ana. Unwelcome in his island home after his transformation, Karemanua swam from one island to another until he was finally allowed to settle on Ulawa.[33] As a popular mythological figure in this region, Karemanua has been rendered on the posts of canoe houses, on shark caskets and on limesticks. This limestick is one of twenty examples in the British Museum collection from the Solomons.

Forty-four lime containers from the Solomon Islands belong to the British Museum. Most prevalent are containers made of bamboo etched with geometric designs. One of the most unusual and oldest lime containers in the collection is a brown wooden lime box comprised of a seated anthropomorphic figure (Pl.154) (B.H.22). The image is 25 cms high; its cylindrically-shaped hollow head constitutes the container. The limbs of the image have suffered much breakage, but the figure appears formerly to have been carved in a seated position with its legs drawn up toward the body and elbows touching knees. Large ears with circular ear ornaments extend at right angles to the head. The projecting brows, tight ovoid mouth, and sensitively sculpted nose are reminiscent of facial features of other early canoe and freestanding images attributed to the region of Roviana (cf. Pls.130, 143, 144). Large shell-inlaid eyes pierced and punctuated with blunt serrations around the edges also characterize images collected from this region during the early mid-nineteenth century.

A label attached to the figure identifies it as 'A Betel Nut Chewer's Chinam (lime) Box from the Solomon Islands, H.N. (or H.?) Denham, 1855'. Denham's name reappears in the files of the Pitt Rivers Museum, Oxford, as the donor of a canoe carving from the Solomon Islands (P.R. IV, 54, 2095). That carving is attributed to Admiral H.N. Denham together with the date 1855. Naval records reveal the existence of an Admiral Sir Henry Denham who commanded the *Herald 8*, a surveying ship which was in the Pacific from 18 February 1852 to 1859.[34] In view of this information, it seems plausible that the lime box figure was acquired in 1855 by Admiral Denham; if this is true, it represents one of the oldest documented pieces in the Solomon Islands collection of the British Museum.

Personal Ornaments

KAPKAPS

Personal ornaments made of wood, shell, beads, and woven grasses from all parts of the Solomon Islands are comprehensively represented in the British Museum and constitute a volume of material too large to be dealt with in an essay of this length. Of particular types in the collection, one is the large group of over sixty *kapkaps*, circular tridacna clam shell discs overlaid with a lace-like fretwork of tortoise-shell (Pl.155). *Kapkaps* were traditionally worn on the forehead attached to a fibre band or as breast ornaments. Subtle variations distinguish *kapkaps* from the different islands, but the openwork motifs rendered in tortoise-shell share a common centrifugal or radial pattern in which a central axial motif is surrounded by concentric zones of designs. The *kapkap* illustrated here (1944 Oc.2, 1341) displays a small four-pronged design in the centre surrounded by the dominant central motif, a six-lobed star. Groups of concentric bands alternate with U-shaped motifs and serrated designs to fill the remaining space.

Over fifty of the *kapkaps* in the collection, formerly in the possession of Harry G. Beasley, came originally from the islands of Buka and Bougainville, where they were collected by the Right Revd H. Voyce of the Methodist Mission, Siwai District, Bougainville. These *kapkaps* came into the British Museum in 1944. Other examples were acquired much earlier from Codrington, Brenchley, and Woodford.

Clubs

Almost every early donor of artefacts from the Solomon Islands contributed to the large collection of wooden clubs obtained from all parts of the islands. There are over one hundred and ninety clubs from the Solomons in the British Museum.

Among the types of clubs represented are six sickle-shaped *roromaraugi* parrying clubs from San Cristobal;[35] five *qauata*, parrying clubs with leaf-shaped blades attributable to the same island; eight *supe*, diamond-shaped hand clubs characteristic of Malaita; nineteen long pointed clubs with faceted blades from Ysabel, Florida, and Guadalcanal; and seventeen clubs with paddle-shaped blades collected from Ysabel and Florida. Five of the latter were obtained in 1865 by Julius Brenchley. Fourteen clubs from Buka and Bougainville and twenty-six from Rennell (Sinker and Bradley collections) represent other major acquisitions.

The club selected for illustration (Pl.156) is one of a large group collected on the 1865 Brenchley expedition (6298). The broad leaf-shaped blade bisected by a raised ridge and the long cylindrical shaft are characteristic features of the clubs which Brenchley obtained on Florida and Ysabel islands. A number of these clubs are not decorated in any way; this is one of the exceptions – ornamented by two carved anthropomorphic heads just above the hand grip, as well as a face incised in low relief on the blade.

In the Pitt-Rivers Museum, Oxford, there is a similar club decorated in the same manner and attributed to Ysabel. The club (Codrington 65), collected by the Revd R. H. Codrington, bears the name RAU-NI-ABA.[36] According to Codrington, 'in Florida and thereabouts, a paddle-shaped club is a favorite walking weapon, *rau ni Aba*, the leaf, so-called, of Aba, a place in Guadalcanal where they are made.'[37] This statement constitutes a fragmentary bit of evidence suggesting that clubs of this type may have been made on Guadalcanal and then sold to residents of Florida and Ysabel.

Shields

Among the many battle shields from the Solomon Islands in the British Museum, three are outstanding for their unusual ornamentation. Two, a rectangular shield of bark (8016) and an oval wicker shield (1954, Oc.6.197; Pl.157) are decorated with intricate designs formed by small square pieces of nautilus shell about one centimetre in width. The pieces of shell are set in parinarium nut glue on the shield surface which is painted red and black. The inlaid bark shield, obtained by the Museum in 1872, is one of three of its type existent in museum collections. Wicker shields decorated with shell-inlaid designs are more numerous, but hardly commonplace, there being approximately nineteen examples in museum and private collections.[38] The British Museum acquired its inlaid wicker shield in 1954.

The decorative theme of the shell-inlaid wicker shields is very consistent: a tall anthropomorphic figure with raised arms occupies the centre of every shield. Small heads always appear below or on either side of the central figure. (The heads recur on the bark shields, but the central figure does not.) Allusions to headhunting form a likely explanation for the presence of detached heads on the shields (cf. Pl.134). No detailed information regarding the function of these shields is available from the period when they were collected (1850s–1860s, when collection date is known), but the fragile nature of the decoration, as well as the relatively small number of these elaborately ornamented shields, suggest a ceremonial function and, probably, ownership exclusive to chiefs or other social group leaders.

A third decorated shield in the collection (6306) was obtained by Brenchley from Boli, Florida (Pl.158). It is constructed of wicker and heavily embellished with woven patterns of grasses as well as concentric rows of attached pieces of shell cut into circular and triangular shapes. Brenchley describes and illustrates the shield in his book, *Jottings During the Cruise of H.M.S. 'Curacoa'* (London, 1873), where he noted that 'there was only one more shield of the (this) kind'. Its owner apparently fled when it became known that the European visitors wanted it.[39] A similar though less profusely decorated shield exists in the Bishop Museum, Honolulu (1859).

In conclusion, it may be said that the Solomon Islands collection now in the British Museum is an extremely comprehensive one incorporating a wide range of artefacts in many media. Particularly impressive is the amount of material acquired during the early to mid-nineteenth century, though there is a regrettable dearth of full historical documentation regarding village and island provenances and details of functions for these early images. The lack of historical data notwithstanding, the existence of so many artefacts from this period in a single collection of ethnographica from the Solomon Islands is of great value. Further detailed typological studies of the clubs, *kapkaps*, canoe ornaments, and other artefacts in the collection will more productively utilize the resources of the collection to illuminate the history of art and ethnographica from this island group.

Notes

1 Letter from the Trustees of the Christy Collection to the British Museum, November 7, 1865.

    I am grateful to Dorota Starzecka, Assistant Keeper in the Department of Ethnography at the British Museum for helping me to consult the accession files and other documents pertaining to the Ethnographical Collections. I also wish to thank Penny Bateman of the Students' Room, Museum of Mankind (Ethnography Department) for her help to me in my research conducted during the spring of 1977.

    Information regarding groups of material or single items from the Solomon Islands collection in the British Museum has been drawn from the Extracts and Temporary Register of accessions in the Ethnography Department unless otherwise indicated. Itemization of artefacts given by the various donors is not feasible here, owing to the size of the donations.

2 M. Steinhauer, *The Catalogue of a Collection of Ancient and Modern Stone Implements and of Other Weapons, Tools, and Utensils of the Aboriginals of Various Countries in the Possession of H. Christy*. London, 1862, pp.65–71.

3 Augustus W. Franks, *British Museum. Guide to the Christy Collection of Prehistoric Antiquities and Ethnography. Temporarily Placed at 103 Victoria Street, Westminster*. London, 1868, p.15.

4 Julius Brenchley, *Jottings During the Cruise of H.M.S. 'Curacoa' in 1865*. London, 1873, preface, p.xv.

5 Walter Ivens, *Melanesians of the S.E. Solomon Islands*. London, 1927, preface.

6 'The Narrative of Mendana by Alvaro de Mendana'. *The Discovery of the Solomon Islands by Alvaro de Mendana in 1568*. Translated by Lord William Amherst and Basil Thomson. London, 1901, Vol.I, p.109.

7 C. F. Claret de Fleurieu, *Discoveries of the French in 1768 and 1769 to the S.E. of New Guinea*, London, 1791, p.139.

8 *Ethnographical Document 1131*. Letter from Captain R. Broadhurst-Hill 29 April, 1965. Ethnography Department, British Museum.

Up until the end of the nineteenth century, headhunting was a focal institution of life in the Western District (especially on Roviana, Choiseul, and Vella La Vella). Woodford (*JRGS* 10 1888 p.360) for example, stated that on Roviana during the 1880s 'no canoe house was completed and no canoe launched without a head being obtained'. Other occasions requiring the taking of a head on Roviana allegedly included marriage, yam harvests, and in consequence of certain omens (Paravicini, *Reisen*, p.179).

9 R. M. Codrington, *The Melanesians*. Oxford, 1891, p.296.

10 C. F. Claret de Fleurieu, *Discoveries of the French*, p.94. For further information about Bougainville's voyage, see Colin Jack-Hinton, *The Search for the Islands of Solomon 1567–1838*. Oxford, 1969, pp.255–61.

11 Personal Correspondence, L. T. Hope, 26 April 1977. Archives of the Council for World Mission, Section 1 B, Box 8, Folders 2–4. Letters from James Smith to London Missionary Society Headquarters: 18 June 1831; 4 October 1831; 21 December 1831; 2 October 1832; 16 January 1833; 17 August 1822.

12 Lieutenant B. T. Somerville, 'Ethnological Notes in New Georgia Solomon Islands', *Journal of the Royal Anthropological Institute*, 26, (1897), p.371.

13 Somerville, *Ibid*, p.384.

14 James Edge-Partington, *An Album of the Weapons, Tools, Ornaments, Articles of Dress, etc. of the Natives of the Pacific Islands*. London, 1898, Vol.I, caption for Plate 210, No.2.

15 Gerald C. Wheeler. *Ethnographical Document 1096. Ethnographica from Alu and Mono. Collected from 1908 to 1909*. Ethnography Department, British Museum, ref.1075; G. C. Wheeler, 'The Mono-Alu People of Bougainville Straits, West Solomon Islands'. MS 170822. Religion 1, p.132, n.2. (School of Oriental and African Studies, London University)

15a Cf. Starzecka and Cranstone, *Solomon Islanders*, illustrations 12, 13 (pp.24–5).

16 Henry B. Guppy, *The Solomon Islands and Their Natives*, London, 1887, 152; Codrington, *Melanesians*, p.317, n.1.

17 Walter Ivens, *Melanesians of the S.E. Solomon Islands*. London, 1927, pp.384–85.

18 R. H. Codrington, *Melanesians*, p.374.

19 B. T. Somerville, *JRAI* 26 (1897), p.374.

20 A. M. Hocart, 'Fishing in Eddystone Island', *JRAI* 67 (1937), p.35.

21 A. M. Hocart, *Ibid.*, pp.35–36, 39.

22 Walter Ivens, *Melanesians*, pp.130–39

23 Sidney M. Mead, 'Material Culture and Art in the Star Harbour Region, Eastern Solomon Islands', *Ethnography Monograph I*, Royal Ontario Museum, Toronto, (1973), p.18. See also: Charles E. Fox, *The Threshold of the Pacific*. London, 1925, pp.115, 129; Ivens, *Melanesians*, pp.209–10.

24 R. H. Codrington, *Melanesians*, p.262.

25 Alfred B. Penny, *Ten Years in Melanesia*. London, 1887, pp.195–96.

26 A. B. Penny, *Ibid.*, pp.55–58; Codrington, *Melanesians*, pp.124–26.

27 Guso Piko, 'Choiseul Currency', *The Journal of the Cultural Association of the Solomon Islands*, 4 (1976), p.105.

28 James Edge-Partington and T. A. Joyce, 'Notes on Funerary Ornaments from Rubiana and a Coffin from Santa Anna', *Man*, 4 (1904), p.129.

29 Harold W. Scheffler, Personal Communication, November, 1973.

30 T. Russell, 'A Note on Clamshell Money of Simbo and Roviana from an Unpublished Manuscript of Professor A. M. Hocart', *The Journal of the Solomon Islands Museum Association*, 1 (1972), pp.23, 27, 28; B. A. L. Cranstone, *Melanesia, a Short Ethnography*. London, 1961, Plate 5, Fig.6.

31 G. Piko, *J. Cult. Assoc. Sol. Is* 4 (1976), p.105.

32 W. Ivens, *Melanesians*, p.53.

33 Charles Fox, *Threshold*, pp.74–75.

34 L. S. Dawson, *Memoirs of Hydrography*. Eastbourne, n.d. According to Dawson, Sir Henry Denham's ship made surveys of Port Jackson, Lord Howe Island, Herald Bay, and several islands in the Fiji group. I am grateful to Mrs Mary Patrick, Research Assistant of the National Maritime Museum Library, Greenwich, for providing this information.

35 Cf. Starzecka and Cranstone, *Solomon Islanders*, Fig.6, p.16.

36 For names of clubs and accompanying illustrations, see Mead, 'Material Culture', pp.43–45.

37 R. H. Codrington, *Melanesians*, p.306.

38 D. Waite, 'Shell-Inlaid Shields from the Solomon Islands', article in preparation.

39 Brenchley, *Jottings*, pp.280–81.

Bibliography

Amherst, Lord William and Basil Thomson. *The Discovery of the Solomon Islands by Alvaro de Mendana in 1568*. Translated from the original by Amherst and Thomson. 2 volumes. Hakluyt Society; London, 1901.

Brenchley, Julius. *Jottings During the Cruise of H.M.S. 'Curacoa' in 1865*. London, 1873.

Broadhurst-Hill, Captain R. Letter, 29 April, 1965. *Ethnographical Document 1131*. Ethnography Department, British Museum, London.

Christy Collection, Letter from Trustees, 7 November, 1865.

Codrington, R. H. *The Melanesians*. Oxford, 1891.

Cranstone, B. A. L. *Melanesia, a Short Ethnography*. London, 1961.

Dawson, L. S. *Memoirs of Hydrography*, (Eastbourne, n.d.)

Edge-Partington, James. *An Album of the Weapons, Tools, Ornaments, Articles of Dress, etc., of the Natives of the Pacific Islands*, Vol.I. London, 1898.

Edge-Partington, James and T. A. Joyce, 'Notes on Funerary Ornaments from Rubiana and a Coffin from Santa Anna', *Man*, 4 (1904), pp.129–31.

Fleurieu, C. F. Claret de. *Discoveries of the French in 1768 and 1769 to the Southeast of New Guinea*. London, 1791.

Fox, Charles E. *The Threshold of the Pacific*. London, 1925.

Franks, Augustus W. *British Museum. Guide to the Christy Collection of Prehistoric Antiquities and Ethnography. Temporarily Placed at 103 Victoria Street, Westminster*. London, 1868.

Guppy, Henry B. *The Solomon Islands and Their Natives*. London, 1887.

Hocart, A. M. 'Fishing in Eddystone Island'. *Journal of the Royal Anthropological Institute*, 67 (1937), pp.33–41.

Ivens, Walter. *Melanesians of the Southeast Solomon Islands*. London, 1927.

Jack-Hinton, Colin. *The Search for the Islands of Solomon 1567–1838*. Oxford, 1969.

Mead, Sidney M. 'Material Culture and Art in the Star Harbour Region, Eastern Solomon Islands', *Ethnography Monograph I*. Royal Ontario Museum; Toronto, 1973.

Paravicini, Eugen. *Reisen in den Britischen Salomonen*. Leipzig, 1931.

Penny, Alfred B. *Ten Years in Melanesia*. London, 1887.

Piko, Guso. 'Choiseul Currency', *The Journal of the Cultural Association of the Solomon Islands*. 4 (1976), pp.96–110.

Russell, T. 'A Note on Clamshell Money of Simbo and Roviana from an Unpublished Manuscript of Professor A. M. Hocart', *The Journal of the Solomon Islands Museum Association*, 1 (1972), pp.21–29.

Smith, James. Letters to Headquarters of London Missionary Society. 18 June, 4 October, 21 December 1831; 2 October 1832; 16 January 1833; 17 August 1833. Archives of the Council for World Missions, Section B. London Missionary Society, Box 8, Folder 2–4.

Somerville, Lieutenant B. T. 'Ethnological Notes in New Georgia, Solomon Islands', *Journal of the Royal Anthropological Institute*, 26 (1897), pp.357–412.

Starzecka, Dorota C. and B. A. L. Cranstone. *The Solomon Islanders*. London, 1974.

Steinhauer, M. *The Catalogue of a Collection of Ancient and Modern Stone Implements and of other Weapons, Tools, and Utensils of the Aboriginals of Various Countries in the Possession of H. Christy*. London, 1862.

Waite, Deborah B. 'Shell-Inlaid Shields from the Solomon Islands'. Article in preparation.

Wheeler, Gerald C. 'Ethnographica from Alu and Mono. Collected from 1908 to 1909', *Ethnographical Document 1096*. Ethnography Department, British Museum.

Wheeler, G. C. 'The Mono-Alu People of Bougainville Straits, West Solomon Islands', MS 170822. London University, School of Oriental and African Studies.

Woodford, C. M. 'Exploration of the Solomon Islands', *Journal of the Royal Geographic Society (Proceedings)*, X, pp.351–76; XII, pp.393–418.

127 Canoe. British Museum, 1927. 10–22.1,
wood. Vella La Vella Island. Collected by
R. Broadhurst-Hill, 1910. Donated by
Trustees of Lady Lever Art Gallery,
Cheshire.

128 Canoe prow with figurehead. Detail of
Plate 127.

129 Canoe prow figurehead. British Museum,
1968, Oc.3.1, wood. d. L. T. Hope. Collected
by donor's grandfather *c*.1830–40. Gr.h. 23 cm.

130 Canoe prow figurehead. British Museum,
1661A, wood. Christy Collection. Gr.h. 18 cm.

131 Two standing figures. British Museum,
   1661. Christy Collection. Gr.h. 37.7 cm.;
   39.5 cm.

132 Figurehead mounted on figures. British
   Museum. 1661, 1661A.

133 Canoe prow carving. British Museum,
   1914–311, wood. d. A. M. Hocart. Collected
   by Hocart in 1908. h. 9.4 cm.; l. 10 cm.

134 Canoe stern carving. British Museum, 1944
   Oc.2. 1792. Ex-Beasley Collection, 4308.
   wood. l. 68 cm.

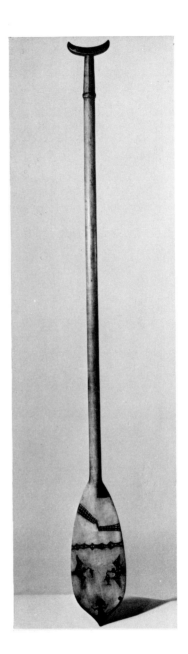

135 Canoe stern carving. British Museum, 1927.
10–3. 46, wood. d. G. C. Wheeler. Collected
by Wheeler from Faleta village, Alu island,
Bougainville Straits in 1908–9. h. 25.5 cm.

136 Canoe paddle. British Museum, 1950,
Oc.4.6. Ex-Oldman Collection. wood.
l. 146.5 cm.

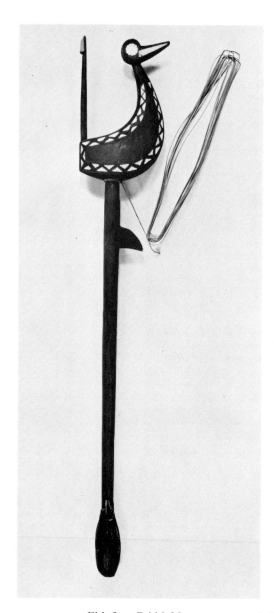

137 Fish float. British Museum, +2017. d. The
    Revd R. B. Comine, 1883. l. 73 cm.

138 Fish float. British Museum, 6317. wood.
    d. Julius Brenchley, 1870. Collected by
    Brenchley on Ulawa in 1865. l. 84.5 cm.

139 Fish net float. British Museum, 87. 2–1, 23.
    wood. d. H. J. Veitch, Esq., 1887. l. 12 cm.

140 Post image. British Museum, 1894–189.
Ulawa. Collected by Admiral Davis of HMS
Royalist, 1892–3. h. 75 cm.

141 Fish/anthropomorphic figure. British
Museum, 1904. 6–21.14. San Cristobal.
wood. Collected by Admiral Davis of HMS
Royalist, 1892–3. h. 65.5 cm.

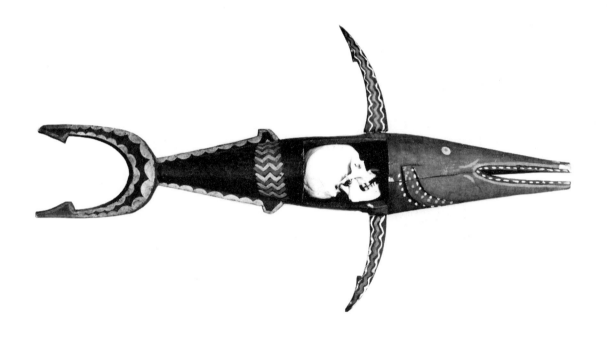

142 Fish casket (*airi*). British Museum, 1904.
6–21.14. San Cristobal. wood. Collected by
Admiral Davis of HMS *Royalist* 1892–3.
l. 142.2 cm.

232

143 Figure. British Museum, +436D. Ex-
R. P. Whitfield Collection. wood. Presented
by A. W. Franks, 1877. h. 32 cm.

144 Figure. British Museum, 5163. wood.
Presented by A. W. Franks, 1869. Purchased
in 1868. h. 25.5 cm.

145 Tindalo image. British Museum, 1900,
3–13,1. stone. Florida Islands. d. The Rev[d]
Alfred Penny. h. 11.5 cm.

146 Openwork plaque (*mbarava*). British
Museum, +3528. Tridacna clam shell. Ex-
Enrico Giglioli Collection. Obtained by
Giglioli in 1867. l. 25.5 cm.

147 Openwork plaque (*mbarava*). British
Museum, 1915–21. Tridacna clam shell.
Collected by C. M. Woodford, Roviana
Lagoon, Roviana. l. 25 cm.

234

148 Serenbule sticks. British Museum, l. to r.:
1904. 6–21.3; 1904. 6–21,4; 1904. 6–21.5.
Clam shell. Roviana Lagoon, Roviana.
Collected by Admiral Davis of HMS
Royalist, 1892–3. h. 41.2 cm.

149 Bird Bowl. British Museum, 6356. wood.
San Cristobal. d. Julius Brenchley, 1870.
Collected by Brenchley, 1865. l. 36.2 cm.; h.
13.4 cm.

150 Bird Bowl. British Museum, 6354. wood.
Ulawa. d. Julius Brenchley, 1870. Collected
by Brenchley, 1865. l. 60.5 cm.; h. 19 cm.

151 Bird bowl. British Museum, 7631. wood.
Oruna Bay, San Cristobal. d. G. F. Wood,
1872. l. 33.5 cm.; h. 16 cm.

152 Bowl. British Museum, 6357. wood. San
Cristobal. d. Julius Brenchley, 1870.
Collected by Brenchley, 1865. l. 33.5 cm.;
h. 14 cm.

153 Limestick. British Museum, 1940. Oc.3.18.
bone. Collected by Walter G. Ivens. l. 42.5 cm.

154 Lime container. British Museum, B. H.22.
wood. Collected by (Admiral) H. H.
Denham, 1855. h. 25 cm.

155 Kapkap. British Museum, 1944, Oc. 2, 1341.
Ex-Beasley 2761. Tridacna clam shell and
tortoise shell. d. 13.2 cm.

156 Club. British Museum, 6298. wood. Ysabel.
d. Julius Brenchley, 1870. Collected by
Brenchley, 1865. l. 112.5 cm.

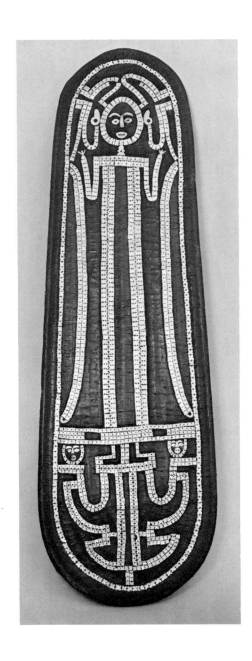

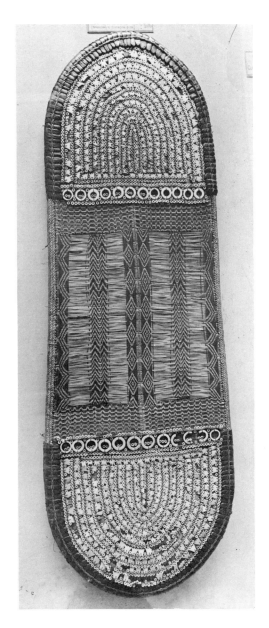

157 Shell-inlaid wicker shield. British Museum, 1954 Oc.6.197. Ex-Wellcome Historical Medical Museum. l. 86.5 cm.

158 Wicker shield. British Museum, 6306. Boli, Florida. d. Julius Brenchley, 1870. Collected by Brenchley, 1865. l. 91.5 cm.

Index

sketch to, 88; and drawing of apotheosis of
Cook, 89; his Cook voyage collection, 94; and
Banks, 97; draws ethnographic artefacts,
168–9; depicts Hawaiian feather image, 171,
177, 178; his drawings of gourd rattles, 182–3
Wellington, New Zealand, Alexander Turnbull
Library, 96; National Museum, 173, 176
West, Benjamin, 171
Wheeler, Alwynne, 22
Wheeler, Gerald C., his collection of Solomon
Islands artefacts, 202–3; obtains canoe-
carvings, 208–9
Whitfield, R. F., 212
Wilkinson, Francis, 23
Williams, John, 206
Willis, Peter, 29
Wiseman, Sir William, 201

Witt Library, 13
Wood, Charles F., acquires Solomon Islands
ethnographica, 201; writes of his experiences,
202; his bird bowl, 215–16
Woodford, Charles M., collects Solomon Islands
ethnographica, 202; writes of his experiences,
202; and attribution of standing images, 207,
212; obtains canoe carving, 208; fish floats, 209;
kapkaps, 218
Woollett, William, *Fleet of Otaheite*, 89, 92

Yale Centre of British Art, Paul Mellon
Collection, 88
York Island (*now* Moorea), 23
Ysabel Island, 205; canoes of, 204; canoe paddles
from, 209; clubs, 218, 219